Nonstate Actors in International Politics

Also of Interest

†Available in hardcover and paperback.

Westview Special Studies in International Relations

Nonstate Actors in International Politics: From Transregional to Substate Organizations
Phillip Taylor

One of the most notable trends in the study of international relations is the resurgence of interest in international organizations, particularly those outside the United Nations. Regional international governmental organizations, multinational corporations, international labor unions, and transnational ethnic groups have become increasingly salient actors in world politics. OPEC, NATO, EEC, and PLO, for example, are all widely understood acronyms, and even a casual review of the crises in Iran and Afghanistan reveals the pervasive involvement of NATO, the European Community, the Islamic Conference, the International Olympic Committee, and more than one hundred other international governmental and nongovernmental organizations. Although international organizations are not likely to replace nation-states as the primary actors in world politics, their growing involvement in global political and economic issues challenges the assumptions of the traditionalists' state-centric model, as well as those whose interests begin and end with the United Nations.

This book goes beyond the traditional UN-focused studies of nonstate actors to provide students with a comprehensive analytical survey of the many other organizations that help shape today's events. A common framework is used to examine what each nonstate actor does, how it organizes to achieve its ends, and how it makes multilateral/international decisions. The degree of integration in each nonstate actor is evaluated.

Phillip Taylor is associate professor of political science and director of international studies at Old Dominion University. He is the author of *When Europe Speaks with One Voice: The External Relations of the European Community* (1979) and coeditor of *Third World Policies of Industrialized Nations* (1982).

Nonstate Actors in
International Politics
From Transregional to
Substate Organizations

Phillip Taylor

Westview Press / Boulder and London

Westview Special Studies in International Relations

Copyright © 1984 by Westview Press, Inc.

Published in 1984 in the United States of America by Westview Press, Inc., 5500 Central Avenue, Boulder, Colorado 80301; Frederick A. Praeger, President and Publisher

Library of Congress Cataloging in Publication Data
Taylor, Phillip.
    Nonstate actors in international politics.
    (Westview special studies in international relations)
    Bibliography: p.
    Includes index.
    1. International Agencies. 2. International relations.
I. Title. II. Series.
JX1995.T38 1984   341.2   83-25997
ISBN 0-86531-344-X
ISBN 0-86531-345-8 (pbk.)

Printed and bound in the United States of America

10   9   8   7   6   5   4   3   2   1

To the memory of

Angelina Petronella Gijsbers-Verboeket

Moge ze ons op onze verdere levensweg geleiden
en ons hart steeds opnieuw helpen openhouden
voor het eenvoudig goede en zuivere waarin ze
ons is voorgegaan.

Contents

PART 1
INTRODUCTION

PART 2
ECONOMIC INTERNATIONAL GOVERNMENTAL
ORGANIZATIONS

Figures and Tables

Figures

Tables

Preface

One of the most notable trends in the academic study of international relations is the resurgence of interest in international organizations, particularly those outside the United Nations. Regional international governmental organizations, multinational corporations, international labor unions, and transnational ethnic groups became increasingly salient actors in world politics in the 1970s. Interest in these nonstate actors has not been confined to the academic community. Decisionmakers in government and business as well as average citizens are more aware of these groups than ever before. OPEC, NATO, the EEC (Common Market), and the PLO are now highly visible and widely understood acronyms. One could not have followed (even casually) the events of the crises in Iran and Afghanistan without having been impressed by the pervasive involvement of the United Nations, NATO, the European Community, the Islamic Conference, the International Olympic Committee, and over one hundred other international governmental and nongovernmental organizations.

No one should infer that international organizations have replaced or will soon replace nation-states as the primary actors in world politics. The United States, the Soviet Union, and Iran were, and are, the central actors in the crises that began in November and December 1979. However, the plethora of nonstate actors and their growing involvement in global political and economic issues challenge the assumptions of the traditionalists' state-centric model and demand greater vision from those whose interests begin and end with the United Nations. Our understanding of what is happening in the world today in part depends on expanding the scope of research into the activities of these many groups and encouraging that research by teaching this area in colleges and universities. This book is designed to fill the need for the latter.

The purpose of this book is to provide a basic text on nonstate actors that exist outside the United Nations and its associated international bodies. Hence, the content differs from the many texts on "international organization" that focus almost exclusively on the United Nations and contain only one or perhaps two chapters on "regionalism" or the European Community alone. The approach of this book differs as well from the few texts on "regional systems" in world politics. Although there are several advantages to the regional approach (common historical, cultural, and geopolitical factors of nation-states that share memberships in several regional bodies), there exists more explanatory power in a comparative study of nonstate actors with similar functional intent or activities. Therefore, this text provides a comparative survey of all economic organizations, security alliances, political organizations, and cultural/ideological groups and treats nongovernment nonstate actors separately. This functional approach has more utility than the regional one in that the latter cannot easily provide examinations of supraregional actors, such as OPEC, NATO, the Islamic Conference, and multinational corporations.

Phillip Taylor

Acknowledgments

No book is published without the hard work of many people. In writing this volume, I had the good fortune to be aided by a number of very helpful individuals. I am especially grateful to Lynne Rienner, Jeanne Remington, Susan McRory, and Christine Arden at Westview Press for their support of this project. Additionally, I am indebted to Van Buggs, Joe Shipley, and especially Linda Stephenson for typing the manuscript. The personal assistance of my colleague Don Zeigler and a grant from the ODU School of Arts and Letters made possible much of the original art work in this text. Several of my former graduate students provided valuable research assistance: Peter Black, Dolf Carlson, Henry Gerber, Henry Goddard, Georgios Iacovou, Tracey Johnstone, Mike Messina, Peter Reitz, E. T. Smith, Connie Vilhauer, and Barbara Wallbrecher. I gratefully acknowledge their help at various times over the past two years. Of course, I absolve everyone named above for any errors, and I accept full responsibility for the final product.

P.T.

Part 1

Introduction

1
Nonstate Actors and the State-Centric Model

The primary actors in world politics are nation-states; any attempt to suggest otherwise is completely erroneous. There will be no effort in this volume to suggest that nonstate actors have replaced or will soon replace sovereign states as the major units of analysis in foreign policy or the broader study of international relations. National governments make and enforce their own laws, declare war, provide for their own security, determine the scope and mode of formal international communications and diplomatic discourse, and determine (when able to do so) the terms and conditions of trade, monetary policy, and so on. However, given the development of increasing economic interdependence and the inability of nations (including the superpowers) to provide adequately for their own security in an age of thermonuclear weapons, nation-states have had to cooperate, accommodate, adjust, and defuse conflict and to seek solutions to problems (such as air and water pollution) not limited by national boundaries. These concerns motivated the creation of a plethora of international organizations, particularly since the end of World War II.

The proliferation of international organizations has not altered the fundamental role of nation-states in world politics. States have the options to join or refuse membership in international organizations and may belong to different organizations that are occasionally at cross-purposes with one another. They may choose to participate in or abstain from any decision taken in an international organization in which they are members or to cause that decision to represent their own view when the "least-common-denominator" approach is utilized in that organization. Effectively, they may veto any action they find objectionable when the unanimity voting principle is applied. Many nations accede to the charter of an international organization while reserving the right to renege on their obligations under the charter, should any action or decision prove a detriment to their national security, prestige, or national honor (or words to that effect). In short, nations yield very little sovereignty when they join international organizations, and yet they are the most important actors, even when acting in concert with fellow members of an international body.

Although nation-states are the most important units of analysis in the study of international relations, there is no historical basis on which to assume they will remain so for all time. Indeed, many international political scholars now argue that nation-states are but "first among equals."[1] There are, however, other scholars (often referred to as "traditionalists") who maintain that knowledge of interstate relations is sufficient to understand and explain world political behavior. These scholars contend that international organizations and other nonstate actors are unimportant in the study of world politics. The assumptions of this school of thought are generalized in the "state-centric model."[2] Those assumptions are worth examining in some detail, given that collectively they are as misleading as any argument for the preeminence of nonstate actors over state actors.

The State-Centric Model

There are seven postulates to the state-centric model. First, global politics are based exclusively on the interaction of nation-states. States are viewed as both actors and targets of action by another state or states. Second, although states vary considerably in size and power and these differences vary over time, each nation-state is believed to be the sovereign equal of any other state. This has become a major tenet of twentieth-century international law. Third, there is no concern for what Rosenau has termed "linkage politics";[3] that is, the interrelationship between domestic and foreign policies is virtually ignored. Indeed, nations are seen as homogeneous political entities in which a central government controls all "legal" forces of violence and coercion. Fourth, nation-states are independent and distinguishable from one another. There is no perceived or actual higher "earthly" authority over them. Fifth, the world is divided into formally recognized geographic compartments called states. The governments of these states possess exclusive control over the totality of their defined territory and the citizen residing in that territory. Sixth, nation-states are the secular repositories (and sacred ones as well where that distinction is sometimes lost) of the highest human loyalties. Nationalism is the most important driving force in international events. Finally, and most importantly, governments of nation-states, through their foreign-policy agents, are the only participants in world politics. All other groups interact in international relations through a recognized national government.[4]

The state-centric model has many shortcomings. Rather than systematically recounting the criticisms of the state-centric model (most should be quite obvious anyway), I find it more productive to state the major faults of the model and the assumptions on which it is based. First, the state-centric model ignores the existence and importance of regional international organizations. This particular omission is serious. The member-states of many such organizations, especially those that have joined to form common markets, have relinquished some sovereignty to permit the executive bodies (commissions) decisionmaking and enforcement powers in specified areas. Although these areas fall into the "low politics" (economic and social policies) category rather than that of "high politics" (expanding the scope of decisionmaking in areas such as security or diplomacy), membership in these organizations changes (or limits) many national decisionmaking processes and the decisions taken. The need to consult and coordinate has become, in many instances, a requirement.

The second major shortcoming of the state-centric model is as serious as the first. Given that power and conflict are preoccupations of political scientists, it is crucial to note that most of the incidents of international conflict since 1945 have involved largely, or exclusively, nonstate actors.[5] These nonstate actors include multinational corporations (e.g., ITT and the copper companies in Chile), stateless groups (the Palestine Liberation Organization, the Basques, and the Kurds), terrorist organizations (the Irish Republican Army, Black September, and so on), regional international organizations (the Organization of American States), and the United Nations Security Council and General Assembly.

A third shortcoming is an inability to account for the tremendous economic import of multinational corporations or the political import of stateless or transnational ethnic groups. The potential political power of multinational enterprises (MNEs) cannot be overemphasized. Charges by developing countries of neocolonialism and a whole body of "dependency theory" literature represent this concern. Many MNEs have such great wealth that were the annual gross sales of the largest MNEs (the "seven sisters," General Motors, and IBM, for example) equivalent to the gross national products of nation-states, they would rank among the top ten nations of the world. International terrorism has increased markedly since 1970. Not only have terrorist groups defied control by their own governments, but acts of terrorism have spread far beyond the geographical regions of these organizations and have become a global phenomenon.

Fourth, the state-centric model ignores, and therefore cannot account for, the important process of economic integration among nation-states.

This process is important politically and socially as well, particularly as nation-states become increasingly economically interdependent.

Finally, the state-centric model cannot explain or appreciate the greater importance that nation-states themselves have given international organizations. The perceived import often tends to be far greater than the actual one; yet the phenomenon of perceived import itself has great symbolic significance.

Nation-states are less inclined to employ unilateral military and economic measures in the contemporary environment of "balance of terror" and increased reliance on imports of energy sources and raw materials. As a consequence, more states are opting for security alliances and collective diplomatic measures. For reasons of convenience or expediency, these measures are attempted through international organizations or made necessary by the actions of transnational substate actors. The scope and intensity of nonstate actor involvement in international events are illustrated well in the crises that began in Iran in November 1979 and in Afghanistan in December 1979.

Nonstate Actors in the Iran and Afghanistan Crises

On November 4, 1979, a mob overran the U.S. Embassy compound in Teheran, Iran.[6] Militant students occupied the Embassy and announced that the captured U.S. personnel would be held hostage until the shah of Iran was returned. Despite assurances from the Bazargan government that the hostages would be released, the Ayatollah Khomeini announced support for the militants, and Bazargan resigned. The newly appointed "overseer" at the Iranian Foreign Ministry, Abdul Bani-Sadr (who would later become president of Iran) set three conditions for the release of the hostages: (1) the United States must admit that the property and fortune of the shah were stolen; (2) the United States must promise to refrain from further intervention in Iranian affairs; and (3) the United States must extradite the shah to Iran for trial.

Forty-eight days later, a second major crisis occurred in the Gulf area. On December 22, the Soviet Union began an invasion of Afghanistan, eventually committing 85,000 Soviet combat troops. President Hafizullah Amin was ousted from power and executed for "crimes against the state" in a coup supported by Soviet troops. The USSR brought in the former deputy prime minister, Babrak Karmal, from his exile in Eastern Europe to be the new president. This crisis both exacerbated and occurred in response to the Iranian crisis. The Soviets feared the fundamentalist Moslem revolution in Iran would spill over into Afghanistan and, perhaps, into South Asian provinces of the USSR.

The move may have been prompted also by U.S. preoccupation with Iran.

The majority of foreign policy actions taken by the United States in response to these crises were unilateral actions. U.S. naval and marine forces were moved into the Gulf and Indian Ocean in large numbers. President Carter ordered economic sanctions against Iran and the Soviet Union. On November 12, the president directed a ban on U.S. purchases of Iranian oil under provisions of the Trade Expansion Act. Two days later, he issued Executive Order 12170 declaring a national emergency in respect to Iran, and froze approximately $8 billion of Iranian assets in U.S. banks at home and abroad. After the crisis had continued for several months without any substantive moves by Iran to resolve it, in April 1980 Carter issued Executive Orders 12205 and 12211, which prohibited most exports to and all financial dealings with Iran. In addition, restrictions on travel to Iran were imposed under the Immigration and Nationality Act. Soon after, all Iranian diplomats and military personnel were declared persona non grata and ordered to leave the United States. A rescue attempt on April 24 failed, and eight U.S. soldiers and airmen were killed when two rescue aircraft collided on the ground.

In response to the Soviet invasion of Afghanistan, President Carter announced on January 5, 1980, a sharp curtailment of grain shipments to the USSR, suspension of high-technology sales, and limits on fishing privileges for Soviet fishing vessels in U.S. waters. Although these and other unilateral actions were the most numerous of all U.S. responses to the crisis, they were not the most important actions taken.

A large number of nonstate actors played important parts in the Iranian and Afghanistan crises; the most significant of these was the United Nations (UN). From the beginning, the United States found the United Nations to be a useful policy tool for the crisis, even though it had long been considered a natural ally of the Third World. Six days after the embassy takeover in Teheran, the UN Security Council urged Iran to release the hostages immediately. On November 14, Iran requested a Security Council meeting to consider the United States' "threats of war," but the United States blocked such a session pending release of the hostages. On November 22, UN Secretary-General Kurt Waldheim became personally involved. Waldheim offered to appoint a commission of international legal experts to investigate Iran's grievances, if the hostages were freed. When the offer was rejected by Iran, Waldheim requested an urgent meeting of the Security Council. This time the United States supported such a meeting, as the session was clearly intended to consider the hostage question. Moreover, it was only the second time in nineteen years that a UN Secretary-General had requested a Security Council meeting. Despite Iran's refusal to send a representative and Khomeini's charge that the Council was but a tool of the United States, and after four long difficult sessions over the wording of the resolution, the Security Council on December 4 unanimously approved a resolution urgently demanding that Iran release the U.S. hostages. Five days before the resolution passed, the United States decided to involve yet another organ of the United Nations. The International Court of Justice (ICJ) was asked to judge Iran for violations of three conventions and one treaty, as a result of seizing the embassy and holding the hostages. Again, Iran boycotted the proceedings and announced it would ignore any decision, as the Court "had no jurisdiction in this matter." The ICJ began deliberations on December 11. On December 15, it ruled unanimously that Iran must release the hostages and declared the inviolability of diplomatic envoys, a fundamental basis of relation between states.

The United States returned to the Security Council to remedy the Iranian crisis on December 31. Having first expressed reservations about the effectiveness of trade embargoes against Iran and twice delaying a demand for UN sanctions due to Waldheim's ill-fated trip to Iran, the United States won an 11 to 0 vote in the Security Council to give Iran one week in which to release the hostages or face UN-imposed economic sanctions. On January 13, however, the delayed resolution that would have imposed sanctions against Iran was vetoed by the Soviet Union. U.S. Ambassador Donald McHenry called the Soviet action "a cynical and irresponsible effort to divert attention away from its invasion of Afghanistan." The Soviets countered that sanctions would destroy the Iranian revolution and charged that the United States was aggravating the Iranian crisis by resorting to the United Nations, an ironic assertion given the raison d'être of that organization.

The Security Council and the World Court were not the only UN bodies involved in the crisis. The UN General Assembly adopted, without dissent, a code outlawing the taking of hostages. At the bequest of the United States, Secretary-General Waldheim went to Iran on January 1, 1980, to seek the release of the hostages. After he was refused permission to see either the hostages or Khomeini, Waldheim returned to New York disappointed after only three days in Teheran. Later, Waldheim appointed a five-member commission of international jurists that visited Iran on February 23. However, it too was prevented from seeing the hostages and returned on March 11 without releasing an official report on its many days of hearing Iran's grievances against the United States.

The United Nations served a more important purpose during the Afghanistan crisis. On January 3, the United States and forty-two western and Third World nations joined in calling for an urgent meeting of the Security Council. The debate in that body began the following day, and a resolution demanding the immediate withdrawal of Soviet troops from Afghanistan received a favorable 13 to 2 vote on January 7. As expected, however, the Soviets cast one of the dissenting votes and vetoed the resolution. Soviet delegate Troyonovsky labeled the resolution "a flagrant intervention in the internal affairs of a sovereign state." After a communication failure in the Philippine Foreign Ministry that caused a twenty-four-hour delay, the Security Council sent the resolution to the General Assembly where the Soviets could not exercise a veto. An emergency debate on the resolution, backed most vehemently by several Asian nations, began on January 10. The Soviet Union won a tactical victory by causing a four-day delay in the debate. Their hope was to retard as long as possible the political momentum built up among Third World nations against the invasion. However, the General Assembly vote on January 14 was a surprisingly resounding defeat for the USSR. The resolution to "strongly deplore" Soviet intervention in Afghanistan and to call for "immediate, unconditional, and total withdrawal" passed 104 to 18 to 18.

Other UN agencies responded strongly to the Afghanistan crisis. The World Bank halted disbursement of funds for fourteen projects underway and eight projects being appraised in Afghanistan. In February, the UN Human Rights Commission adopted, by a 27 to 8 vote, a resolution condemning the Soviet intervention as "aggression against human rights and a violation against the freedom of peoples." The Commission also called for immediate and unconditional withdrawal by the Soviets.

The United States did not confine its unilateral efforts in the two crises to the United Nations. Indeed, the Carter administration knew that actions such as trade embargoes and an Olympic boycott would not succeed without cooperation and assistance from U.S. allies and many nonaligned countries. Important consultations occurred in the Organization for Economic Cooperation and Development (OECD), the General Agreement on Tariffs and Trade (GATT), and the Economic Summit of the Big Seven in Venice, Italy, in June 1980. But the most important fora for international action outside the United Nations were NATO and the European Community. When the crises occurred, the perception of the U.S. government was that its allies, unilaterally, had done "everything they could except hurt themselves." To increase allied support for actions against Iran, President Carter sent a delegation of ranking Treasury and State Department officials to Western Europe in early December 1979 to discuss multilateral economic measures against Iran. A few days later, Secretary of State Vance visited Britain, France, Italy, and West Germany, and attended the NATO foreign ministers' meeting in Brussels. Vance's mission was to encourage further proposals for economic retaliation against Iran, to coordinate a full-scale economic embargo in and through the United Nations, and to discuss Iran's system for evading the U.S. freeze of Iranian assets. The United States won support in the NATO meeting for the release of the hostages and for a plan seeking economic sanctions against Iran. Following the Soviet invasion of Afghanistan, Deputy Secretary of State Christopher held an urgent meeting in London on December 31, 1979, with high-level officials of the British, French, West German, Italian, and Canadian governments. The discussions in the meeting centered on whether the NATO countries should continue their representations in Afghanistan and what additional help might be provided to friendly countries bordering Afghanistan. Christopher then pressed for multilateral actions against the Soviets at the NATO emergency meeting on January 2, 1980.

NATO did not become intimately involved in the Iranian crisis. Iran, many member-states believed, was outside NATO's sphere of interest. The Afghanistan crisis was quite different. Because Soviet troops and armor were mobilized not only in and near Afghanistan but in the Warsaw Treaty Organization (WTO) countries as well, NATO took a profound interest in the crisis. Many NATO analysts had argued that the invasion occurred partly in reaction to the NATO decision to deploy new nuclear missiles in Western Europe. In mid-January, British Foreign Secretary Lord Carrington represented all NATO countries in his ten-day tour of countries affected by the Afghanistan crisis. The NATO supreme commander, General Bernard Rogers, reported that, in his view, the crisis posed serious implications for European security—a statement that irritated many European leaders (especially West German Chancellor Schmidt). At a mid-January NATO meeting, the NATO Council considered the possibility of an Olympic boycott, restrictions on sales of high technology to the USSR, and reductions in credits and subsidies on sales to the Soviet Union. In addition, all states (except France) pledged that they would not undercut or undermine each other on any steps they might have taken individually. The Soviets responded with a "European strategy" of their own, strenuously attempting to open gaps between Western Europe and the United States. The Soviet strategy played on the feeling in some European capitals that the United States had overreacted to the invasion of Afghanistan.

Secretary of State Vance met the foreign ministers of Britain, France, Italy, Japan, Canada, and West Germany in Bonn on February 25, in another effort to shore up the alliance and coordinate policies toward Iran and the Soviet Union. This meeting followed his bilateral meetings in Bonn, Rome, Paris, and London five days earlier. As in previous meetings, the allies issued strongly worded statements and moved closer to an agreement on a boycott of the Moscow Olympics, but U.S. efforts to achieve agreements on economic sanctions against Iran and the Soviet Union were frustrated in the NATO forum. The Carter administration found that it had to deal with its Western European allies through the European Community (EC) if it hoped to achieve these measures.

The nine member-states of the European Community first became actively involved in the crises in early January 1980. All nine agreed not to undermine curtailment of U.S. grain shipments to the Soviet Union but were divided as to whether they should halt sales of other commodities, fearing that a complete curtailment of food sales would bring a return of cold war conditions. However, the executive body of the European Community, the Commission, acted independently of the member-states' governments, and suspended export subsidies and the granting of licenses for grain and dairy products to the USSR. The Commission refused to go along with the general trade sanctions requested by the United States, however. Later in January, the European Community decided to donate $20 million to Pakistan to assist the Afghanistan refugees there.

On February 19, 1980, while meeting under the political cooperation arrangement created separate from but adjacent to the EC structure, the foreign ministers of the nine member-states offered to guarantee the neutrality of Afghanistan if the USSR withdrew, but the Soviets refused. In March, the EC foreign ministers took up the question of actions against Iran for the first time. Although a diplomatic break with Iran was seriously considered, no action was taken.

In mid-April, the United States demonstrated its frustration with inaction by its allies. The Carter administration pressured the EC for a ban on all exports to Iran and for "strong diplomatic moves." The EC ignored the call for sanctions but issued its strongest denunciation of Iran, as did the Council of Europe meeting in Lisbon on April 10. On April 12, the EC member-states' ambassadors to Iran and the Japanese ambassador to Iran met with Iranian President Bani-Sadr to personally protest the holding of U.S. hostages. And in a summit meeting of the heads of state and government of the nine member-states in Luxembourg on April 22, the EC decided that the member-states would cut their diplomatic staffs in Teheran and would impose economic sanctions by May 17 if the hostages were not released. Two days later, Canada and Japan followed suit on this move, which was intended to conform to the UN Security Council resolution vetoed by the USSR on January 13. Although the decisions appeared to be a victory for the United States, the May 17 deadline passed without substantive action by the allies of the United States.

U.S. actions in and through NATO and the EC were clearly the most aggressive and important, but those regional international governmental organizations (IGOs) were but two of many such organizations the United States consulted and attempted to involve in the search for solutions to the two crises. It is fair to say that the U.S. government contacted in some fashion virtually every IGO. Some examples may help to illustrate the scope of those efforts. In November, Charles T. Schultze, chairman of the Council of Economic Advisors, conferred with OECD members in Paris. The Arab League refused to permit the Iranians to address the November 22 conference and rejected an attempt by Libya and Syria to draw the League into the conflict. At the request of the United States, the Organization of American States (OAS) unanimously urged Iran to release the hostages.

In December, the Organization of Petroleum Exporting Countries (OPEC) discussed the Iranian situation but appeared to be most concerned with the U.S. freeze of Iranian assets, fearing that similar actions might be taken against other OPEC members in the future. At the January special meeting of the Islamic Conference, the Islamic foreign ministers, led by Saudi Arabia and Iraq, strongly criticized Iran for holding the hostages, but also approved a resolution opposing U.S. economic sanctions against Iran. The same conference produced the strongest criticism of the Soviet Union by a nonaligned group. The resolution calling for immediate and unconditional withdrawal of Soviet forces from Iran followed intensive consultations between Saudi Arabia, Kuwait, and Iraq on ways to keep the Gulf free of foreign intervention.

U.S. efforts to achieve coordinated actions were least successful with its OAS partners. Both Argentina and Brazil refused to join the grain embargo against the USSR. The Soviets managed to lessen the impact of the U.S. grain embargo by buying grain from South America through private exporters as early as late January 1980.

Private transnational groups (banks, corporations, and labor unions) had important roles in the crises; many were unwillingly drawn into the subsequent events. The Carter administration's decision to freeze Iranian assets threatened serious harm to the international banking and payments systems. Almost immediately, currency markets were thrown into turmoil. Reactions from the international business community were strong; for example, the director of the Union of Arab Chambers of Commerce, Burhan Dajan, warned that the freeze would adversely affect U.S.-Arab economic relations. The freeze affected U.S. banks, as well as their subsidiaries and many non-U.S. banks. UBAF Arab American Bank of New York, European-American Banking Corporation, Morgan Guaranty Trust Company, the Chemical Bank, Crocker National Bank, and Wells Fargo Bank NA, among others, filed suits involving Iranian funds. Suits in Britain, France, and West Germany were filed both by banks and the Iranian government. Morgan Guaranty Trust succeeded in attaching Iran's 25-percent interests in Fried, Krupp GmbH and Deutsche Babcock AG. European and Japanese banks were warned by the U.S. government that should they fail to take strong action to safeguard their loans to Iran, they would not share in the distribution of Iranian assets seized by U.S. banks, and many European banks declared loans to Iran to be in default. This prompted a high-level team of U.S. officials to make a quick tour of European cities in an attempt to reduce friction among bankers caused by the freeze.

The roles of multinational corporations (MNCs) in, and as a result of, the crises were pervasive and often crucial. To relate all that is known (much is not public knowledge) would entail more time and space than is practical here, but a few examples should suffice. When the Iranian crisis began, the State Department strongly advised the sixteen U.S. MNCs operating in Iran to immediately evacuate their U.S. employees. The Fluor Corporation was the first to respond, moving its fifty-two employees out of Iran and halting work on the oil refinery it was building. Many other MNCs (though not all) followed Fluor's lead. When President Carter announced a ban on all oil from Iran, all U.S. oil companies operating in or trading with Iran supported him fully. Following the Soviet intervention in Afghanistan and the president's decision to freeze shipments of grain, high-technology products, and strategic goods intended for the USSR, a great many more MNCs were affected. The Aluminum Company of America (ALCOA) was the first of many U.S. firms to suspend completely all trade with the Soviet Union, despite the general feeling among industrialists that economic measures would pose more serious problems for them than for the Soviets. ALCOA later scrapped plans to build a smelter plant in Siberia. The National Broadcasting Company, Coca-Cola Company, and others canceled contracts related to the Moscow Olympics. In one of the more concerted efforts, Armand Hammer, chairman of Occidental Petroleum Company, personally met with Soviet Premier Brezhnev to explain the reasons for the phosphate ban against the Soviet Union.

Labor unions were important independent actors during the initial months of the crisis. Five days after the U.S. Embassy was seized in Teheran, International Longshoremen's Union (ILU) leader Thomas W. Gleason announced a union boycott of all Iranian ships. The International Transport Workers joined the ban on November 25, and the ban was extended against servicing all ships and aircraft bound for Iran. Following the Afghanistan crisis, the ILU directed its members to stop handling Soviet ships and cargoes in all U.S. ports. Teamsters at Dulles International Airport in Washington, D.C., delayed a Soviet Aeroflot jetliner for two hours to protest the invasion of Afghanistan. Unionized baggage handlers and ground service personnel then refused to service any Soviet aircraft. A serious incident occurred on January 31, 1980, when air traffic control personnel at Kennedy International erased radar data used to guide Soviet aircraft, and jeopardized a Soviet plane carrying Soviet Ambassador Dobrynin. The actions of the ILU and others caused some consternation in the U.S. government. A State Department spokesman announced, somewhat testily, that foreign policy decisions would be left to the president and his branch of government, and not be made outside of it.

Other international nongovernmental organizations (INGOs) figured importantly in their reactions to the two crises. The Helsinki Watch Committee, the International League for Human Rights, the College of Cardinals, and the Committee for American-Iranian Crisis Resolution took actions ranging from visiting the U.S. hostages to issuing formal resolutions condemning Iran, the Soviet Union, and the United States (for the screening of Iranian students in the United States). The most important INGO was the International Olympic Committee (IOC). The United States decided in mid-January to boycott the Moscow Olympics if the Soviets did not withdraw their troops from Afghanistan by mid-February. The Soviets had relegated great political import to their hosting the summer Olympic games, and it was thought that sending a team to Moscow was tantamount to acquiescence to Soviet actions in Afghanistan. Consequently, U.S. government officials began to exert great pressure on the IOC and the U.S. Olympic Committee (USOC). The United States also asked for support from its allies and from the forty-nine-nation Supreme Council for Sport in Africa. The USOC voted unanimously in late January to ask to IOC to postpone, cancel, or transfer the Moscow games, but the IOC refused. U.S. Secretary of State Vance personally pleaded for the removal of the games from Moscow at the IOC's meeting at Lake Placid, New York, February 9–11. Again, the IOC refused. President Carter then directed efforts at the USOC and the U.S. allies to achieve a boycott of the Moscow Olympics. Threatening to use the Emergency Powers Act, Carter succeeded at home when the USOC House of Delegates voted 1604 to 797 on April 12 to boycott the 1980 Olympics. The vote followed a personal appeal by Vice-President Mondale. The IOC met in Switzerland in late April to head off the boycott and was more successful than was the United States in its efforts to convince other nations to stay away from the Moscow Olympics. However, the IOC provided an important forum from which the United States attacked politically and diplomatically the Soviet invasion of Afghanistan.

Stateless groups or transnational ethnic groups are nonstate actors that played more destructive than constructive roles in efforts to resolve the two crises. In fact, they often served only to prolong or exacerbate the conflicts. The best known of these groups, the Palestine Liberation Organization (PLO), seemed out of character in the initial days of the Iranian crisis. The PLO let it be known that it was willing to intercede with Iran to secure the release of the hostages. The U.S. government announced that it would accept help "from anyone." Abu Jihad (leader of Al Fatah) and Abu Walid made such a mission to Teheran on orders from PLO leader Yasir Arafat. On November 24, however, a PLO spokesman denied that the PLO ever intended to intercede for the United States. A few days later, the United States charged that the PLO had trained the militants who captured the U.S. Embassy in Teheran and had provided technical assistance in the subsequent mining of the embassy compound perimeter. The charge appeared more plausible when late in December hundreds of Iranians prepared to leave for Lebanon to aid the Palestinian guerrillas there. That effort was thwarted by Lebanese President Sarkis, who ordered his security forces to bar Iranians from entering Lebanon to fight Israel.

Transnational ethnic groups were partly responsible for the initiation and prolongation of both crises. The Pushtans and Baluchis in Afghanistan and Pakistan had demanded political autonomy for years in their respective regions. Their continued activities helped to weaken the Amin government and to prompt Soviet armed intervention. In Iran, the new revolutionary government experienced serious destabilizing threats by several groups committed to political autonomy or separation. The Azerbaijanis, Kurds, Baluchis, and Arab Iranians perceived the dominant Persian group as the "real imperialist enemy" in Iran, and political violence was frequent and pervasive. The revolts were particularly threatening to Khomeini, because by opposing the new constitution they attacked the theological underpinnings of the revolution. It is probable that one of the major reasons for Khomeini's support for the seizure of the U.S. Embassy and hostages and his vociferous campaign against "satan America" was an effort to distract the separatists and unite Iran against a common external enemy. In part, the continued resistance of ethnic minorities made release of the hostages and resolution of the crisis politically impractical for the shaky Iranian government.

Most of the political violence in Iran following the crisis occurred in the northwest province of Azerbaijanistan. Turkish speaking and Sunni Moslems, the Azerbaijani followers of Ayatollah Shariat-Madari opposed both the establishment of an Islamic republic and the concentration of power in the hands of Khomeini and the Persian Shiite majority. In early December 1979, Azerbaijanis occupied local government buildings and the governor's mansion in Tabriz and gained effective control of Azerbaijanistan Province. Demonstrations and clashes with Khomeini supporters in the holy city of Qom left three dead and prompted Khomeini to appeal on statewide radio for national unity. Following unsuccessful negotiations between Khomeini and Shariat-Madari, thousands of Azerbaijanis demonstrated in the streets of the provincial capital, Tabriz, and demanded the removal of non-Azerbaijani troops from the area. Azerbaijani and Iranian government troops clashed in Tabriz and twelve revolutionary guards were taken hostage. Renewed fighting broke out in early January. At least ten were killed, and many more were wounded. Iranian authorities summarily tried and executed eleven Azerbaijanis, after Iranian government troops overran Shariat-Madari's fortified opposition party's headquarters in an assault that killed two more individuals. Rioting erupted following the executions. Battles over control of the radio-television station in Tabriz left three dead and sixty injured. Control of the station changed several times. In early February, air force officers were arrested in Tabriz for allegedly supplying arms to the outlawed Moslem People's Party and for plotting a coup of the government.

The Kurds in Kurdistan Province also opposed the new Iranian constitution. Like the Azerbaijanis, the Kurds enjoyed a modicum of political autonomy under the shah, and expected far more after the revolution. The Kurds opened a new offensive against the government on November 13, after their leader, Sheik Ezzedin Hosseini, sent a message of solidarity to Shariat-Madari. However, Khomeini's "fear of the United States" strategy appeared to work in late November. The Kurds announced a truce and vowed to join the Iranian army should the United States attack Iran. The truce, however, was short-lived. Like the other Iranian ethnic minorities, the Kurds boycotted the constitutional election. Uprisings throughout the province in early December brought strong government reprisals. Helicopters bombed villages near the city of Rezaiyeh; elite commandos surrounded the main market city of Sanandaj. Heavy fighting and casualties returned in a four-day battle, January 30 through February 3, 1980. Subsequent street battles were waged in March when the Kurds sabotoged the oil fields in Kurdistan, and again in April in Sanandaj.

The Baluchi revolt began in late December 1979. Three people were killed and forty-eight wounded in clashes between Baluchis and Persians in Zahidan. The Iranian government declared a state of emergency in the southeast area of the country and moved troops into Baluchistan. Ensuing battles between minority Seistanis and Baluchis caused eleven more deaths and at least eighty injuries. As gun battles and opposition to the Iranian government increased, leaders of both sides blamed "U.S. and Communist agents" for the trouble.

The last major ethnic group revolt occurred in the southwest province of Khuzistan. On January 4–6, 1980, a battle between Sunni Arabs and Shiite Persians in the Gulf City of Linegh left 43 killed and 110 injured. Ensuing clashes led to the beginning of the Iranian-Iraqi border dispute in April. The fighting spilled over into Beirut on April 15–17 between Shiite Moslems and the Iraq-supported Arab Liberation Front of the PLO. Violence had been extended previously as far away as Kuwait, Thailand, and the Philippines, where Moslem separatist groups demonstrated and planted bombs at U.S. embassies. The most explosive incident external to Iran occurred in London on April 30. Iranian Arabs from Khuzistan Province seized the Iranian embassy and held 13 hostages until British forces stormed the embassy and freed the hostages on May 5.

Conclusions

The events described in the preceding case study do not include all that occurred during the crises in Afghanistan and Iran. Indeed, one might even argue that given our focus on the involvement of nonstate actors in the crises, the most important actions (or those that occurred bilaterally between the protagonists or with other nation-states) were not adequately presented. The analysis does help, however, to illustrate the scope of involvement by nonstate actors and, at a minimum, the importance the United States placed on utilizing or having to take into account so many nonstate actors in its responses to the crises. Moreover, the analysis illustrates a major shortcoming of the state-centric model. Clearly, that model would not have encouraged one to appreciate the salience of so many nonstate actors in either crisis. The case study analysis also challenges the assertion that interstate relations with international organizations are little more than a collection of bilateral relationships. For instance, the member-states of the European Community were determined to respond collectively to requests from the Carter administration for assistance in the crises. That imperative to speak with one voice often rendered British actions equal only to how far the French or West Germans were willing to go, or the French perhaps more cooperative than they might otherwise have been.

The study of nonstate actors in world politics will promote a greater understanding of contemporary international relations. That study should be based on a clear typology of nonstate actors, what those actors do, and how they organize to perform those functions and make decisions. These concerns are outlined next in Chapter 2. Chapter 3 completes the framework for this analysis with a survey of theories of international integration. The discussion of these theories should assist in subsequent analysis and evaluation of nonstate actors and their roles in world politics.

Notes

1. From Richard W. Mansbach, Yale H. Ferguson, and Donald E. Lampert, *The Web of World Politics: Non-State Actors in the Global System* (Englewood Cliffs, N.J.: Prentice-Hall, 1976), p. 25.

2. See Robert O. Keohane and Joseph S. Nye, Jr., *Power and Interdependence: World Politics in Transition* (Boston: Little, Brown and Co., 1977), Ch. 1.

3. See James N. Rosenau (Ed.), *Linkage Politics* (New York: Free Press, 1969), pp. 1–15.

4. Mansbach, Ferguson, and Lampert, *World Politics*, pp. 2–6.

5. See, for example, J. S. Nye, *Peace in Parts: Integration and Conflict in International Organization* (Boston: Little, Brown and Co., 1971); also, Mansbach, Ferguson, and Lampert, *World Politics*, pp. 275–278, 281.

6. The information contained in the remainder of this chapter was taken from numerous articles that appeared in the *New York Times* and *Washington Post*, as well as from personal interviews conducted in the Bureau of International Organizations Affairs and Bureau of Politico-Military Affairs, U.S. Department of State.

2
A Framework for Analysis

The value of the study of nonstate actors in world politics continues to increase for students of international relations. As the number of nonstate actors increases and their involvement in world affairs broadens, our need to understand who these actors are and how and why they affect political and economic outcomes in our world also increases. Such a study must proceed from a solid framework for analysis; this chapter contains a brief presentation of such a framework.

The first step in constructing a framework for the analysis of nonstate actors is to define clearly the units of analysis. To this end, it is more useful to construct a typology of the units rather than to attempt an exhaustive list of all nonstate actors. The second step is the most important one. Having identified and classified the units of analysis, one should ask, "What do nonstate actors do?" The identification of the purpose(s) and function(s) of a nonstate actor is crucial for two reasons. First, it is difficult to understand any political actor without first determining its reasons for existence or its stated goals and objectives. Evaluative terms such as organizational effectiveness and system maintenance are virtually inapplicable without this information. Second, the normative reasons for studying international organizations and other nonstate actors centers on the question, "What good or ill do they do?" It is the quest for answers to this question that makes the study important in and of itself and more than an abstract intellectual exercise.

The third step is to look for structures and processes. Knowledge of how groups organize to fulfill a purpose, perform certain functions, and produce specific decisions is important to our understanding of the behavior of any actor in world politics. These three steps, taken and applied consistently and coherently, permit comparative analysis and evaluation of nonstate actors. Moreover, the approach establishes the groundwork for theory-building and the application and testing of existing theories.

The Units of Analysis

The simplest definition of nonstate actors is that they are entities other than nation-states that interact in the international political system. Unfortunately, that definition is both too simplistic and too broad. It would include, for example, substate groups that perhaps only once or incidentally enter the international arena. It might also include individuals acting in some capacity other than as officials of a nation-state's government. Although many scholars argue for including both in a definition of nonstate actors, and although individuals and groups solely composed of citizens of one state often become salient actors in international politics (when acting independently of their respective nation-states' governments), these individuals and groups are relatively less important over time. The nonstate actors that constitute the units of analysis in this text are those that are (1) transnational (i.e., consisting of individuals or groups residing in two or more states) and (2) formally organized. This definition is somewhat restrictive, but given the plethora of nonstate actors today, it is necessary to focus on those that are relatively larger and more permanent.

The creation of a typology of nonstate actors may be approached in many ways. One way might be to classify nonstate actors on the basis of their size, memberships, geographical location, purpose, function, importance, longevity, and so on. One of the more common classifications of international organizations places all organizations whose members are nation-states into one group, namely, international governmental organizations (IGOs), and those whose members are not nation-states into another, namely, international non-governmental organizations (INGOs). Another common method is to group them according to the geographical scope of their memberships: regional groups and supraregional (or global) groups. A more specific typology can be achieved by combining these categories, making the latter (geography of membership) subclasses of the former (IGOs and INGOs). This yields four categories: regional IGOs, supraregional IGOs, regional INGOs, and supraregional INGOs. These four classes are useful, but they still compress too many dissimilar organizations into categories too broadly defined. Further classification is necessary.

A third common technique is to classify groups by the functions they perform. Although this exercise is more difficult, given the many multifunction organizations or those whose actual or latent function differs from the group's stated purpose, it can be achieved. By considering the functions or tasks they perform, we can place nonstate actors (if not neatly, then conveniently) into four general categories: economic, security, political, and cultural/ideological functional groups. The functions of those in the economic category include increasing intragroup trade, economic development, elimination or reduction of dysfunctional economic competition, "control" of dominant nonmember-states and multinational corporations, and the like. Security groups contain members who join for mutual security (i.e., pledge to come to each other's aid should any or all sustain an attack from outside the group) or collective security (i.e., members who eliminate conflict by transforming old enemies into new allies of the same organization). Political organizations are those that seek to increase intragroup communication, settle disputes among member-states through multilateral diplomatic means, caucus to "speak with one voice" to more powerful nonmember-states or within other international organizations, and so on. Cultural/ideological task-oriented groups reflect the ethnic, national, religious, kinship, and/or philosophical bonds that members of those groups wish to preserve or expand through concerted unified efforts.

When the four functional classes are added as subclasses to the four membership categories, a typology of sixteen categories is created. This arrangement is illustrated in the 4 × 4 matrix format in Table 2.1. Economic supraregional IGOs include the General Agreement on Tariffs and Trade (GATT), the Organization for Economic Cooperation and Development (OECD), the Organization of Petroleum Exporting Countries (OPEC), and other commodity cartels. Economic regional IGOs consist of common markets such as the European Community (EC), the Andean Common Market (ANCOM), and the Association of South East Asian Nations (ASEAN), free trade associations (e.g., the European Free Trade Association [EFTA] and Latin American Free Trade Association [LAFTA]), and development banks. Economic supraregional INGOs are best represented by multinational corporations (the major oil companies, auto manufacturers, and communications firms). Economic regional INGOs include organizations like the Union of Arab Chambers of Commerce.

The major security supraregional IGOs are the United Nations Security Council (UNSC) and the North Atlantic Treaty Organization (NATO), and the major security regional IGOs are the Warsaw Treaty Organization (WTO), the Central Treaty Organization (CENTO), and the ANZUS Pact. Security INGOs are few in number. International consortia or arms procedures/marketing agents and multinational corporations such as Lockheed, McDonnell-Douglas, and Mirage fall into the security supraregional INGO group. Security regional INGOs include the Jewish Defense League (JDL), the Irish Republican Army (IRA), and the Ulster Protestant Vanguard (UPV).

Political organizations are frequently considered to be multipurpose organizations, but it is their political function that is most salient. The

TABLE 2.1. Nonstate Actors by Membership and Function

		ECONOMIC	SECURITY	POLITICAL	CULTURAL/ IDEOLOGICAL
INTERNATIONAL GOVERNMENTAL ORGANIZATION	SUPRAREGIONAL	OECD GATT OPEC CIPEC	UNSC NATO	UNGA	ISLAMIC COUNCIL
	REGIONAL	EC ANCOM ASEAN ECOWAS EFTA LAFTA DEV. BANKS	WTO CENTO ANZUS (SEATO)	OAS OAU COUNCIL OF EUROPE	ARAB LEAGUE NORDIC COUNCIL
INTERNATIONAL NON-GOVERNMENTAL ORGANIZATIONS	SUPRAREGIONAL	EXXON SHELL ITT IBM GM	INT'L ARMS CONSORTIA	INTERNATIONAL LABOR UNIONS	AMNESTY INT'L IOC HELSINKI WATCH COMMITTEE
	REGIONAL	UNION OF ARAB CHAMBERS OF COMMERCE	JDL IRA UPV	PLO	IBOs BASQUES KURDS AZERBAIJANIS PUSHTANS

most visible political supraregional IGO is the United Nations General Assembly (UNGA). Examples of political regional IGOs are the Organization of American States (OAS), the Organization for African Unity (OAU), and the Council of Europe. International Labor Organizations (such as the World Federation of Trade Unions [WFTU] and the World Confederation of Labor [WCL]) are examples of political supraregional INGOs. The most salient political regional INGO is the Palestine Liberation Organization (PLO).

Cultural/ideological organizations are similar to political organizations; often these groups perform the same functions. The distinction is a matter of personal choice, as is the determination of where any group is placed in our typology of nonstate actors. Again, the distinction should be made on the basis of which function is perceived to be the most important or salient. Therefore, the best example of a cultural/ideological supraregional IGO is the Islamic Council; the Arab League and Nordic Council are considered to be cultural/ideological regional IGOs. There are many cultural/ideological supraregional INGOs. The International Olympic Committee (IOC), the Helsinki Watch Committee, and Amnesty International are the best known examples. The final category, cultural/ideological regional INGOs, contain transnational ethnic groups such as the Ibos, Basques, Kurds, Azerbaijanis, Baluchis, and Pushtans.

The typology of nonstate actors just presented should not be taken as the only possible arrangement; indeed, it is not intended to represent even the epitome of any such effort. Students of world politics will differ as to which actors properly belong to any given classification, even among those scholars who employ the same general typology. The system explained here is only a means to better operationalize the definition of types of nonstate actors discussed in this text. It must be pointed out again (as it was in the preface to this book) that this volume is devoted to those organizations outside the United Nations and its specialized agencies. Hence, not all the groups depicted in Table 2.1 will be examined in this text.

What Nonstate Actors Do

All IGOs and most INGOs declare formally the purposes of the organization in the charter or convention that legally binds the members of that organization or in a published statement of principles. Logically, the first step in analyzing what nonstate actors do is to examine the stated purposes of the organizations. One of the most significant outcomes of the analysis should be an evaluation of performance and behavior compared to those announced purposes. The charter that establishes an IGO normally contains specific goals and objectives as well as "competences" assigned to the organization and the institutions created for that organization. The intended functions of an INGO may not appear in a public document (at least not totally) and therefore must be garnered from public statements of the group's leaders or by examining the long-term behavior of a given organization. Many nonstate actors perform either more or fewer tasks than the organization was created to accomplish. Often, a multipurpose organization will take on additional functions not originally intended for that organization. The resultant complexity underscores the need to examine initially and very carefully the behavior intended for any given organization upon its creation.

As explained earlier in this chapter, state actors perform many functions. Two functions are common to all international organizations. First, nonstate actors are created and maintained as means of cooperation among states or groups in two or more states to perform tasks in areas where cooperation is deemed advantageous to all or most of the members of the organization. Second, nonstate actors provide multiple channels of communication among the members to facilitate accommodation or consensus formation when needs or problems arise.

Nonstate actors perform at least one and often many of the following more specific functions: (1) to provide security, to promote or maintain peace; (2) to increase the economic standards of its members; (3) to preserve or promote ethnic or ideological identity; (4) to promote political and social goals among nations (e.g., human rights and social welfare); (5) to coordinate common positions and "speak with one voice" on issues before the United Nations and other international organizations; (6) to respond collectively to other nonstate actors (e.g., common markets or international labor to multinational corporations, international interest groups to economic IGOs). The identification of the functions performed by any given nonstate actor is an essential step in the analysis and evaluation of that actor. If one accepts the functionalists' premise that "form follows function" (or even if one doesn't), the next logical step is to identify the structures created to perform organizational tasks and to analyze the decisionmaking process(es) of that organization.

Structures

The performance of international/multilateral tasks requires that nonstate actors create institutions to coordinate policies, manage funds and programs, and facilitate decisionmaking. With the exception of regional IGOs, international organizations often create very elaborate institutional structures to fulfill these needs. Institution building is an essential task when new international organizations are created; it frequently becomes an ongoing feature of the integration process as organizations expand the scope of competences assigned the organization.

The typical structure of an IGO contains at least a council, a secretariat, and an executive body or commission. Other institutional features of most IGOs are an assembly or parliament, an economic and social committee, and a court or board to adjudicate disputes and/or interpret provisions of the charter. This typical structural arrangement (illustrated in Figure 2.1) breaks down as follows:

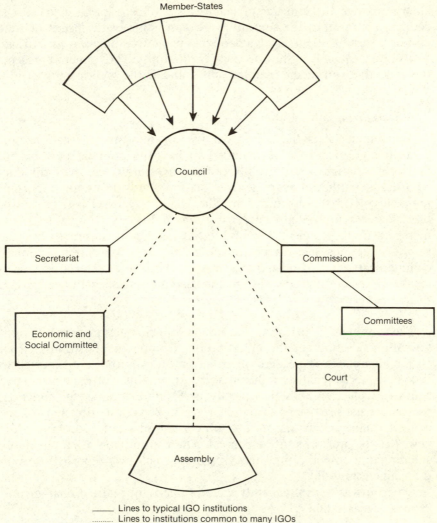

Figure 2.1   Typical Structure of an International Organization

The Council

The council performs the rule-making function of the organization. It is usually composed of one official of ministerial rank (or his deputy) from each of the member-states. The official is most often the foreign minister, except when the subject for discussion is within the specific competence of another cabinet member (energy, finance, agriculture, social welfare, industry and commerce, and so on) or, as in security alliances, when the minister of defense is the more logical choice. The council may meet at the summit level (consisting of the heads of state and/or government), as always happens in the Organization for African Unity and frequently in the European Community. The council represents the collective will of the member-states and is the highest authority in IGOs.

The Secretariat

The secretariat is the administrative organ of an international organization. Generally, it is intended to have no political powers, but due to the continuity and visibility of this institution and the individual who heads it (the secretary-general), it frequently takes an important political role in the organization. The secretary-general is a citizen of one of the member-states chosen by and politically acceptable to the members of the council. The secretariat's major tasks are to manage routine functions such as personnel, payroll, transportation, supplies, communications, and other types of support. The secretariat is always located in the city considered to be the headquarters of that organization.

The Commission

The commission performs the policy-implementation and program-formation functions of the organization. Composed of nationals from all member-states, its leaders often become (or, indeed, are expected to become) internationalists rather than representatives of their respective countries. The commission typically performs a "watchdog" function, overseeing the provisions of the charter, implementing decisions of the council, managing funds and ongoing programs, and recommending new rules or programs to the council. The commission often has many standing and ad-hoc committees, some of which may report directly to the council as well.

Other institutions frequently incorporated by international organizations are as follows:

The Assembly

Assemblies or parliaments in IGOs never serve the same function (legislation) that such bodies perform (or nominally perform) in national governments. They are, at best, advisory bodies that represent political parties or factions from all the member-states. A frequent practice is for each member-state to send a few members of its foreign ministry or national parliament to the international assembly; only recently has one IGO, the European Community, permitted direct elections to its assembly, the European Parliament. Assemblies may be given some control over the operating portion of the budget, and the commission (but never the council) may be nominally accountable to the assembly, but these are relatively minor powers. In no IGO is the council required to involve the assembly in the decisionmaking process.

The Economic and Social Committee

Economic and social committees are advisory assemblies of representatives of business, labor, agriculture, and professional interest groups. They serve to channel (but not replace) the "lobbying" activities of these groups. Economic and social committees can be important sounding boards and public fora in IGOs, but they generally lack any real power as an institution. They are institutionalized bodies that must pass resolutions that reflect a consensus of the many diverse interests represented in that body. Seats in the economic and social committee are proportional for each member-state based on the relative size of its population, and individuals are selected for those seats by the respective member-states.

The Court

In those IGOs with an international court, that institution may be little more than a board of arbitration (e.g., the Community Tribunal in the Economic Community of West African States), a body that renders advisory opinions to other principal bodies of the organization (as does the ICJ in the United Nations), or a court empowered to decide disputes between bodies of the organization and rule on whether acts of these institutions and the member-states are compatible with the charter provisions (as does the EC's European Court of Justice). Judges on the court represent all or the major member-states and are appointed by their respective national governments.

The structures of the many INGOs (multinational corporations, labor unions, and transnational ethnic groups) are so varied as to defy presentation of a typical example. The institutional arrangements of these nonstate actors will be considered individually later in the text.

Decisionmaking Processes

A nonstate actor's decisionmaking process is an important determinant of its behavior. The decisionmaking process reflects the degree of integration of an organization, as well as its functions and structures. In most IGOs, it is the council that makes decisions, but there are many factors that influence how decisions are made and the international character of these decisions. The major factors follow:

1. The charter of the organization will enumerate those areas for which the organization may make decisions on behalf of the member-states. The scope of these areas is important. Further, the charters of many IGOs prohibit the national governments from making decisions in areas reserved for the organization's competences.

2. The relationship between the council and other bodies, particularly the commission, is most important. A few organizations assign the power of initiative to the commission, others require prior consultation with other institutions, and a small number permit the organizations' courts to practice a form of judicial review. The extent to which there exists a formalized dialogue between the council and the commission is a feature important to the analysis of a given organization's behavior.

3. The access afforded other institutions, interest groups (both national and international), and individual citizens in the decisionmaking process, concomitant with the perceived need of these actors for access, is a measure of the character of the decisionmaking process. It reflects the degree of integration in that organization, the relative degree of "democratization" of the organization, and the extent to which decisions are taken by the organization or are a collection of national decisions.

4. The rules governing voting in the council must be an essential focus of the analysis. Majority rule and weighted voting systems based on the relative population sizes of the member-states are frequently provided but seldom employed. When significant majorities or unanimity are required, several outcomes may be expected. First, relatively fewer decisions will be taken. A requirement for unanimity means that any one member-state may veto any action, even though it may be desired by all others. Second, the decisions will be relatively less ambitious. They will reflect a compromise or the least common denominator (or the wishes of the most conservative member). Finally, the decisionmaking process may be extremely time consuming, requiring marathon negotiating sessions or weeks and months of political maneuvering to deal with problems, even those that may have been perceived initially as a crisis.

Again, decisionmaking in multinational corporations and transnational ethnic groups is quite different from that in most IGOs. Depending on the nature of the corporate structure and the network of subsidiaries or the personal force of the individual leader and the degree of intragroup factionalism, decisionmaking in these actors tends to be far more hierarchical or monolithic (and, perhaps, more efficient). The decisionmaking processes of these groups will be discussed on a case-by-case basis in Part 5 of this text.

Summary

The analysis and evaluation of nonstate actors must be based on a framework specifically constructed for the study of these groups. At a minimum, that framework should lead the student to a better understanding of what nonstate actors are, what they do, and how and why they behave as they do. Logically, this understanding requires a clear definition of the units of analysis, an examination of purposes and functions, and a study of the institutions and decisionmaking processes created to perform those functions and achieve organizational goals. This approach works well for both individual and comparative analysis. For those wishing an evaluative component for the analysis, a survey of theories of international integration is presented in Chapter 3.

3
Theories of
International Integration

Nonstate actors exist by integrating the governments of nation-states or groups of citizens of many states into a common organization. This chapter presents a survey of several efforts to explain the process of political integration necessary to the creation and continued existence of nonstate actors. It is hoped that this discussion will provide a basis for explaining an international organization's progression and probable future. I should point out initially that international integration theories contain an explicit value judgment: integration and the continuing process of integration are good things; disintegration and stagnation are not.

International integration has been a major area of concern in international relations for the past twenty years, and theories concerning the possibilities, stages, and dynamics of integration of nation-states into larger units are numerous. Almost as numerous are the attempts to categorize various schools of thought. For example, Altiero Spinelli suggests three "designs" for political integration: the functionalists, the confederalists, and the federalists.[1] Steven Warnecke concentrates on U.S. "sources" in his delineation of three major academic theories:[2] those of Karl Deutsch,[3] of Ernst Haas,[4] and of Leon Lindberg and Stuart Scheingold.[5] Charles Pentland has suggested four schools: the pluralists, the functionalists, the neofunctionalists, and the federalists.[6] The latter are probably the most frequently suggested categories; I have chosen them as a means of organizing the following discussion of the utility and inadequacies of international integration theory.

Pentland's four schools are not mutually exclusive, nor are they necessarily at odds with one another. Indeed, it is useful to view each of the four as having relatively more explanatory capabilities, depending on which aspect or stage of the integration process is under investigation. For example, the pluralists have more to offer to explain the impetus for and initial stages of regional integration, but they fail to address (or address too briefly) what maintains and keeps the process going or to what end the process is intended. The functionalists and neofunctionalists concern themselves little with the initial or final stages of regional integration, but concentrate instead on the dynamics of operating and expanding the process. Similarly, the federalists' concerns are of greatest utility in considering final stages and end-products, while offering little insight into initiating the process or linking means to ends. Viewed in this way, each school makes an essential contribution to understanding the entire process of regional integration.

The Pluralists

The pluralists' approach to integration sees a "community of states" engaged in a "continuous process of sensitive adjustment to each other's actions, supported usually (although not necessarily) by the socio-political behavior and attitudes of their populations."[7] This approach centers on several variables important to the formation of the community of states: historical, cultural, economic, social, political, and diplomatic exchanges among those states.

Of the major integration theorists, Karl Deutsch best represents the pluralist approach. In his *Political Community and the North Atlantic Area*, Deutsch puts forth several underlying definitions central to his approach:[8]

1. Security community: A group of people that has become "integrated."

2. Integration: "The attainment within a territory of a sense of community and of institutions and practices strong enough and wide-spread enough to assure for a long time dependable expectations of peaceful change among its population."

3. Sense of community: "A belief on the part of individuals in a group that they have come to agreement on at least this one point that common social problems must and can be resolved by processes of peaceful change."

4. Peaceful change: "The resolution of social problems normally institutionalized by institutionalized procedures without resort to large scale physical force."

5. Amalgamation: "The formal merger of two or more previously independent units into a single larger unit with some type of common government after amalgamation."

Deusch enlarges upon his central concept of the "security community" as follows:

> A political community is not necessarily able to prevent war within the area it covers. . . . Some political communities do, however, eliminate war and the expectation of war within their boundaries. . . . A security community, therefore, is one in which there is real assurance that the members of that community will not fight each other physically, but will settle their disputes in some other way.[9]

The concept of the security community centers on the linkage between transactions and conflict. According to the pluralists, this linkage process involves certain characteristics. First, some form of communication must be taking place. Normally this communication involves positive inter- actions, although hostile or negative communications represent a type of communication system also. Second, something of common interest must be present about which two parties can communicate. The mutual interest presumes both the physical capabilities to communicate (exchange messages, trade, etc.) and an identification of interests to allow meaningful communication to occur. Third, interacting nations are important to each other, and their basic relationship (as defined by the communication) is therefore different from those with whom they do not interact. Fourth, high international interaction is unlikely to be accompanied by high tension and conflict. In such cases, behavior tends to be institutionalized, and patterns of interaction arise. These patterns soon develop into standard procedures, which in turn develop into formal (international) organizations.[10] The process suggests that as communication between the units increases, the complexities inherent in such activities increase, causing the groups in the potential community to formalize their in- teractions to handle these complexities, which results in greater colla- boration. This mutual cooperation facilitates the formation of formal institutions to further simplify the relationships or to make decisions jointly for the states now involved as one unit. Once that stage has been reached, it is argued, further integration becomes more likely. Michael Sullivan suggests that the most insightful proposition of the pluralists is that truly integrated communities may not necessarily be those declared integrated by formal agreement, and that "using concepts from communication theory, Deutsch contended that those nations that contain high and consistent levels of communication, and transactions with each other may be more integrated than those that have signed agreements."[11] Surely, the relationship that has evolved between Canada and the United States is the best example of integration. In many ways, these two nations have more common economic, communications (mass media), cultural, ecological, and legal (e.g., relaxed restrictions at border crossings) policies than do the signatories of the Treaties of Rome.

The Functionalists and Neofunctionalists

Those belonging to the functionalist school of political integration theory have drawn from the social theories of Spencer, the metaphorical organicism of Radcliffe-Brown and Durkheim, and the "requisite analysis" or structural functionalism of Parsons, Levy, Almond, and Apter.[12] The notions that "form follows function" and that "structures exist to satisfy functional needs" were expressed very early by David Mitrany,[13] and later by other international integration functionalists, namely, Inis L. Claude, James P. Sewell, and Paul G. Taylor.[14] These theorists focused on the world international system. As for those who concerned themselves with regional integration and Europe in particular, Altiero Spinelli describes them as follows:

> There were the Functionalists who believed that first of all it is important to confide the administration of certain concrete public activities to a suitable European administration. This administration would receive its common directives from the national states which would have formulated them in appropriate treaties and in subsequent inter-governmental decisions. Within the framework of these directives the European administration would be separated from and independent of the various administrations.[15]

It is perhaps a bit simplistic, but not inaccurate, to say that the functionalists argue for a sort of economic determinism. They do this by tying economics to the process of integration in such a way that political integration is an automatic result of economic integration. In theory, economic cooperation between states results in working relationships rather than political relationships, and these relationships can be established only through international organizations. The transfer of functions to the international organization leads to a transference of loyalty and support from the national to the supranational entity and, finally, to the creation of a political community.

The neofunctionalists agree that the process of political integration results from economic integration (or its "functional equivalent"), but they do not see the process as automatic. Those of the neofunctionalist school (notably Ernst Haas, Philippe Schmitter, and J. S. Nye[16]) assert that political variables cannot be extracted from the process and that, indeed, political actors, technocrats, and bureaucrats often manipulate the process and give it a political push (or what Haas refers to as "cultivated spillover"). The central analytical concept for the neofunctionalists is spillover, a force caused by functional interdependence or inherent linkages of tasks that press political actors to define their common tasks and then to go on to other activities. Spillover is commonly thought of as a process in which integrative activity in one sector leads to integrative activity in other sectors. Or, as M. P. Sullivan notes, it occurs when "certain procedures and behaviors occurring in the communication process spill over into others: cooperative processes in the matter of trade, for example, may affect relations between the parties in the matter of extradition."[17]

Put simply, spillover is said to occur when integrative success in one policy sector spills over into other, related policy sectors, causing the member-states to integrate their once separate activities in the new policy sectors. At the macro level, the best example of spillover was the creation of the EEC and Euratom out of the successes of the ECSC in the 1950s. Subsequent microexamples are numerous. When tariff barriers were first reduced in the EEC, the profit margins and competitive positions of many European firms became more strongly affected by the different systems of taxation in the member-states. This led to the adoption of a common system of calculating the value-added tax. Similarly, the agricultural surpluses generated by the initial common pricing system pressed the member-states toward a common structural policy in agriculture. An example of deliberative ("cultivated") spillover was the 1960 package deal that hastened internal tariff cuts in the EEC to satisfy those eager to advance the common market and that, at the same time, lowered the external tariff to satisfy those concerned about a loss of foreign trade.[18] These examples illustrate an important observation: spillover involves an increase in both the scope of authority and the level of authority for central institution decisionmakers.

The neofunctionalists view international integration as an ad hoc, step-by-step process characterized by gradual, continuous movement toward regional integration. Ernst Haas sees political integration as the process whereby certain crucial elites, those in government, interest groups, and political parties, "are persuaded to shift their loyalties, expectations and political activities toward a new center, whose institutions possess or demand jurisdiction over the pre-existing national states." His central theoretical conclusion is that integration is favored by societal circumstances (e.g., an industrialized economy, politically mobilized masses, and pluralist democracy) that favor or permit leaders of central institutions to propose or pursue collective policies that increase elite expectations and demands.[19] Haas provides several criteria for judging whether community sentiment, which is the basis for political union, can be considered to flourish:

1. Interest groups and political parties at the national level endorse supranational action in preference to action by their national government, or if they are divided among themselves on this issue, only the case of national opposition to supranational action could be considered incompatible with community sentiment.

2. Interest groups and political parties organize beyond the national level in order to function more effectively as decision makers *vis à vis* the separate national governments or the central authority, and if they define their interests in terms larger than those of the separate national state from which they originate.

3. Interest groups and political parties in confronting each other at the supranational level succeed in evolving a body of doctrine common to all or a new nationalism, i.e., supranationalism.

4. Interest groups and political parties, in their efforts at supranational organization, coalesce on the basis of a common ideology surpassing those prominent at the national level.

5. Interest groups, political parties, and governments show evidence of accepting the rule of law and faithfully carrying out supranational court decisions, administrative directives, and rules even when they oppose these, instead of obstructing or ignoring such decisions; further, when opposing federal policy they channel their objections through the legal avenues provided instead of threatening or practicing secession.

6. Governments negotiate with one another in good faith and generally reach agreement while not making themselves consistently and invariably the spokesmen of national interest groups; furthermore, community sentiment would seem to prevail if governments give way in negotiations when they find themselves in a minority instead of insisting on a formal or informal right of veto.[20]

In his latest work, Haas argues that integration theories are becoming obsolescent because the assumptions on which they are based are becoming less relevant to the behavior of international organizations. He suggests that the behavior of nonstate actors can no longer be explained on the basis of disjointed incrementalism, but rather on a new decisionmaking rationality he calls "fragmented issue linkage." Further, this condition is unlikely to lead to any permanent structure of institutions in international organizations.[21]

Another prominent neofunctionalist, J. S. Nye, defines the significant aspects of political integration as institutional, policy, and attitudinal integration, and adds Deutsch's "security community" as a fourth aspect. Nye's neofunctionalist model concentrates on seven process mechanisms: the functional linkage of tasks, rising transactions, deliberative linkages and coalition formation, regional group formation, elite socialization, the identitive appeal, and the involvement of external actors. His basic hypothesis is that "most political decision-makers will opt for the status quo at any level so long as the process forces or popular pressures are not so strong as to make the choice unbearable for them."[22] Nye's seven process mechanisms are meant to be indicators of continued, arrested, or reversed institutional, policy, attitudinal, and "security community" regional integration. According to the model, the response of political decisionmakers to these process mechanisms depends on the strength of the mechanisms and on certain integrative conditions: structural conditions (economic equality of units, elite value complementarity, pluralism, capacity of the member-states to adapt and respond), and perceptual conditions (perceived equity of distribution of benefits, perceived external cogency, low or exportable visible costs).[23]

The Federalists

Although the pluralists' emphasis on pre-integration forces and the beginnings of integration makes the pluralist school of greater value in understanding that stage of the integration process, and the functionalists' and neofunctionalists' views are helpful for understanding the dynamic maintenance of the process (how it keeps going), the federalists offer the most with regard to measurement of objectives and the end-product orientation of the process. Generally, the federalists stress political solutions, political institutions, and an acceptance of the nation-state as a political given that needs to be accommodated, rather than abolished or circumvented, in any scheme to reorganize world politics. As Charles Pentland notes, the federalists argue that "since the classic mechanisms of international adjustment have proved impermanent or unreliable for maintaining peace and security, real institutional limitations must be placed on the autonomy of states—however difficult this may be. While autonomous states can be influenced by diplomacy and communications, they can only be controlled if they give up some of their autonomous powers. Hence, in the federalist view, the need for a supranational state."[24]

Those in the federalist school, notably C. J. Friedrich, W. H. Riker, Peter Hay, George Liska, and Amitai Etzioni,[25] take an approach to international integration most aptly described by Spinelli:

> There are the Federalists who asked that the political institutions of a democratic Europe be constructed first by taking certain powers of initiative, deliberation, decision and execution from the national executives, parliaments and judiciaries and confiding them to a European executive,

TABLE 3.1. Comparative Summary of the Four Schools of International Integration

	PLURALISM	FUNCTIONALISM	NEOFUNCTIONALISM	FEDERALISM
I. The End Product				
Structure	Community of states	Administrative network responsive to community needs	Supranational decisionmaking system	Supranational state
Evidence	Probability of peaceful conflict resolution; communications (flows intensity)	Degree of 'fit' between structures & functions; need--satisfaction	Locus of decisions (scope & level)	Distribution of power (formal & informal
II. The Process (levels of analysis)				
System	Self-sustaining growth of interdependence & informal structures	Technical self-determination; imperatives of functional needs & technological change	Political development; growth of central institutions through "forward linkage"	Constitutional revolution: dramatic redistribution of power and authority
State	Increase of capacity for decisionmaking information, & responsiveness	Reluctant cooperation to solve technical & economic problems	Bargaining process where governments pursue interests among other groups	Bargaining resulting in Hobbesian contract among elites of states
Individual	Social learning through communications & interaction (elite & mass)	Habits of cooperation derived from satisfaction of utilitarian needs by new institutions	Effects of successful decisionmaking & conflict resolution on elite attitudes	Differentiation of loyalties according to level of government

III. Major Variables Measured

PLURALISTS	FUNCTIONALISTS	NEOFUNCTIONALISTS	FEDERALISTS
(1)unbroken links of social communication (2)mobility of persons (3)multiplicity of persons of communications and transactions (4)interchange of group roles (5)mutual predictability of behavior (6) flow of goods, information, services, population and symbols between states	(1)international trade and trade agreements (2)technological change and cooperation between states (3)creation of international organizations (4)creation of interdependencies (5)social-welfare agreements between states (6)"technical self-determination"	(1)size of unit (2)rate of transaction (3)pluralism (of governments) (4)elite complementarity (5)governmental purposes (6)powers of union (7)decisionmaking style (8)rate of transaction (9)adaptability of governments (10)perception of governments (11)external pressures	(1)Power politics (division of, separation of, etc.) (2)political identification (3) process of decisionmaking (4)control over means of violence (5)national political elites (6)government/citizen relationship (7)equity of governmental members (8)"constitutionalism" (9)decentralization and diversity

Source: Compiled from Charles Pentland, *Integration Theory and European Integration* (New York: Free Press, 1973), p. 190; and Gerhard Mally, *The European Community in Perspective* (Lexington, Mass.: Lexington Books, 1973), pp. 25-39.

parliament and judiciary. The institutions would derive their legitimacy from the consent of European citizens directly expressed through European citizens without interference from the member states in matters of federal competence.[26]

Table 3.1 contains a comparative summary of the four schools described.

The Eclectics

There is no popular acceptance of an added typology, the eclectic school. However, many international integration theorists agree that some utility exists in all the schools discussed previously. Indeed, as earlier mentioned, J. S. Nye borrowed the "security community" concept from Deutsch and the concern with elite socialization from the pluralist school, and the works of George Liska and Amitai Etzioni on international integration appear to combine functionalist and federalist perspectives.

Perhaps the best example of eclectic international integration theory is the work of Leon Lindberg and Stuart A. Scheingold.[27] Like Nye, Lindberg and Scheingold attempt to refine the concepts advanced by Haas in light of the historical experience of the European Community's first ten to fifteen years. Lindberg and Scheingold describe the European Community as "an ambiguous pluralistic system" and, in an assessment of two decades of polity building in the three European Communities that focuses on the development of the varieties of mass public and elite attitudinal and behavior supports, they discuss the role in integration of four different coalition-formation mechanisms; functional spillover, side-payments and logrolling, actor socialization, and feedback. The authors also suggest some specific models of change, such as forward linkage, output failure, equilibrium, and "spillback."[28] Although these models are strongly neofunctionalist in character, their eclecticism comes primarily from the liberal borrowing from Karl Deutsch.

Another neofunctionalist who has demonstrated in his more recent work some borrowing from the pluralists and significant modification to the neofunctionalist model is Philippe Schmitter. Schmitter concluded in the late 1960s, from the experience in Europe and elsewhere, that "spillover" was much less automatic than he or other neofunctionalists had once supposed. Consequently, he extended the concept of spillover to include several "strategic options" available to actors in particular policy sectors (see also Figure 3.1):

1. Spillover: i.e., to increase both the scope and level of his commitment concomitantly

2. Spillaround: i.e., to increase only the scope while holding the level of authority constant

3. Buildup: i.e., to increase the decisional autonomy of capacity of joint institutions but deny them entrance into new issue areas

4. Retrench: i.e., to increase the level of joint deliberation but withdraw the institution(s) from certain areas

5. Muddle-about: i.e., to let the regional bureaucrats debate, suggest, and expostulate on a wider variety of issues but decrease their actual capacity to allocate values

6. Spillback: i.e., to retreat on both dimensions, possibly returning to the status quo ante

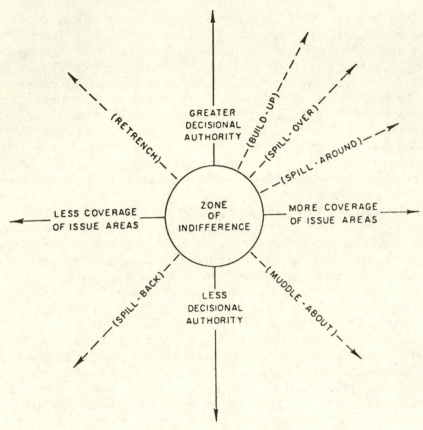

Figure 3.1   Schmitter's Alternative "Actor Strategies"

Source: Derived from Philippe C. Schmitter, "A Revised Theory of Regional Integration," in Leon Lindberg and Stuart Scheingold, eds., *Regional Integration: Theory and Research* (Cambridge, Mass.: Harvard University Press, 1971), p. 241.

7. Encapsulate: i.e., to respond to crisis by marginal modification within the zone of indifference[29]

Schmitter's concept of spillover does not differ from the explanation given previously. By spillaround, Schmitter means that regional decisionmakers would be given authority by national leaders to regulate additional aspects of a particular policy sector or an entirely new policy sector without an accompanying increase in autonomy or in rule-making or rule-enforcement power. For example, the scope of EC Commission authority in external relations has increased due to the expansion of the European Community and the increase from nineteen Yaoundé associate states to fifty-two African-Caribbean-Pacific (ACP) states. However, the level of authority granted the Commission did not significantly increase for the Lomé Convention relative to the Yaoundé agreements.

The build-up concept is similar to spillaround except that central institution decisionmakers are given more autonomy or rule-making authority, but only in those areas over which they previously had some control. They are not given any additional competences. The European Parliament was given more control over the operating budget (of the European Community's institutions) in 1970. Although parliamentary control was increased, it was over only that small portion of the European Community budget for which it previously had had some input. The increase in the level of authority without the Council's permitting the Parliament any decisionmaking authority over the major portion of the EC budget is an example of buildup.

Schmitter's terms "retrench," "muddle-about," and "spillback," are all negative in character. "Retrenchment" brings an increase in decisionmaking authority but a decrease in the number or scope of policy areas. The increase in authority may mean only an increase in the level of joint deliberation (e.g., from the Council of Ministers to the European Council), but this is accompanied by a withdrawal from certain common areas (e.g., British, French, and Italian withdrawal of their currencies from the European Community's common currency float). "Muddle-about" refers to an increase in the scope of authority with a concomitant decrease in the level of authority given regional decisionmakers. The Council of Ministers, for example, may permit an increase in the Commission's fields of investigation and debate, but it gives them no power to act on those issues. Such is the present situation for industrial and energy policies in the EC. Directorate General III (Industrial and Technological Affairs) and Directorate General XVII (Energy) have been permitted to research and recommend new policy areas, but not a single mandate for action has come from the Council of Ministers since 1970. "Spillback" denotes disintegration, a decrease both in the level and the scope of decisionmaking authority given regional institutions. Historical examples of spillback in the European Community include the national solutions to the 1958 coal crisis in the ECSC, the isolation of the French and West German agricultural markets after the changes in currency values in 1969, and the immediate reaction of the EC member-states to the Arab oil embargo.

Schmitter's final strategy, "encapsulation," pertains to another of his concepts, the "zone of indifference." He suggests that regional actors operate inside certain loosely defined limits within which their activities (or absence thereof) go uncontested. As long as regional bureaucrats work within the zone of indifference and incur no new costs, they are tolerated. Encapsulation, then, is the response of regional actors to crises by marginally modifying their actions without exceeding the zone of indifference. Encapsulation occurs when regional actors respond to crises by reasserting previous strategies. Perhaps the best examples are the decisions of the European Community to negotiate the Lomé Convention and to begin the Eur-Arab Dialogue in response to the 1973 oil crisis.

Schmitter's expanded neofunctionalist model, particularly his "strategic options," will be employed to evaluate the degree of integration in the nonstate actors analyzed in this text. International organizations and the major individual policy sectors within them will be examined as to whether they have exhibited the characteristics of spillover, spill-around, buildup, retrenchment, muddle-about, spillback, or encapsulation. The choice of Schmitter's model will facilitate the attempt to explain the direction of integration in each case, and to compare nonstate actors and the policy sectors within them.

Notes

1. See Altiero Spinelli, *The Eurocrats: Conflict and Crisis in the European Community* (Baltimore: Johns Hopkins Press, 1966), pp. 10–17. See also David Calleo, *Europe's Future: The Grand Alternatives* (New York: Horizon Press, 1965).

2. Steven Warnecke, "American Regional Integration Theories and the European Community," *Integration* 1 (1971), p. 9.

3. In particular, Karl Deutsch, *Nationalism and Social Communication* (Cambridge: Harvard University Press, 1966), and *International Political Communities: An Anthology* (New York: Doubleday, 1966).

4. Haas's seminal work is *The Uniting of Europe: Political, Social, and Economic Forces 1950–1957* (Stanford, Calif.: Stanford University Press, 1958). See also Ernst Haas, "The Uniting of Europe and the Uniting of Latin America," *Journal of Common Market Studies* 5 (June 1967), pp. 315–343; "The Study of Regional Integration: Reflections on the Joy and Anguish of Pretheorizing," in Leon N. Lindberg and Stuart A. Scheingold (Eds.), *Regional Integration: Theory and Research* (Cambridge: Harvard University Press, 1971), pp. 3–42.

5. Leon N. Lindberg and Stuart A. Scheingold, *Europe's Would-be Polity: Patterns of Change in the European Community* (Englewood Cliffs, N.J.: Prentice-Hall, 1970).

6. Charles Pentland, *International Theory and European Integration* (New York: Free Press, 1973). Pentland's typology of the four major schools is based on the end-product to which the integration process is expected to lead and on which major conditions are seen as bringing about the process of change. According to Pentland, the federalists and neofunctionalists believe the end-product of integration to be the state-model (respectively, a federal state and a supranational government), and the pluralists and functionalists think that the

community-model is the end-product. Both pairs are divided, however, in terms of the types of independent variables employed to explain the process of change. Federalists and pluralists focus on the direct processes or political variables, and functionalists and neofunctionalists concentrate on indirect processes, particularly the socioeconomic variables.

7. Ibid., p. 29.

8. Karl Deutsch, *Political Community and the North Atlantic Area: International Organization in the Light of Historical Experience* (Princeton, N.J.: Princeton University Press, 1957), pp. 5–6.

9. Karl Deutsch et al., "Political Community in the North Atlantic Area," in *International Political Communities: An Anthology* (Garden City, N.Y.: Doubleday, 1966), pp. 1–2.

10. Roger W. Cobb and Charles Elder, *International Community: A Regional and Global Study* (New York: Holt, Rinehart and Winston, 1970), pp. 8–9.

11. Michael P. Sullivan, *International Relations: Theories and Evidence* (Englewood Cliffs, N.J.: Prentice-Hall, 1976), p. 210.

12. See H. Spencer, *The Principles of Sociology*, vol. 1 (New York: Appleton, 1897); E. Durkheim, *The Rules of Sociological Method* (Glencoe, Ill.: Free Press, 1938); A. R. Radcliffe-Brown, *Structure and Function in Primitive Society* (Glencoe, Ill.: Free Press, 1951); T. Parsons, *The Social System* (Glencoe, Ill.: Free Press, 1951); M. J. Levy, Jr., *The Structure of Society* (Princeton, N.J.: Princeton University Press, 1952); G. A. Almond, "Introduction," in G. A. Almond and J. S. Coleman (Eds.), *The Politics of the Developing Areas* (Princeton, N.J.: Princeton University Press, 1960); and D. E. Apter, *The Politics of Modernization* (Chicago: University of Chicago Press, 1965).

13. David Mitrany, *The Progress of International Government* (New Haven Conn.: Yale University Press, 1933).

14. See Inis L. Claude, Jr., *Swords into Plow Shares* (4th ed.) (New York: Random House, 1971); James Patrick Sewell, *Functionalism and World Politics* (Princeton, N.J.: Princeton University Press, 1966); P. G. Taylor, "The Concept of Community and the European Integration Process," *Journal of Common Market Studies* 7 (1968), pp. 83–101; and P. G. Taylor, "The Functionalist Approach to the Problem of International Order: A Defense," *Political Studies* 16 (1968), pp. 393–410.

15. Altiero Spinelli, *The Eurocrats: Conflict and Crisis in the European Community* (Baltimore: Johns Hopkins Press, 1966), p. 13. "European functionalists" appear to have lost interest in the European Community and now direct their attention to the Economic Council for Europe (ECE). See, for example, A.J.R. Groom, "Functionalist Approach and East-West Cooperation in Europe," *Journal of Common Market Studies* 1-2 (1975), pp. 21–60.

16. See Ernst Haas, *The Uniting of Europe: Political, Social, and Economic Forces 1950–1957* (Stanford, Calif.: Stanford University Press, 1958); E. Haas and P. C. Schmitter, "Economics and Differential Patterns of Political Integration: Projections about Unity in Latin America," in *International Political Communities: An Anthology* (Garden City, N.Y.: Doubleday, 1966), pp. 259–300; J. S. Nye, *Peace in Parts: Integration and Conflict in Regional Organization* (Boston: Little, Brown and Co., 1971).

17. Sullivan, *International Relations*, p. 212.

18. J. S. Nye, "Comparing Common Markets: A Revised Neo-Functionalist Model," in Leon Lindberg and Stuart A. Scheingold (Eds.), *Regional Integration: Theory and Research* (Cambridge, Mass.: Harvard University Press, 1971), pp. 200–202.

19. Haas, *The Uniting of Europe*, p. 16.

20. Ibid., pp. 9–10.

21. Ernst Haas, "Turbulent Fields and the Theory of Regional Integration," *International Organization* 30:2 (Spring 1976), pp. 173–212.

22. Nye, "Comparing Common Markets," p. 97.

23. Ibid., pp. 55–107.

24. Pentland, *International Theory*, pp. 149–150.

25. See C. J. Friedrich's *Trends of Federalism in Theory and Practice* (London: Allen and Unwin, 1968); W. H. Riker's, *Federalism: Origin, Operation, Significance* (Boston: Little, Brown and Co., 1964); and Peter Hay, *Federalism and Supranational Organizations: Patterns for New Legal Structures* (Urbana: University of Illinois Press, 1966). Although not explicitly federalist, George Liska's *Europe Ascendant: The International Politics of Unification* (Baltimore: Johns Hopkins Press, 1964) and Amitai Etzioni, *Political Unification: A Comparative Study of Leaders and Forces* (New York: Holt, Rinehart and Winston, 1965) employ a body of federalist assumptions. Liska sets out to analyze the means and forces forging Europe's unity by focusing on the concept of "statecraft." His analysis of the shortcomings of functional strategies and his prescriptions for moving from functional to political phases make the work federalist in character. In *Political Unification*, Etzioni attempts to construct a general theoretical framework based on Parson's structural-functional systems theory. He posits twenty-two propositions, which he attempts to test (rather, to illustrate) in case studies of the European Community and three other regional organizations. Although his work is intended to be a functional analysis, Etzioni's use of the single-state analogy, his emphasis on the continuing role of the component units, and his insistence on the role of supranationality make the work equally federalist in character.

26. Spinelli, *The Eurocrats*, p. 11.

27. See, especially, Lindberg and Scheingold, *Europe's Would-be Polity*, and idem, *Regional Integration*.

28. Lindberg and Scheingold, *Europe's Would-be Polity*, pp. 34–39.

29. Philippe C. Schmitter, "A Revised Theory of Regional Integration," in Lindberg and Scheingold (Eds.), *Regional Integration*, p. 242.

Part 2

Economic International
Governmental Organizations

4
The European Community

The European Community is the most highly developed and most important regional intergovernmental organization in existence. The Community (also referred to as the European Economic Community, European Common Market, EEC, or EC) is an economic and political union of nine European nations[1] that provides for an ever closer union of the member states for an unlimited period of time. Its permanent institutions not only apply and administer the treaties that constitute the legal foundation of the union, but also make and revise policy as the integration process continues.

The European Community is actually the combination of three communities that share the same institutions. The three communities are the European Coal and Steel Community (ECSC), the European Economic Community (EEC), and the European Atomic Energy Community (Euratom). The ECSC was created by the Paris Treaty of April 18, 1951, and the EEC and Euratom by the Treaty of Rome of March 25, 1957. The stated purpose for the creation and maintenance of the three communities is to put an end to national prejudice, discrimination, and armed conflict in Europe; to open up the economic frontiers that had previously divided Europe into small, protected markets; to harness the constructive energies of the European peoples; to make the European Community a single economic area; to recover collectively some of the world influence the Western European nations had lost separately; to become a strong force for peace and a generous provider for the world's poorer nations; and to contribute to world stability and law and order.[2]

The European Community is, without question, an important world actor. Collectively, its member-states have a population greater then either the United States or the Soviet Union, as well as a share of international trade and aid to developing nations that exceeds that of the United States. Although the EC is not a "superpower" politically or militarily, its economic strength in an emerging era of increasing global economic interdependence lends it potential importance as an international actor. This chapter will provide a brief history of the

47

European Community, an explanation of the structure of its institutions and decisionmaking procedures, and a summary of what is known of its present state of integration.

[handwritten margin note: Us not mad about economic Trade that World be because lost of the political stabilization]

History and Development

The end of World War II and the resultant suffering and devastation reawakened the movement to unite the nations of Europe. If for no other reason, Europeans were determined to find a way to prevent another war on the continent and the effects brought on by unlimited nationalism. The difficulties in post-war economic recovery exacerbated the problems imposed by narrow national boundaries, and the inability to compete with U.S. trade in the world market enhanced the arguments for European union. The U.S. Marshall Plan, which began in 1948, gave those who favored European union a first glimmer of hope.

One aim of the Marshall Plan was to promote economic integration. The organization created by the Marshall Plan, the Organization for European Economic Cooperation (OEEC), was to be a supranational body, but resistance by the British kept it from being what France and the Benelux countries hoped for and what the United States had designed it to be. Moreover, the OEEC was limited in scope and suffered due to the unanimity rule. This meant that when decisions as to common action could be negotiated, they occurred almost always at the level of the lowest common denominator. The Hague Conference of May 1948, sponsored by the International Committee of the Movement for European Union, ended in agreement only to support traditional forms of cooperation among European states. The conference did assist, however, in laying the groundwork for the Council of Europe, which was formed in May 1949. The European federalists and those who supported some immediate form of European unification were confronted by nation-state rivalries and those favoring a gradual approach to the question. It seemed as though these obstacles could be overcome only by a substantial shock to post-war Western Europe.

[handwritten margin note: OEEC went another direction later 1976 to become OECD(?).]

The shock came in May 1950. Robert Schuman, the French foreign minister, formally proposed that Franco-German coal and steel production be combined under a common high authority in which participation would be offered to all other European countries. Schuman justified his plan in economic terms, but his primary motive was political. He later admitted that the French proposal was "to end Franco-German hostility once and for all."[3]

The Schuman Plan was approved by the French cabinet in hopes that by entrusting part of their sovereignty to a supranational authority, individual nations would lay the basis for an eventual political union in Europe. Negotiations between the nations responding to the Schuman Plan (France, Germany, Italy, Belgium, the Netherlands, and Luxembourg) began in Paris on June 20, 1950, and culminated in the signing of the Joint Declaration on April 18, 1951. This action formally initiated the European Coal and Steel Company (ECSC). The ECSC High Authority began operations on August 10, 1952. The ECSC Treaty provided for the abolition of customs duties and other restrictions in the movement of coal and steel between the member-countries. It also contained a set of common rules meant to control cartels and to regulate mergers, measures to harmonize transport rates, and measures to control production and prices during economic crises.[4]

The drive toward further European unity suffered a setback when, in 1954, the proposed European Defense Community and creation of a European Army were defeated in the French National Assembly. These proposals were replaced, in part, by the creation of the Western European Union (WEU) and the admission of West Germany into NATO in 1955. Although political and military integration plans were thwarted, economic integration in the ECSC was sufficiently successful for the foreign ministers of the six nations meeting in Messina, Sicily, in June 1955 to call for even further economic integration. The eventual outcomes were two new treaties that were signed in Rome in March 1957 and entered into force on January 1, 1958. Known collectively as the Treaty of Rome, the treaties added to the ECSC the European Atomic Energy Community (Euratom) and the European Economic Community (EEC). The three communities each had separate executive bodies (commissions) but shared some common institutions—the European Court of Justice, the European Parliamentary Assembly (later called the European Parliament), and the Council of Ministers—which made all important policy decisions for all three communities.

Euratom progressed little in the beginning. Differences between the member-states as to the scope and direction of its research activities and serious budgetary difficulties hampered Euratom's development.[5] Despite initial progress, the ECSC was overtaken by a serious coal crisis in 1958, competition from cheaper imported oil, and difficulties in the steel industry. By contrast, the EEC was an immediate and unexpected success. In its first four years, tariffs on industrial goods were cut by 40 percent, significant progress toward a common external tariff was achieved, and the member-states agreed on initial steps toward the free movement of workers and capital and on rules for competition. Further, agreement was reached on financial and marketing arrangements for a common agricultural policy.[6]

Successful integration in the economic sectors brought about yet another attempt at political unity. The "Plan Fouchet" proposed foreign and defense policy coordination through a treaty for political union. The de Gaulle–initiated proposal was negotiated for two years, but it collapsed in 1962 due to French refusal to include the British and Dutch insistence on it. This cleavage was exacerbated the following year by the French veto of British entry into the European Community.

The Community experienced its greatest crisis in 1965. The Commission proposed that the financing of the Common Agricultural Policy (CAP) should be made independent of the member-states. At about the same time, it also recommended a substantial increase in the budgetary power of the European Parliament. The immediate break occurred in June when several of the member-states (notably Italy) refused to commit themselves to a definite settlement on financing the CAP, an issue on which France was most adamant. But deeper issues lay behind the conflict. The major problem involved the willingness of the member-states to introduce majority voting in the Council of Ministers during the third stage of transition provided in the Treaty of Rome (which began in 1959).[7] In September 1965, French President de Gaulle announced that he would not accept majority voting, proposed changes to decrease the power of the Commission, and ordered a boycott of Community institutions. When France walked out of the Council of Ministers, the European Community came to a standstill.

The crisis was finally resolved by a compromise reached in Luxembourg in January 1966. France agreed to resume active participation in the Community after the six member-states agreed to disagree concerning majority voting in the Council of Ministers. The "gentlemen's agreement" in the Luxembourg Compromise had the effect of maintaining the unanimity rule and immediately increasing the power of the Council of Ministers and decreasing that of the Commission. The weighted voting system still remains a formal part of the Council of Ministers, but it is virtually never used. To date, each member-state retains the right of veto in the Council. France did not win completely. In return for the Luxembourg Compromise, France softened its demands concerning the CAP, getting from the other states only a program of work that promised progress toward completing the CAP.

Economic integration progressed despite further conflict between the member-states (Britain's second attempt to enter the Community was again answered by a French veto in December 1967). The customs union was completed ahead of schedule, the decision to progressively introduce a value-added tax and a five-year economic program was worked out, and some progress was made on the common transport policy. Further, on July 1, 1967, the merger of the commissions of the three communities into one Commission was accomplished. In the external affairs of the European Community, significant successes occurred also. The Community spoke with one voice in the Kennedy Round of GATT, which concluded successfully in 1967. The six member-states renegotiated the Yaoundé Convention with the African "associate states" and added a substantial number of trade agreements, notably with Morocco and Tunisia, in 1969.

In many ways, 1969 was a watershed for the Community; two important events occurred in that year. First, the election of Georges Pompidou as French president to succeed de Gaulle paved the way for British entry and enlargement of the Community. Second, the European Council meeting in the Hague in December 1969 called for "completing, deepening, and enlarging the Community." It formally declared the Community's twelve-year transition period to be at an end on December 31, 1969, and approved a plan to finance, by 1975, a Community budget totally from proceeds of the common external tariff and a small part of the proceeds of the value-added tax. The agreement also gave limited control of the Community budget to the European Parliament.

The Hague Summit also produced proposals for the creation of an economic and monetary union and a renewed attempt at political union. The economic and monetary union proposal prompted a report the following year by a committee chaired by Luxembourg Prime Minister Pierre Werner. The "Werner Report" set a target date of 1980 for a high degree of coordination of national economic policies, a harmonization of budgetary policies, a Community currency, a unified capital market, and Community intervention into regional policies.[8] Also in December 1969, a marathon Council session produced agreement on financing a common agricultural policy.

Membership negotiations opened in 1970 to include the United Kingdom, Denmark, Ireland, and Norway. Also in 1970, the common foreign-trade policy became operational and political cooperation meetings began. The following year produced a common fisheries policy and the generalized system of preferences for ninety-one developing nations. The Accession Treaty enlarging the Community was signed in 1972, but the people of Norway rejected membership in a popular referendum and Norway declined membership. In 1973, Ireland, Denmark, and the United Kingdom began actively participating in the Community, giving the EC the membership and character it has today.

The European Community expanded significantly the scope of its external relations with the signing of the Lomé Convention in February 1975. Initially forty-six (now fifty-eight) African, Caribbean, and Pacific (ACP) countries joined in a comprehensive trading and economic cooperation relationship with the Community. The first Lomé Convention granted the ACP countries duty-free access on a nonreciprocal basis to all industrial and nearly all agricultural exports to EC member-states.

In addition, it set up industrial cooperation efforts, an export stabilization program (STABEX) for ACP products, and greatly increased EC development assistance for those developing nations. The second Lomé Convention (Lomé II), signed in October 1979, increased slightly the scope of the participants and benefits under STABEX and the European Development Fund (development assistance).[9]

The most heralded accomplishment of the European Community in the 1970s was direct elections to the European Parliament in June 1979. The 410 directly elected members took their seats in the newly constituted Parliament on July 17, in Strasbourg, France. Although the scope of the Parliament's powers was not increased, many in the Community feel that direct elections will give the Community's 260 million citizens a stronger voice in EC affairs, thus marking an important step toward political integration in the Community.[10]

Another important accomplishment was the creation of the European Monetary System (EMS). The EMS is based on a European Currency Unit (ECU) and incorporates a compulsory intervention mechanism designed to achieve greater stability of European exchange rates. After years of negotiations and frequent impasses created by French and British reservations, the EMS went into force on March 12, 1979. The agreement falls far short of the once-hoped-for "European Economic Union" and is weakened by Britain's refusal to participate in it.[11]

The final important development of the 1970s occurred in May 1979. Greece and the European Community signed an accession treaty to make Greece the tenth member of the Community. Full active membership began in 1981.[12]

The Institutions

The six major institutions of the European Community are the Council of Ministers, the Committee of Permanent Representatives, the Commission, the European Parliament, the Court of Justice, and the Economic and Social Committee (and Consultative Committee). In general, the Council of Ministers fulfills a legislative role, the Commission an executive role, the Court of Justice has the power of judicial review on the EC Treaties, and the Parliament, Economic and Social Committee, and Consultative Committee are advisory groups to the Council and Commission. The Committee of Permanent Representatives has the responsibility of preparing the deliberations of the Council. All institutions are located in Brussels, Belgium, except for the Court of Justice, which is located in Luxembourg, and the European Parliament, which meets both in Luxembourg and in Strasbourg, France.[13] (See Figure 4.1.)

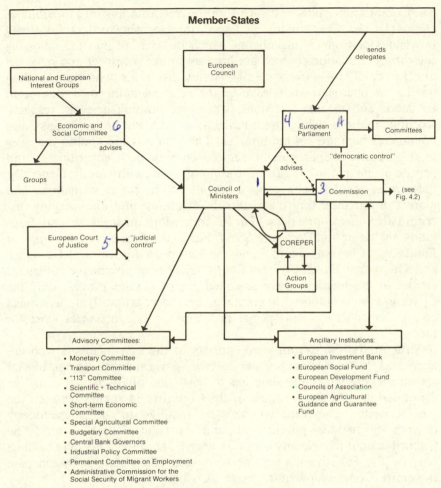

Figure 4.1 The Community's Institutional Structure

✳ The Commission ⑥

The Commission is the "guardian of the treaties." It is responsible for seeing that treaty provisions and institutional decisions are properly implemented. It has the authority to investigate, issue an objective ruling, and notify the government concerned (subject to verification by the Court of Justice) of the required corrective action. As the executive arm of the communities, the Commission is directly invested with specific powers by the treaties. It also has been granted substantial additional powers by the Council to implement enactments based on the Treaties (these powers are referred to as "derived Community law").

The Commission's powers can be summarized as falling into three major areas. (1) The Commission prepares implementing orders for treaty provisions or Council enactments, which in turn fall into the following categories: regulations (which are binding in every respect and have the direct force of law in every member-state), directives (which are binding on the member-states but leave to the national authorities' discretion the mode and means), decisions (which are binding in every respect), recommendations (which are binding as to ends but not to means), and opinions (which are not binding). (2) The Commission applies the rules of the treaties to particular cases (concerning both governments and private firms) and to the administration of Community funds. Generally, these rules involve such actions as preventing cartel formations and market dominance, limiting state subsidizations, and discouraging discriminatory fiscal practices. The Commission manages several large funds, including the European Social Fund, the European Development Fund, the "Cheysson Fund," and the European Agricultural Guidance and Guarantee Fund. (3) The Commission administers the safeguard clauses in the treaties. These so-called escape clauses provide only the Commission the authority to grant waivers ("derogations") at the request of a member-state when special problems or circumstances exist for them.

Structurally, the Commission consists of thirteen members who are appointed by agreement of the member-governments. By an official agreement, each member-state has at least one of its nationals on the Commission, and the president of the Commission rotates between the member-states. The commissioners are required to act independently of both the national governments and the Council of Ministers. The Council cannot remove any commissioner from office. This may be done only by the Parliament's passing of a vote of censure, in which case the entire Commission must resign as a body.

The commissioners have working for them a General Secretariat, a Legal Department, a Statistical Office, nineteen functionally specific directorates-general, and a small number of specialized services. Their staffs total over 7,000 civil servants from the nine member-states. The major importance of the Commission is that it is the initiator of Community policy and the exponent of Community interest. It is responsible to see that Community policy forms a single consistent whole.[14] (See Figure 4.2.)

The Council of Ministers

The Council of Ministers is the Community's main decisionmaking body. It is made up of representatives of the member-states. As a rule,

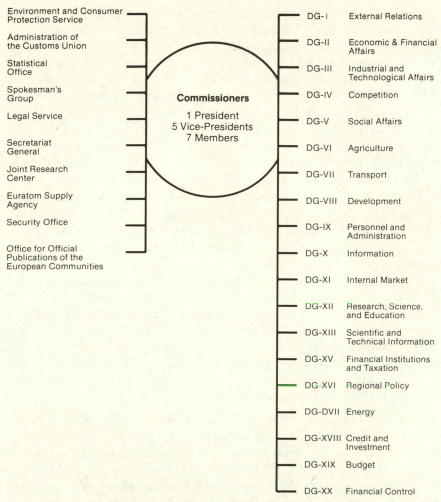

Figure 4.2 Organizational Structure of the Commission

each government sends one minister, although it may send more than one on occasion. Membership varies according to the subject matter under consideration. The member-states' foreign ministers are considered the main representatives of the Council, but meetings are often composed of ministers of agriculture, transport, finance, industry, and so on. The Council usually meets three or four times monthly. It has a permanent secretariat (with a staff of 1,200) and the Committee of Permanent Representatives to assist in the preparations for meetings. The chairmanship of the Council rotates among the member-states every six months. The present rotation began in the first half of 1973 with Belgium and follows this order: Belgium, Denmark, Germany, France, Ireland, Italy, Luxembourg, Netherlands, United Kingdom.

In theory, decisionmaking in the Council is executed by means of a weighted majority vote. The larger states, Germany, Italy, France, and the United Kingdom, have ten votes each, Belgium and the Netherlands five each, Ireland and Denmark three each, and Luxembourg two. Of this total of fifty-eight votes, forty-one are required for passage. Should the vote concern anything that did not come first as a proposal from the Commission, those forty-one or more votes must have been cast by at least six member-states. In practice, almost all decisions are made by seeking unanimity, although the treaties require this in only a few instances (such as admission of a new member). The gentlemen's agreement of the Luxembourg Compromise is still in force. Rather than give up veto powers, the member-states have preferred the practice of seeking unanimity on Council decisions during marathon sessions. These sessions continue around the clock without interruption until consensus is reached by "splitting the difference" or, as is more usually the case, by "finding the lowest common denominator." All Council decisions on matters included in the Treaties must be based on a Commission proposal. Commission proposals can be amended by the Council, but this requires a unanimous vote.[15]

The Committee of Permanent Representatives

The Committee of Permanent Representatives (COREPER) consists of the nine member-states' ambassadors to the individual communities and the staffs of the ambassadors, which are composed of experts in various fields of Community interest. These staffs are arranged in multinational action groups and working committees. Basically, their role is to do the groundwork for the Council meetings by reviewing all Commission proposals and reporting to the Council areas of agreement among the national viewpoints. As such, the COREPER provides a function similar to that of a congressional committee. Although the COREPER does not hold formal hearings, the Commission can and does provide them further information and support for the Commission proposals. Given the great volume of Council business, COREPER recommendations carry great weight and influence. The COREPER has been an important institution since 1958. Its existence was not provided for in the treaties (it did not even exist for the ECSC), but the Treaty of Accession in 1973 confirmed its existence and gave it a legal basis.

⚹ The European Parliament

The major role of the European Parliament is that of a consultative body and watchdog over the Commission, charged to ensure that it does not adhere to any one national position or lose sight of the "Community interest." The Parliament consists of 410 directly elected members: 81 for each of the four largest countries (Germany, France, Italy, and the United Kingdom), 25 for the Netherlands, 24 for Belgium, 16 for Denmark, 15 for Ireland, and 6 for Luxembourg. The Parliament is truly "Community" in character, having European-level political party groups but no national groupings. Seats in the first directly elected Parliament, by European party groups, broke down as follows: Socialists, 111; Christian Democrats, 106; Conservatives, 63; Communists, 44; Liberals, 41; Democrats for Progress, 21; Independents, 12; and miscellaneous, 12.[16]

The Parliament meets seven or eight times a year for a week at a time. Between sessions, its various functional committees meet *in camera* to discuss issues concerning the Community and obtain information from other Community institutions. The Parliament has the right to put written and oral questions to commissioners and the Council of Ministers. In 1973, a "question time" was introduced to increase the dialogue with the executive organs.[17]

The Parliament has limited but gradually increasing budgetary powers. In 1970, the "free" part of the budget (money to maintain EC institutions' functioning) was brought under "the final word of the Parliament." Although the funds involved are small by comparison to the total Community budget, they have great political significance. Control of operating funds is a matter to which all Community institutions are quite sensitive.[18] The budgetary powers of the Parliament are likely to increase in the future. The directly elected European Parliament and the accompanying increase in political power substantially enhance the chances of a much stronger role for the Parliament in the near future.

⚹ The European Court of Justice

The Court of Justice consists of nine judges. They are appointed at the consent of the national governments for terms of six years. The nine judges are assisted by four advocates-general. The Court ensures the observance of law and justice in the interpretation and application of the Treaties and in the laws passed to implement the Treaties. The Court may give judgment on appeals brought by a member-state, the Council, the Commission, or any person or company affected by a

Community decision. In that sense, the Court of Justice is the Community "Supreme Court." The Court's decisions are binding and final, and cannot be appealed in the national courts.[19]

✳ The Economic and Social Committee

The Economic and Social Committee (ESC) is a consultative body that influences decisionmaking in the Community, although it has no powers of decision or initiative. The Commission and the Council are required to consult the ESC on most major policy proposals. In addition, the ESC sends published opinions to the Commission, many parts of which are included in later Commission proposals sent to the Council. The Committee consists of 144 members selected from labor, business, agriculture, consumer, and family organizations. Seats are allocated by nation: twenty-four each from Germany, France, Italy, and the United Kingdom; twelve each from the Netherlands and Belgium; nine each from Denmark and Ireland; and six from Luxembourg. Most of the ESC's members are high officials in interest groups that have offices and staffs located in Brussels as well as throughout Europe.

The ESC is divided into three groups. Group I contains business organizations, such as the Union des Industries de la Communauté Européenne (UNICE). Group II is the labor unions' section; its largest member is the European Trade Union Confederation. Group III is made up of agricultural groups (e.g., the Committee of Professional Agricultural Organizations [COPA] in the EEC), professionals, consumer groups, and family groups.

The ESC functions only for the EEC and Euratom matters. A similar group, the "Consultative Committee," advises the Council and Commission on ECSC affairs. Similar to the ESC in constitution, the Consultative Committee has eighty-one members.

✳ The "European Council"

In recent years, an unofficial institution has developed in the Community. Motivated by a concern to deal at the highest level with difficult political problems that had stalemated the Council of Ministers, the heads of state and of government of the member-states began holding periodic summits to discuss Community issues and problems. This body, popularized as the "European Council," is an extremely important actor in the Community. So far as institutional structures are concerned, however, it may be little different than the Council of Ministers, attended by prime ministers rather than foreign ministers. As with the Council of Ministers, the European Council's chairman rotates between the member-states every six months; the nation chairing the Council of Ministers also chairs the European Council. When the European Council meets (generally every four months), both the COREPER and the Council of Ministers serve to prepare the meeting.

The Decisionmaking Process

By virtue of the treaties, the Commission can make regulations and decisions and can submit resolutions to the Council, but these must be made collegiately. Majority voting is used in the Commission, and the minority always abides by the majority decision. The Commission draws up decisions and proposals in two stages. After consulting with political circles (e.g., the European Parliament, top civil servants, and the Economic and Social Committee and various employers and workers groups), the appropriate directorate-general prepares an opinion on its own, generally through a long, time-consuming series of meetings. When general policy guidelines (based on the prepared opinions) have been determined and approved by the commissioners, the second procedure is initiated. The directorate-general in question holds meetings with groups of experts from the national governments and often informally confers with representatives of the COREPER. In addition, members of the Commission meet with representatives of interest groups and other Community institutions in committees, many of which have become institutionalized (e.g., the Short-Term Economic Policy Committee, the Budgetary Policy Committee, the Medium-Term Economic Policy Committee, the Nuclear Research Advisory Committee, the Committee on Vocational Training, the Committee on the Free Movement of Workers, and the Committee on Social Security for Migrant Workers). The results of these meetings are reported to the responsible commissioner, who, in turn, reports them to the entire Commission.

When the Commission sends either a memorandum of general scope or a proposal on a particular point, the Council will first refer it to the COREPER. The COREPER can only recommend action to the Council; all actual decisions must be made by the Council of Ministers. On matters of relatively less importance and when the COREPER and Commission are unanimously in agreement, the Council will adopt the decision without debate. On more important matters or those having political implications, the Council will debate the issue. At such times, members of the Commission attend the Council meetings (as a right) to defend their proposals. Consultation with other Community institutions (i.e., the Parliament and ESC) generally takes place before the debate, but usually only if required by the treaties. Decisions and regulations of the Council are binding, subject only to review by the European Court of Justice.[20]

The Present State of Integration

The European Council (heads of state and of government of the nine member-states of the European Community) issued in its final communiqué of the 1972 Paris Summit the resolve "of transforming, before the end of the present decade and with the fullest respect for the Treaties already signed, the whole complex of the relations of Member States into a European Union" and "requested the institutions of the Community to draw up a report on this subject before the end of 1975." The reports, published by the Commission, the European Parliament, the Economic and Social Committee, and the European Court of Justice, and specifically commissioned reports by Belgian Prime Minister Leo Tindemans and by the Dutch government (the latter known as the "Spierenburg report"), all strongly advocate European union. The recent reports of the Community institutions indicate greater consensus, a stronger resolve by political leaders, and higher expectations for European union than ever before.

Yet, since the 1972 Paris Summit, European integration seems to have approached a standstill. Despite the optimistic tone of the various reports on European union, direct elections to the European Parliament, the creation of the EMS, and the communalistic rhetoric that has come out of the European Council, attempts at reaching economic and monetary union have met an impasse (or, perhaps, nine separate impasses). The nine member-states differ in their various market mechanisms, labor structures, and consumer mentalities to the extent that goal conflicts abound. The Community members cannot decide whether the European Community should concentrate on fighting inflation or focus on fighting unemployment by expanding economic growth. No consensus exists as to whether it is best to take steps to minimize energy costs or to safeguard energy sources. Were the nine member-states able to reach agreement on the basic goals, they would still be at odds concerning the means to be employed to reach those goals. The accession of Greece, and later of Spain and Portugal, should serve only to exacerbate these differences.

The actor strategy in Schmitter's model that best describes the general state of integration in the Community is encapsulation (marginal modification within the zone of indifference). Little progress has been made in the Community's internal affairs. The European Parliament recently called the lack of progress toward a common transport policy "disappointing" and characterized the lack of political will to arrive at a common position on energy a sign of "weakness and impotence" of the Community and of renewed competition between the nation-states. The parliamentary report further charged that "the lack of progress toward economic and monetary union was largely attributable to the failure of the Council [of Ministers] to take decisions."[21] The parliamentarians' assessment of the state of integration in the economic and monetary affairs of the Community was negative:

> Coordination of [the] economic policies of the Member States [is] incon-sistent; [there are] now more restrictions in movements of capital that at [the] beginning of [the] '60's; only limited progress [has occurred] in EC structural policy and fiscal harmonization. [The] European Monetary Cooperation Fund plays [a] subsidiary role. Ireland, Italy, and [the] United Kingdom play no part in the EC's exchange-rate mechanism. Cooperation between the central banks of the Member States [is] satisfactory.[22]

The unsuccessful attempt to achieve a passport union in the Com-munity provides another example of the state of integration in the Community's internal affairs. Indeed, the original effort has now been reduced to an attempt to standardize the size, color, and format of the member-states' passports. Even this effort is now bogged down due to disagreements over which languages should be used, in what order they should appear, and what color the external cover should be.

Attempts at further integration in the European Community have been frustrated by various conditions, personalities, and external prob-lems that fall into two broad categories: political barriers and economic barriers. With the exception of the agreement to begin the European Monetary System (and it, too, is suspect because Britain has refused to participate in it), the European Community has stagnated internally. Failure to progress (stagnation) is very often assessed as retrenchment; Community political leaders have tended, at least publicly, to read stalemate as failure. Once the attempt to find policies for further integration reaches the policy decision state (i.e., the agenda of the Council of Ministers), numerous barriers block the ideological com-mitment to advance integration in each policy sector. These barriers are as follows.[23]

Political Barriers

1. Different attitudes exist among the member-states vis-à-vis various nonmember-states (e.g., the Middle East nations, the United States, former colonies).
2. Different internal political pressures exist within the member-states (e.g., antimarketeer forces in Denmark, Scottish nationalism in Britain, large Communist parties in France and Italy).

3. There are different national perceptions as to the equality of the member-states (i.e., large versus small states).
4. There are different national perceptions as to the question of collective security (e.g., Ireland advocates neutrality, France wants an alternative to dependency on the United States in NATO, and Germany and Denmark would welcome more U.S. involvement).
5. National and Community-level interest groups exert political pressures on ideological and economic questions.

Economic Barriers
1. The member-states have different economic problems: growth rates, strength of currencies, unemployment, and inflation rates vary greatly.
2. The states have different economic philosophies (e.g., France and Italy concentrate on keeping employment high, whereas Germany and Denmark are more concerned with controlling inflation).
3. There are differences as to energy (e.g., France and Belgium want to minimize prices, Denmark has sought to guarantee supplies of energy with less attention to price, and Britain's attitude changes as it develops North Sea oil).
4. The member-states differ in their various market mechanisms, labor structures, and consumer mentalities.
5. There is an element of uncertainty caused by the state of the world economy, due particularly to the Third World's demand for a new international economic order.
6. Since 1972 all the member-states have been experiencing economic recession characterized by relatively high unemployment and inflation.

These political and economic barriers have been of sufficient strength in all but one major policy sector to block further progress (integration) in those sectors. The one exception has been the area of external relations. This is not to say that no such barriers exist in external relations; indeed, they not only exist, but many have had substantial effects. However, the barriers have been relatively the weakest of all those in the Community's policy sectors. The drive toward continued integration in the Community, powered by the ideological commitment to European union, has spilled around those policy sectors in which the political and economic barriers were strongest and has followed the path of least resistance—in this case, the policy sectors having to do with external relations. Progress past the weaker barriers is often assisted by certain "facilitators": (1) Costs (such as losing jobs) can be exported at present and postponed to the future. (2) External agreements can be justified as means to improve domestic economies through increased trade. (3) Assisting developing countries is supported on grounds of historical relationships, ideological or humanitarian concern, and so on. (4) Collective security is a convincing argument in many of the states.

Philippe Schmitter has suggested that regional actors would increasingly seek common external positions and increasingly rely on central institutions to find those common positions.[24] That all or even the majority of the Community's external relations are results of compulsive negotiations of common positions by the member-states would certainly be difficult to substantiate. There are, however, instances in which Schmitter's externalization hypothesis is most plausible. Although the Community nearly broke apart when the OPEC embargo and price hike occurred late in 1973, the best examples of externalization are the Community's long-term reactions to the Arab oil boycott.

There is a general consensus that the Community member-states were motivated by the OPEC price hikes and Arab oil embargo to initiate the Eur-Arab Dialogue and to participate in the North-South Dialogue. It may be argued that they were compelled to do so by the sudden realization of their dependence on and vulnerability to energy and raw material producers. It may also be argued that such considerations motivated, at least in part, the negotiations that led to the Lomé Convention and the ongoing negotiations of the International Energy Agency of OECD. What is perhaps most interesting (and most supportive of Schmitter's externalization hypothesis) is that the Community member-states decided to negotiate "with one voice" in all four fora. Further, they ensured such an outcome through structural arrangements. In these cases and in several others, the member-states do not take part in the direct negotiations with nonmember countries, but are represented by the Commission (as in the GATT and International Energy Agency, or IEA) or by the Commission and Council of Ministers serving as cochairmen or codelegates (as in the Eur-Arab Dialogue and the Conference on International Economic Cooperation, or CIEC).[25] The structural arrangement requires the Community to negotiate from a common position, which, in turn, demands a two-level negotiating process. The Community member-states may find themselves having to hammer out common positions daily at the Community level in reaction to events occurring at the negotiating level with nonmember-states.

A second important observation pertaining to externalization is that linkages develop between multilateral negotiations in which the Community is involved. Some doubt exists as to how much attention the Community (particularly the Commission) gave to similar types of negotiations conducted with different countries during the same or different time periods. There appeared to be little or no institutional effort to acquaint Commission negotiators with the results of previous similar negotiations or with related events in other international fora. This may account, if only in a small way, for the frustration of the nineteen African Yaoundé associates and the African, Caribbean, and Pacific (ACP) states at seeing their trade advantages eroded by Community agreements in GATT negotiations (which offered generalized tariff preferences to all developing states and consequently lessened the comparative advantage of associate and ACP exports). This phenomenon seemed to have been reversed dramatically in the spring of 1976. The Community member-states made a decision to deemphasize their involvement in the Fourth General Meeting of the United Nations Conference on Trade and Development (UNCTAD IV), preferring instead to concentrate on the North-South Dialogue. When it appeared that a failure to reach any agreement at Nairobi in UNCTAD IV might jeopardize the North-South Dialogue, the Community member-states (particularly Germany) scrambled for some (albeit symbolic) gesture of accommodation with the Third and Fourth Worlds. An important further observation is that the member-states each represented themselves at UNCTAD IV but were represented by the Community at the North-South Dialogue. The linkage between the two multilateral negotiators is unmistakable. Regardless of motivations, the apparent preference for the forum in which structural arrangements require a common voice supports the externalization hypothesis.

There are other examples of external-relations events furthering integration among the member-states and having an integrative impact on the Community. Although essentially an intergovernmental exercise, the political cooperation (Davignon Committee) machinery has further integrated the foreign ministries of the member-states. The activities of the Group of Foreign Correspondents and the COREU network (the communications system tying the nine foreign ministries together) are examples. The gradual incorporation of Commission observers into all but one of the political cooperation working groups and the expected establishment of a secretariat for political cooperation in the Council of Ministers' Secretariat-General should enhance that integration. A further example may be found in the Lomé Convention and its predecessors. The Community had always encouraged regional group formation among Third World countries, preferring to negotiate bloc-to-bloc. The Community was directly responsible for the creation of the Associated African States and Madagascar (AASM) among the Yaoundé associates and indirectly responsible for the creation of the ACP states group. The Commission still disburses funds designed to encourage regional organization formation and maintenance for developing countries. The effect has been occasionally dramatic and unexpected. ACP solidarity during the Lomé negotiations forced the Community member-states to come to common Community decisions that they might not otherwise have attempted.[26]

The economic and political barriers just discussed have contributed to an atmosphere of uncertainty and caution in the European Community. Member-state and Community decisionmakers have been largely unable to make decisions favoring further internal integration of the Community for fear of the risks involved. Such attempts have not been totally frustrated, however. Despite (or perhaps due to) the stagnation in the Community's agricultural, industrial, financial, transport, and social sectors, significant progress has been achieved in the external-relations sectors of the Community. It is worth noting that, in his address to the European Parliament on February 12, 1980, Roy Jenkins (president of the EC Commission) chose to discuss the five major accomplishments of 1979. The first was the creation of the EMS; the other four concerned the Community's success in external relations.[27]

Notes

1. The original six member-states are Belgium, the Netherlands, Luxembourg, France, Italy, and West Germany. Denmark, Ireland, and the United Kingdom became active members in 1973.

2. The European Community Information Service (Washington, D.C.), *The European Community: The Facts* (February 1974), p. 2.

3. F. Roy Willis, *France, Germany, and the New Europe 1945–1963* (Stanford, Calif.: Stanford University Press, 1965), p. 80.

4. For background, see Ernst B. Haas, *The Uniting of Europe: Political, Social, and Economic Forces 1950–1957* (Stanford, Calif.: Stanford University Press, 1958).

5. See Jaroslav G. Polach, *Euratom: Its Background, Issues and Economic Implications* (Dobbs Ferry, N.Y.: Oceana Publications, 1964).

6. More on this period may be found in Michael Curtis's *Western European Integration* (New York: Harper and Row, 1969) and Roger Morgan's *Western European Politics Since 1945: The Shaping of the European Community* (London: B. T. Batsford, 1972).

7. Roy Pryce, "Customs Union and Economic Union in the EEC," in John Calmann (Ed.) *The Common Market* (London: Anthony Bland, 1967), pp. 43–57.

8. Glenda G. Rosenthal, *The Men Behind the Decisions: Cases In European Policy-Making* (Lexington, Mass.: Lexington Books, 1975), pp. 101–125.

9. See Phillip Taylor, *When Europe Speaks with One Voice: The External Relations of the European Community* (Westport, Conn.: Greenwood Press, 1979), pp. 153–158; also, "European Community Signs Agreement (Lomé II) with Developing Nations," *European Community News*, No. 36/1979 (October 31, 1979), pp. 1–4.

10. "The Directly Elected European Parliament: First Session," *European Community News*, No. 25/1979 (July 11, 1979), pp. 1–11.

11. "European Monetary System to Go into Force: France Lifts Reserve on System," *European Community News*, No. 7/1979 (March 7, 1979), pp. 1–10.

12. "EC and Greece to Sign Accession Treaty," *European Community News*, No. 36/1979 (October 31, 1979), pp. 1–4.

13. General descriptions of the Community's institutions may be found in A. H. Robertson, *European Institutions: Cooperation: Integration: Unification* (New York: Matthew Bender, 1973); and in Michael Palmer and John Lambert, *Handbook of European Organizations* (New York: Praeger Publishers, 1968).

14. See David Coombes, *Politics and Bureaucracy in the European Community: A Portrait of the Commission of the EEC* (London: George Allen and Unwin, 1970).

15. See P.H.J.M. Houben, *Les Conseils des Ministres des Communautés Européennes* (Leiden: Sijthoff, 1964).

16. "The Directly Elected European Parliament: First Session," *European Community News,* No. 25/1979 (March 7, 1979), pp. 1–10.

17. See Valentine Herman and Juliet Lodge, *The European Parliament and the European Community* (New York: Praeger Publishers, 1979).

18. Emile Noel, "How the European Community's Institutions Work," *Community Topics* 39 (April 1973), pp. 9–10.

19. See Gerhard Bebr, *Judicial Control of the European Communities* (New York: Praeger Publishers, 1962). Also, Stuart A. Scheingold, *The Rule of Law in European Integration: The Path of the Schuman Plan* (New Haven, Conn.: Yale University Press, 1965).

20. Noel, "How the European Community's Institutions Work," pp. 11–12.

21. "Report on European Union," *European Parliament Working Papers*, Document 174/75, July 7, 1975, pp. 5ff.

22. Secretariat of the European Parliament, *Europe Today: State of European Integration* (Luxembourg: European Parliament, 1976), par. 4.163.

23. For a detailed discussion of barriers and facilitators, see Taylor, *When Europe Speaks*, pp. 7–12.

24. Philippe C. Schmitter, "Three Neo-Functional Hypotheses About International Integration," *International Organization* 23 (Winter 1969), pp. 161–166.

25. France does not belong to the IEA, and the United Kingdom for some time had not wanted to participate in the CIEC due to its oil interests in the North Sea. Both had or now have their interests represented in these fora through the Community delegations.

26. Taylor, *When Europe Speaks*, pp. 202–204.

27. "Roy Jenkins Presents the Commission's Program for 1980 to the European Parliament," *European Community News*, No. 10/80 (February 20, 1980), pp. 1–4.

5
The Andean Group and
the Association of
South East Asian Nations

The Andean Group (also known as ANCOM or the Andean Common Market) and the Association of South East Asian Nations (ASEAN) are important economic international governmental organizations (IGOs) for several reasons. First, ANCOM is important for what it attempted to do, and ASEAN for its potential as an economic (and political) world actor. Second, both are important for their respective efforts to emulate the European Community and to develop special ties to it. Although the European Community served as an active model for these IGOs, both share characteristics that make them very different from the EC. Consequently, the efforts of such theories as neofunctionalism and others developed to explain European integration have been largely unsuccessful when applied in ANCOM and ASEAN.

Perhaps the greatest difference is that ANCOM and ASEAN are composed of developing nations. Nationalism developed in different ways in developing countries than in Western Europe, and national consciousness appears to have grown stronger in recent years. Again, unlike Western Europe there is little structural homogeneity in Latin America and Southeast Asia. The highly pluralistic social structures found in Europe are relatively nonexistent in ANCOM and ASEAN member-states. These nations constitute what some have labeled "communities of poverty," having little to trade with each other except the same raw materials and agricultural products they export to First World countries. Consequently, ANCOM and ASEAN have had to develop innovative strategies to cope with these differences. In order to overcome growing exclusivist nationalism and the problem of dependency in the international economic system, ANCOM developed what Edward Milenky has termed "developmental nationalism" or "the use of industrialization as an economic strategy and rallying point for the rejection of all forms of external dependence by a developing country on the advanced countries."[1]

Finally, unlike the European Economic Community, neither ANCOM nor ASEAN is a true common market or economic union. A common market is defined as a customs union (in which tariffs and quantitative restrictions to trade among the member-states are abolished and a common external tariff is established) with no restrictions on economic-factor movements between member-states. An economic union is a common market that features some degree of harmonization of national economic policies. ANCOM is a customs union with some degree of harmonization. ASEAN is even less ambitious. It seeks only to coordinate economic policies and developmental efforts.[2]

The Andean Group

The origin of the Andean Group was a meeting in Bogotá, Columbia, in August 1966 among the presidents of Chile, Colombia, and Venezuela, and the personal representatives of the presidents of Bolivia and Peru. In the resulting declaration of Bogotá, the leaders called for general agreement on trade concessions and complementary industrial agreements to promote balanced economic development within the framework of the Latin American Free Trade Association (LAFTA).[3] The LAFTA foreign ministers approved the guidelines contained in the Bogotá Declaration in September 1967. The group's basic charter, the Agreement of Cartagena (named for the Colombian city where most of the negotiations took place), was signed on May 26, 1969, and entered into force on October 16, 1969. The five charter members were Bolivia (a late entry to the negotiations), Chile, Colombia, Ecuador, and Peru. Venezuela did not join until February 13, 1973.

The primary motivations for the creation of ANCOM were to enable the Andean states to compete on a more equal basis with the LAFTA "big three" (Argentina, Brazil, and Mexico) and to accelerate the process of economic integration among the member-states. The stated objectives in the Cartegena Agreement are (1) to promote equitable and accelerated economic development; (2) to facilitate more effective participation and integration in LAFTA; and (3) to raise the standard of living for the citizens of the member-states. The achievement of these objectives hinged on the following steps: (1) joint planning, including industrial sector agreements; (2) harmonization of economic and social policies; (3) a program of trade liberalization more ambitious than that of LAFTA; and (4) a common external tariff.[4]

History and Development

The case for ANCOM's success potential early in its development was convincing. The member-states made up an area approximately two-thirds that of the United States and had a combined gross national product of $30 billion, larger than Argentina's or Mexico's and nearly half that of Brazil (1972 figures). In addition, they exported 70 to 100 percent of the world's trade in copper, tin, molybdenum, tungsten, and bismuth, 65 percent of the world's iron exports, and nearly 50 percent of its coal exports. Energy production was quite favorable. Hydroelectric power potential, especially in Colombia and Peru, was tremendous. With the accession of Venezuela in 1973, the group had two important OPEC members (with Ecuador).[5]

Acting on the provisions of Articles 33 and 47 of the Cartagena Agreement, the Commission began the system of sectorial programs for joint development in late 1970. This system provides for the assignment to different countries of a monopoly or semimonopoly in the manufacture of certain products for periods of ten to fifteen years (Bolivia and Ecuador were granted longer periods as part of the "special attention" given for their relatively poorer economies).[6] By 1975, petrochemical and metal working programs had been approved, along with motor vehicles, fertilizers, steel, glass, electronics, pharmaceuticals, and pulp and paper. For example, Colombia was assigned light aircraft, Ecuador dairy equipment, and Peru refrigerators and parking meters. The deadline for conclusion of all sectoral programs was set for 1977; however, difficulties arose concerning the timetables themselves and serious dissension over the allocation of other products and industries in the late 1970s. Agreement was reached in September 1977 for sharing the market for motor vehicles through the Andean Automotive Industrial Development Program, and a production target of 400,000 vehicles was set for 1985.

Another important innovative development occurred in 1971 concerning foreign capital and multinational corporations. By Commission directive (known as Decision 24), foreign investors could not qualify for preferential trade arrangements unless they divested themselves of 51 percent of their shares to local investors. In utilities, communications, and retail marketing enterprises, foreign investors were to hold no more than 20 percent of total shares. Certain extractive industries (notably oil) were exempt from Decision 24, but notice was given that nationalization was a "probability" by the end of the century. Under Decision 24, transfers were to be completed within fifteen years for Colombia, Peru, and Venezuela, and within twenty years for Bolivia and Ecuador.

Decision 24 proved to be the cause of the first real shock to Andean integration. After the fall of Allende, the right-wing government of Chile began to encourage foreign multinational enterprise investment and sought for two years to have Decision 24 revised or rescinded. Having failed in those negotiations, Chile withdrew from membership in October 1976.

Two important developments also occurred in 1976. First, an agreement was adopted by the ministers of labor for the integration of social and labor policies to proceed into two stages (1978 and 1980). The agreement is meant to extend the social security benefits each worker enjoys in his own country to the rest of the Andean region. Second, the ministers of agriculture concluded twenty-two resolutions to integrate the agricultural sector. The plan to coordinate national agricultural plans under a standard regional policy was put into effect in 1977.

Major changes to the Cartagena Agreement were accomplished through the Protocol of Arequipa, signed in April 1978. Deadlines for most of the mechanisms contained in the agreement were extended, and exceptions to the sectoral industrial development programs were approved. The common external tariff was to have been phased in beginning December 31, 1979, but that process appears to be indefinitely "on hold."

At a summit meeting in May 1978, the leaders of the member-states signed the "Mandate of Cartagena," which called for accelerating the integration process in many economic sectors and for the creation of a judicial tribunal to be located in Quito. The Latin American Regional Parliament had its first meeting in December 1979. Patterned after the European Parliament, the members are seated by party rather than national affiliation. Direct elections are planned by the mid-1980s.

Institutions

The Cartagena Agreement established two principal institutions, the Commission and the Junta (or Board). The Commission is intended to be the highest authority in ANCOM; the Junta is the permanent secretariat and technical organization. Other bodies are the Consultative Committee, the Economic and Social Advisory Committee, the Andean Development Corporation, the Regional Parliament, and the Judicial Tribunal (the latter three were created by separate conventions). The Junta and other bodies are located in Lima, Peru. (See Figure 5.1.)

The Commission consists of one plenipotentiary representative from each member-state. The presidency rotates annually among the member-states. The Commission, which corresponds to the EC Council of Ministers rather than to the EC Commission, meets three times each year and may be called for special sessions on request of the Junta or any member-state. The Junta serves as both an executive body and a general secretariat. In addition, it performs those tasks given to the

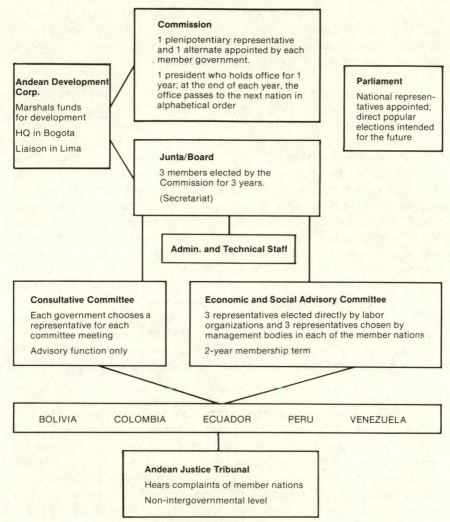

Figure 5.1   ANCOM Organizational Structure

COREPER in the European Community. The Economic and Social Advisory Committee consists of representatives of management and labor and serves the role of "sounding board" to both the Commission and Junta. The Consultative Committee is an ad hoc advisory body that serves the nebulous function of communications channel between the member-states and the Junta.

There are several functionally assigned councils concerned with finance, fiscal policy, tourism, and the like. The Andean Development Corporation serves as the development-financing arm of ANCOM. Its authorized capital has been relatively small ($400 million in 1976). The Andean Reserve Fund began operations in 1978. It is intended to assist to harmonizing exchange, monetary, and financial policies of the five member-states.

The decisionmaking process in ANCOM involves only the Commission and the Junta. The Junta does possess the right of initiative and does most of the preparatory work for the Commission. By Article 11 of the Cartagena Agreement, a two-thirds majority vote is required for Commission "decisions." However, since the agreement envisioned a six-member group, the present five members employ a four-fifths majority rule. The agreement has three annexes that specify two-thirds approval with no negative votes cast (for delegation of power without a second negative vote cast by the same nation on proposals sent back to the Junta for modification and resubmittal), and a two-thirds majority with one or two negative votes, but not by both Bolivia and Ecuador (on matters relating to the special treatment accorded Bolivia and Ecuador).

Proposals submitted by the Junta may be accepted or rejected by the Commission using the two-thirds (four-fifths) rule. It is relatively difficult, however, for the Commission to amend a Junta proposal and then act on that revision. Such actions require a unanimous vote in the Commission. The Junta also enjoys an advantage relative to the Commission in far greater continuity of its highest officials.[7]

State of Integration

The most charitable assessment of the state of integration in ANCOM is that of stagnation. However, were it possible to describe the entire organization in its first decade of existence, the best possible term is "muddle-about" (from Schmitter's actor strategies discussed in Chapter 3). Through the ANCOM Commission, the member-states have significantly increased the scope of the organization's functions, and the number of the component institutions has more than doubled. Yet, due to severe political and economic barriers, the authority of the central institutions to act on behalf of the member-states has been diminished. In addition, the timetable for realizing the goals in the Cartagena Agreement has been procrastinated and often seemingly forgotten.

The barriers to integration are numerous. Economic barriers include relatively small economic sizes and economies of scale, underdeveloped transportation and communications systems, lack of homogeneity in per capita GNP, high rates of inflation, and differing degrees of state participation in the respective national economies.[8] Here, one can cite an important contrast with the European Community. Transportation costs from city to city in one state are often much higher in ANCOM than from country to country in the EC.[9]

Political barriers plague ANCOM integration efforts as well. Peru is a military Yugoslovia-like socialist state, whereas Colombia and Venezuela are conservative-capitalist nations. Ecuador has a military conservative-capitalist government, and Bolivia has had 184 changes in government in the last 146 years (the most recent from far left to center right and back again to the left). The greatest political blow was the politically motivated withdrawal by the right-wing military junta in Chile.[10]

Initially, the accession of Venezuela with its wealth of experience in OPEC was expected to be a catalyst for Andean integration. However, Venezuela may yet choose to dominate and, perhaps, to disrupt ANCOM. Venezuela's entry required some "slippage" in the Cartagena Agreement's provision. Venezuela demanded and got some relaxation in the use of safeguard measures, expanded free trade exemptions on agricultural products, extension of the veto to include the common external tariff, and more control over its own monetary policy than that permitted the other ANCOM states.[11]

The Association of South East Asian Nations

The Association of South East Asian Nations (ASEAN) was created formally on August 8, 1967, at Bangkok when the foreign ministers of Thailand, Indonesia, Malaya, Singapore, and the Philippines signed the ASEAN (or Bangkok) Declaration. The declaration was based on the premise that "cooperation among nation-states in the spirit of equality and partnership would bring mutual benefits and stimulate solidarity which would contribute to building the foundations of peace, stability and prosperity in the world community at large and the region in particular."[12]

The seven objectives of the ASEAN Declaration are (1) to accelerate economic growth, social progress, and cultural development; (2) to promote regional peace and stability; (3) to promote collaboration on matters of common interest; (4) to promote mutual assistance in training and research facilities; (5) to encourage greater utilization of agriculture and industry, expansion of trade, and improvement of transportation and communications facilities; (6) to promote Southeast Asian studies; and (7) to promote closer links with regional organizations that have similar aims.

74

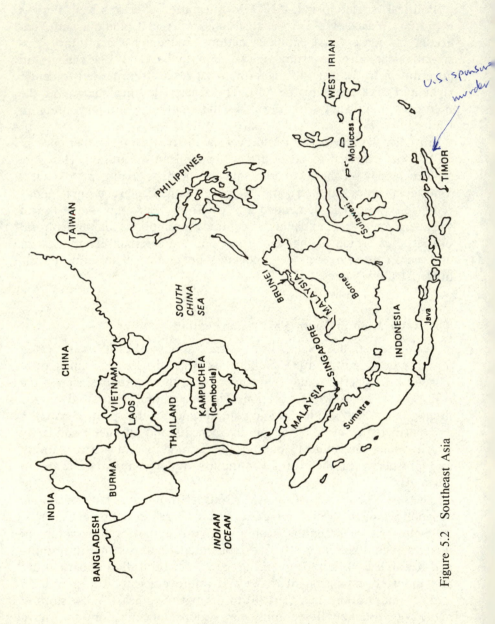

Figure 5.2 Southeast Asia

History and Development

The first attempt at regional integration in Southeast Asia was the Association of Southeast Asia (ASA) created in 1961 by Malaya, the Philippines, and Thailand. ASA was dissolved one year later when the Philippines suspended diplomatic relations with Malaya due to conflict over claims on the Sabah region. In 1963, Indonesia, Malaya, and the Philippines formed the Maphilindo Association for the same purposes that ASA was formed: to promote consultation on economic, social, cultural, and technical matters of common interest to the member-states. The Maphilindo Association was short-lived as well. It failed due to Sukarno's attempts to incorporate Malaya into a "greater Indonesia" and to perceptions in Malaya and the Philippines that Sukarno was "leaning toward Communism."[13]

The two major events that led to the creation of ASEAN were the secession of Singapore from Malaya in 1965 and the fall of Indonesian leader Sukarno in 1966. In August 1967, Thailand invited the foreign ministers of all Southeast Asian nations to a conference to discuss the formation of a regional economic cooperation agreement. For the five who responded, the meeting stalled for two days while the foreign ministers played golf together. This occurrence, which has more than anecdotal significance, has been repeated at each subsequent ASEAN foreign ministers' conference. Playing golf served to build personal friendships important to the attitude of the negotiations. (Since 1967, the most commonly given symbols of friendship have been golf clubs and related equipment.[14]) The signing of the ASEAN Declaration was received with little attention in the West, with general skepticism from most Asian nations, and with animosity in China.[15]

During ASEAN's first four years of existence, few results were achieved or expected. The member-states appeared preoccupied with building and mending ties, particularly those between Malaysia and the Philippines in their dispute over Sabah. In 1972, the ASEAN leaders were shocked by Nixon's visit to China. They resolved to move toward "neutralism" and to seek peaceful relations with China. ASEAN leaders also began to express the feeling that U.S. presence in their countries was ineffective and embarrassing. Thai Premier Kukrit Pramo stated that U.S. military presence was like a woman "being caught in a bedroom with a gentleman who can no longer operate. You find yourself compromised for nothing."[16] Thus, in 1975 Malaysia proposed a "Zone of Peace, Freedom, and Neutrality (ZOPFAN)" so as to include Vietnam, Laos, and Kampuchea as members of ASEAN. The following year, the ASEAN summit (heads of government) produced the ASEAN Concord (principles and framework for an action program in various economic fields), the Treaty of Amity and Cooperation (the first step toward creation of ZOPFAN and a mutual agreement to settle intra-ASEAN disputes through "friendly negotiation"), and the Agreement on the Establishment of the ASEAN Secretariat.

ASEAN began to function as a formal "regional lobby" for negotiations in UNCTAD and the GATT in 1977. Joint meetings were begun with the prime ministers of Australia, New Zealand, and Japan. ASEAN committees were established in the capitals of important trade partner-states (the United States, Canada, and India). In 1980 ASEAN signed the "Joint Declaration of ASEAN-EEC" with the European Communities.[17] That agreement calls for most-favored-nation treatment bloc to bloc; economic, commercial, and development cooperation; and establishment of a joint cooperation committee. At that time, ASEAN had included 6,000 items in its Preferential Trading Agreement; reduced existing tariffs on all intra-ASEAN trade by 20 percent; concluded industrial projects in urea, soda ash, and pulp and paper; and instituted a Food Security Reserve Agreement for the region.

Institutions

The primary institutions are the ministerial meetings and the Standing Committee. The foreign ministers meet once a year, rotating the site of the meeting among the capitals of the member-states. Meetings have been held at the summit level (heads of state and government), and meetings of other ministers (especially economic ministers) have been regularized. The Annual Ministerial Meeting of Foreign Ministers is the policymaking organ of ASEAN. (See Figure 5.3.)

The Standing Committee serves as the executive body. It meets once a month in the capital of the nation hosting the annual meeting. It consists of the foreign minister of the host nation, ambassadors of the other members, the directors-general, and the secretary-general. The Standing Committee oversees the activities of the nine permanent committees and seven ad hoc committees. The permanent committees are functionally assigned: Trade and Tourism, Industry, Minerals, and Energy; Food, Agriculture, and Forestry; Transportation and Communications; Finance and Banking; Science and Technology; Social Development; Culture and Information; and Budget. The ad hoc committees include the Special Coordinating Committee, ASEAN-Brussels Committee, Special Committee of Central Banks and Monetary Authorities, Coordinating Committee for the Reconstruction and Rehabilitation of Indochina, Senior Officials on Sugar, Senior Trade Officials on GATT, and the ASEAN Geneva Committee. The General-Secretariat is also subordinate to the Standing Committee. Since its creation in 1976, it has been headquartered in Jakarta, Indonesia.

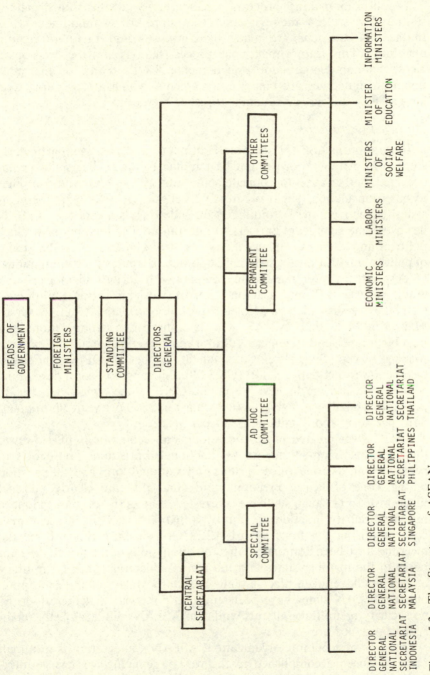

Figure 5.3   The Structure of ASEAN

The decisionmaking process is salient only at the ministerial or summit levels. New members must be approved by unanimous vote. In fact, all decisions are made by consensus and therefore require unanimity. This feature makes the process tedious and the decisions a "least-common-denominator" phenomenon. Still, many of the most important outcomes are bilateral agreements, which are encouraged as long as they are not detrimental to other members.

State of Integration

Integration in ASEAN has been continuous and positive, particularly since 1976. Although one might be tempted to argue that spillover has occurred, perhaps the appropriate actor strategy has been and continues to be encapsulation (slight progressive steps taken within the member-states' collective zone of indifference). Indeed, it appears that ASEAN has overcome significant barriers to integration. The member-states lack political and economic homogeneity. All but Thailand bear the stamp of political institutions from colonial powers. Disputes over international borders remain, and many still contend with serious ideological and ethnic cleavages: Roman Catholics versus Moslems in the Philippines, Orthodox versus Abogon Moslems in Indonesia, and Chinese versus Malays in Malaysia.[18] All ASEAN states have dense populations and high birth rates, and fragile agricultural economies vulnerable to extreme weather (except Singapore). Although a member of OPEC, Indonesia has the lowest per capita GNP (US $240). Singapore is not a developing country and has the highest per capita GNP in the region (US $2,700 per year). The others, in 1980, were Malaysia, $860 per year; Philippines, $410 per year; and Thailand, $380 per year.[19]

ASEAN was created to be and remains an economic IGO. However, there has been some evidence of functional diffraction. The efforts to negotiate and use one voice in other international fora, and the creation of the Zone of Peace, Freedom, and Neutrality are clearly political functions. Some analysts have suggested that ASEAN may adopt a military/security function. Certainly, China was very much a common concern during the first half of ASEAN's existence. Since 1978, the meetings have been dominated often by discussions of the threat Vietnam poses to the member-states and the region. Bilateral talks and military maneuvers have taken place among Thailand, Malaysia, and Singapore, but the ASEAN states have been quick to point out that there is to be no security or military alliance and that ASEAN will steadfastly retain a neutralist posture.[20]

In terms of economic organization, ASEAN's integration is minimal. Little has been accomplished in the way of reducing barriers to intra-ASEAN trade. Indeed, intraregional trade decreased as a percent of total trade from 17.8 percent in 1968 to 15.9 percent in 1977.[21] The prospects for a free trade area are not great, and even less so for a common market/common external tariff for ASEAN. Still, the organization's external economic relations with the United States, Japan, and the European Community make it a potentially important world actor.[22]

Notes

1. See Edward Milensky, "From Integration to Developmental Nationalism: The Andean Group, 1966–1971," *Inter-American Economic Affairs* 25:3 (Winter 1971); and "Developmental Nationalism in Practice," *Inter-American Economic Affairs* 26 (Spring 1973).

2. David Morawetz, *The Andean Group: A Case Study in Economic Integration Among Developing Countries* (Cambridge: MIT Press, 1974), p. 1.

3. Now called ALADI (Latin American Association of Integration). See Chapter 6.

4. Article 3 of the Charter (Subregional Integration Agreement).

5. Alice Taylor (Ed.), *Focus on Latin America* (New York: Praeger Publishers, 1973), p. 51.

6. See Andrew B. Wardlaw, *The Andean Integration Movement: A Report Prepared Under Contract for the U.S. Department of State* (Washington, D.C.: Government Printing Office, 1973), pp. 12–16.

7. Ibid., pp. 7–11.

8. Morawetz, *The Andean Group*, pp. 102–103.

9. Ibid., pp. 22–24.

10. Ibid., p. 5.

11. William Avery, "Oil, Politics, and Economic Policy Making: Venezuela and the Andean Common Market," *International Organization* 30:4 (Autumn 1976), p. 569.

12. *Ten Years of ASEAN* (Jakarta: ASEAN Secretariat, 1977), p. 1.

13. Shee Poon Kim, "A Decade of ASEAN," *Asian Survey*, August 1977, pp. 1–8.

14. *New York Times*, May 14, 1975.

15. The news media (*Hsin hua*) in the People's Republic of China reported it as an "out and out counter-revolutionary alliance against China" and "another instrument for U.S. imperialism and Soviet revisionism." *New York Times*, August 13, 1967.

16. *New York Times*, June 29, 1975.

17. For background, see "Focus: EEC and Asia '78" *Far Eastern Economic Review*, April 21, 1978, pp. 36–66.

18. John Bastin and Harry J. Benda, *A History of Modern Southeast Asia* (Englewood Cliffs, N.J.: Prentice-Hall, 1968).

19. R.J.G. Wells, "ASEAN Intraregional Trading in Food and Agricultural Crops: The Way Ahead," *Asian Survey*, June 1980.

20. See Rodney Tasker, "Seeking a Sense of Direction," *Far Eastern Economic Review*, June 9, 1978, pp. 29–31; and "ASEAN: Five Fingers on the Trigger," *Far Eastern Economic Review*, October 24–30, 1980, p. 32.

21. Kim, "A Decade of ASEAN," pp. 1–8.

22. For a theoretical perspective, see Charles W. Kegley, Jr., and Llwellyn D. Howell, Jr., "The Dimensionality of Regional Integration: Construct Validation in the Southeast Asian Context," *International Organization* 29:4 (Autumn 1975).

6
Other Common Markets, Free Trade Associations, and Development Organizations

There are many regional economic intergovernmental organizations. Although some have failed recently (the Central American Common Market and the East African Community are examples) and others have been absorbed into larger bodies (e.g., CARIFTA into CARICOM), the trend of such organizations appears to be toward proliferation rather than retrenchment.

The extent to which any of these organizations is or may become an important world actor depends upon many factors, but principally upon the character of its memberships as well as the degree of and progress toward integration. Both of these factors are directly related to the scope and intensity of the political barriers each confronts. It is also important to consider the purposes for which each organization was created and any degree of focusing or diffraction in its functions over time. Like ASEAN, those that began with relatively less ambitious goals may appear to be more successful than those that, like ANCOM, started out to form common markets among Third World nations.

The following survey of these regional economic organizations presents common markets (in order of their relative success), free trade associations, and development programs. Each presentation will include brief discussions of background, purposes, institutions, and accomplishments. The chapter will conclude with a comparative analysis of relative states of integration for them all.

Common Markets

The Benelux Economic Union

The Benelux Union was created in 1948 and reconstituted in 1960 by the Treaty of the Benelux Economic Union. Consisting of Belgium, the Netherlands, and Luxembourg (hence "Benelux"), the Union's purposes are to coordinate the economic, financial, and social policies of those states and to supervise common foreign trade policies. The policymaking body is the Committee of Ministers, which meets three times each year and is composed of at least one cabinet-level minister from each nation. Passage of resolutions requires unanimity, but abstentions are not considered negative votes. The executive body (commission) is the Council of the Economic Union. This consists of one chairman from each member-state and the chairmen from each of the eight committees (foreign economic relations; monetary and financial; industrial and commercial; agriculture, food, and fisheries; customs and taxation; transport; social; and movement and establishment of persons). The Benelux Union also has a forty-nine-member (advisory) Consultative Inter-Parliamentary Council, a twenty-seven-member Economic and Social Advisory Council, both a College of Arbitration (to settle disputes over the application of the Treaty) and the Benelux Court of Justice (since 1974), and a General-Secretariat. All institutions are located in Brussels.[1]

The Benelux Union has accomplished the abolition of passports and labor permits (for movement among the three nations) and the removal of intra-Union import duties and most quotas. It also serves as an important caucus for economic and social matters discussed in the European Community and the Organization for Economic Cooperation and Development.

Economic Community of West African States

The Economic Community of West African States (ECOWAS) was created in 1976 by the Treaty of Lagos. It consists of sixteen nations (Nigeria, Liberia, and fourteen Francophone states).[2] The stated purposes of ECOWAS are to eliminate trade barriers, to establish a common external tariff and a common commercial policy, and to eliminate disparities in levels of development among the member-states. Located in Lagos, Nigeria, the central institutions include the Supreme Authority of Heads of State (a policymaking body that meets annually at the summit level), the Council of Ministers (two from each state), the Tribunal, the Executive Secretariat, four specialized commissions (Trade, Customs, Immigration, and Monetary), and the Fund for Cooperation, Compensation, and Development (for member-states adversely affected by ECOWAS trade liberalization).[3]

ECOWAS has achieved a "consolidation" of customs duties, an improvement in telecommunications links, and the abolition of visas for ninety-day visits for citizens of one ECOWAS state to another. In its first five years of existence, ECOWAS has managed to maintain its timetable for moving toward the goal of establishing a customs union by 1990.[4]

Council for Mutual Economic Assistance

The Council for Mutual Economic Assistance (CMEA or COMECON) was created in 1949 and reconstituted to its present structure in 1960. Its members include the USSR, the Eastern European states (Yugoslavia is only an associate member and Albania has not participated since 1961), Cuba, Mongolia, Vietnam, and Laos. There are three "cooperating countries"—Finland, Iraq, and Mexico—that have observer status and special trade arrangements with COMECON. The CMEA was created by the Soviet Union (probably in response, and as an alternative, to the U.S. Marshall Plan) to contribute to the "planned development" of the members, to accelerate economic and technical progress and industrialization, and to raise the well-being of the citizens of the member-states. The central institutions are the Council (a policy organ that meets at the ministerial level once each year and makes decisions by unanimity), the Executive Committee (which meets every two months), several standing commissions in which most of the work is accomplished (experts from various industries, agriculture, health, and nuclear energy), the International Bank for Economic Cooperation and the International Investment Bank, and the General-Secretariat. All institutions and meetings are in Moscow.[5]

From 1949 to 1955, economic progress achieved under CMEA aegis was clearly an instrument of Soviet control. However, the scope of activities and some "democratization" increased under Khrushchev. In 1971 Brezhnev began programs of "socialist integration" and division of labor with COMECON. These programs were resisted by Rumania and East Germany, who sought to diversify their industries rather than create dependency relationships through specialization intended to enhance intra-CMEA trade. An effort by the USSR to circumvent East German and Rumanian resistance by introducing majority rule in the Council failed in 1978. The most recent emphasis has been on nuclear energy development and development assistance to the less developed member-states.[6]

Common African and Mauritian Organization

The Common African and Mauritian Organization (OCAM) was begun in 1961 and reorganized in 1965 and 1974 due to significant changes in membership. Its current membership is Benin, Togo, Upper Volta, Central African Republic, Ivory Coast, Niger, Rwanda, and Mauritius (all moderate Francophone states).[7] Its original purposes were to harmonize economic policies, to coordinate economic development through the Organization for African Unity, and to coordinate efforts to raise the living standards of the citizens of the member-states. Since 1975, the organization has changed its focus or, perhaps, simply lost direction. The common transports and communications bodies are now separate and independent entities. The annual meetings of the Conference of Heads of State and Government (a policymaking organ) are now highly politicized. Rather than permitting discussion of economic programs suggested by the organizations charter, the sessions have concentrated on such issues as the political situations in the Western Sahara, South Africa, and Ghana. Institutional development is minimal. Other than the summit-level Conference, the only central institutions are the Council of Ministers (which meets annually to implement Conference resolutions) and the Secretariat. The headquarters of the Secretariat is Bangui, Central African Republic.

Caribbean Community and Common Market

The Caribbean Community and Common Market (CARICOM) was created in 1973 to replace the Caribbean Free Trade Association (CARIFTA) and to further integration in the region. The member-states are Antigua, Barbados, Belize, Dominica, Jamaica, and seven small island nations. The Bahamas is an ex officio member. The first non-Commonwealth nation, Haiti, applied for membership in 1979. The central institutions of CARICOM are the annual meetings of the heads of state and government and the Secretariat, located in Georgetown, Guyana. CARICOM was created as an "umbrella" organization. It contains, as "associate institutions," the East Caribbean Common Market, the West Indies Associated States, the Caribbean Development Bank, and several small organizations.

During the 1970s, CARICOM accomplished nothing of substance. Its efforts to establish the common external tariff and to coordinate development planning have been thwarted by political divisiveness among the member-states. Intra-CARICOM trade has declined. Indeed, most have followed nationalistic economic policies, particularly those concerning protectionism.

Central American Common Market and East African Community

Two of the oldest regional economic communities, the Central American Common Market (CACM) and the East African Community (EAC), exist now only "on paper" but deserve brief mention for their historical import. The CACM had existed most of this century and was last reorganized in 1961 to be a common market and customs union. Honduras and Nicaragua are nonparticipating members. Among El Salvador,

Guatemala, and Costa Rica, only the last has not been economically paralyzed by serious civil strife.[8]

The EAC was formally established by the Treaty of East African Cooperation in 1967. The organization created by Kenya, Tanzania, and Uganda was a continuation of the British-imposed East African Common Services Organization (High Commission) from 1945 to 1960. The common market, common communications, and transportations bodies, the Tribunal, and the Legislative Assembly have been inoperative since Idi Amin caused a rift between the nations in 1971.

Free Trade Associations

European Free Trade Association

The European Free Trade Association (EFTA) was established in 1960 principally due to the efforts of Britain to form an alternative to the EEC. The original members were Britain, Iceland, Portugal, Switzerland, Austria, and the Scandinavian countries (Finland is an associate member). Britain and Denmark left EFTA in 1973 when both became members of the EC. The organization's stated purpose—namely, the gradual elimination of barriers to nonagricultural trade among the member-states—is quite limited. Located in Geneva, the central institutions are the Council, the standing committees, the joint councils, and a very small Secretariat. The Council is the policymaking body. It meets three times each year at the ministerial level and several times per year at lower levels. There are two joint councils: EFTA-Finland and EFTA-Yugoslavia; these meet concurrently with the Council. The eight standing committees are functionally assigned (e.g., trade, customs, budget, and the like) and serve as separate executive bodies for the organization.

EFTA achieved customs elimination and special trading agreements with the EC in the early 1970s. In 1975, the Council began to hold general discussions on matters beyond the region relative to the world economy: raw materials, monetary policies, unemployment, and inflation. In 1977, EFTA revised the trend toward further integration when the member-states abandoned the objectives of economic policies harmonization. Spain began negotiations for entry into EFTA in 1979, but withdrew the initiative when it began entry negotiations with the EC.[9]

Latin American Association of Integration

The Latin American Association of Integration (ALADI) was originally formed as the Latin American Free Trade Association (LAFTA) by the Treaty of Montevideo in 1961. The purpose of that organization was to eliminate gradually over a twelve-year period trade barriers for products originating in the member-states. Formed by Mexico and ten South American nations (all except the three Guyanas), the organization set up a system of tariff reductions based on several national lists of products and a common list that would gradually replace the national lists. In addition, an intraregional trade growth program was initiated, and a number of industrial agreements and a system of payments and credits was included under the Cooperative and Development Program. The organization achieved substantial success during its first five years, but the following ten years were characterized by stagnation and retrenchment. Many of the member-states felt that the means to overcome the lack of any further integration was to increase the goals and scope of LAFTA substantially. However, serious negotiations to create a Latin American common market in the late 1970s were thwarted by political divisiveness and the inability of the member-states (principally Colombia and Uruguay) to agree on the mechanisms for creating the common market. In 1980, the free association function was abandoned completely and the organization was reconstituted as the Latin American Association of Integration (ALADI). The only remaining function is policy harmonization in matters of development cooperation.[10]

The structural organization of ALADI consists of the Council (which holds annual meetings of the foreign ministers), the Conference of Contracting Parties (which meets annually to approve programs and budgets and elects the Secretary-General), and the Permanent Executive Committee (Commission). The Secretariat is located in Montevideo, Uruguay.

Development Organizations

Organization for Economic Cooperation and Development

The OECD was founded in 1961 to replace the Organization for European Economic Cooperation (the OEEC had been created in 1948 as a condition of the Marshall Plan). Often referred to as the "Capitalists' Club," its members include Turkey and all twenty-three First World nations. Yugoslavia and the EC are nonvoting members. The purposes of the organization are to promote economic growth, employment, and living standards in the member-states; to promote "sound and harmonious" development of the world economy; and to coordinate policies and programs to assist the less-developed countries. The central institutions are the Council, which meets annually at the ministerial level and regularly at the level of the permanent representatives; the Executive Committee (fourteen members elected annually by the Council), which meets once each week; and the Secretariat. The central institutions are located in Paris. There are twenty-five auxiliary bodies (functionally assigned committees) and five autonomous/semi-autonomous bodies. The most salient auxiliary body is the Development Assistance Committee (DAC). This committee serves to encourage harmonization of development-assistance programs and promotes efforts to achieve the goals of the United Nations Conference on Trade and Development (the major forum for North-South negotiations). The DAC also compiles data on trade and economic assistance to the Third World (i.e., the levels, purposes, direction, and nature of national foreign-aid progress).[11] The most important autonomous body is the International Energy Agency (IEA). Created in November 1974 by nineteen of the OECD member-states (France, Australia, Finland, Iceland, and Portugal declined membership), the IEA commits its members to share information on the international oil market, to participate in computer simulations on future developments, and to honor both an emergency oil-sharing plan that encourages the states to assist any member that experiences a 7 percent or greater reduction in oil supply as well as an agreement to force the member-states' oil companies to open their books in times of "extreme emergency" (i.e., another oil embargo).[12]

In its first ten years, the OECD achieved agreements on cooperative measures designed to increase the gross national products (GNPs) of the member-states by 50 percent. Other than the creation of the IEA, OECD's only substantive accomplishment during the 1970s was a code of conduct for multinational corporations. However, the perceived "socialistic" nature of the code angered U.S. corporations: its "voluntaristic" nature caused reactions in the Third World that alternated between cynicism and hostility.

Latin American Economic System

The Latin American Economic System (SELA) was created in 1975 by all twenty-six Latin American nations. Its stated purposes are to create and promote Latin American multinational enterprises, to protect the prices of basic commodities, and to reinforce scientific and technical cooperation among the member-states. The organizational structure is the Latin American Council (which meets annually at the ministerial level), several action committees (temporary bodies designed to carry out specific studies, programs, and projects at the direction of the Council), and the Permanent Secretariat. All meetings and institutions are located in Caracas, Venezuela.[13]

SELA's activities during its first five years have been narrowly defined and limited in scope (relative to the aims of its charter). SELA coordinated earthquake-recovery assistance to Guatemala, initiated a high-protein foodstuffs project and a program to accelerate housing construction in the member-states, and supervised multilateral aid to the new government of Nicaragua. In addition, it has been engaged in bloc-to-bloc discussions on economic matters with the Commission of the European Community.

A Comparison of States of Integration

There are many ways to assess the states of integration in economic IGOs. A structural/functional test might easily (too easily, perhaps) posit that common markets are more highly integrated than are free trade associations, and that the latter exhibit more integration than development organizations. Generally, organizations whose memberships are First World nations tend to be more highly integrated than do those consisting of developing countries. Yet again, the degree to which nation-states have been willing to yield some of their sovereignty to an IGO's central institutions can often be deduced from the level of the organization's council or policymaking body. Those that meet at the ministerial level tend to indicate a greater degree of integration ("transfer of trust") than those that mandate meetings at the summit level. None of these considerations are valid for all cases, nor are they ever sufficient criteria in and of themselves. The application of Schmitter's "actor strategies" model may have comparative validity, but we must remember that it may be successfully applied to different policy sectors within one organization but quite difficult to apply to the organization overall.

Evaluations of states of integration are not ultimate but instrumental aims of the analysis. There is an association between the degree of integration and the importance of an economic IGO as a world actor. That importance is at once economic and political and directly concerns what nonstate actors do in world politics.

Generally, the organizations made up of First World nations are the most highly integrated. The Benelux Union is the most integrated of all those considered in this chapter; most of its accomplishments qualify as "spillover." However, many of its functions have been absorbed into the EC, in which the Benelux nations are members. The OECD has limited aims and is not highly integrated by design. Since decisions are made by consensus, the member-states most supportive of continued integration are members of the EC and have concentrated their efforts in that organization; others, like the United States, Canada, and Japan, have little or no interest in joining common markets or free trade associations. Most of the OECD activities are examples of encapsulation. EFTA, on the other hand, has experienced "spillback." The loss of Britain and Denmark, Spain's decision not to join, disadvantageous competition with the EC, and the abandonment of policy harmonization efforts in 1977 are factors. The case of COMECON, the only Second

World economic organization, is quite different. In general, COMECON has chosen "spillaround." The Soviet Union has attempted to increase the scope of this organization but has been unwilling to permit any greater degree of authority outside of the Soviets' direct control. Clearly, the Soviet Union has always dominated COMECON and derived the greatest benefit from it. COMECON-sponsored projects are usually bilateral between the USSR and one of the East European states. Problems that continue to frustrate COMECON are the nonconvertability of currencies and dependency relationships: dependency on the West for technology and on the Soviet Union for energy supplies and loans.

Among organizations consisting of Third World nations that function as economic IGOs, the performance of ECOWAS is the most promising. Barring serious political disputes or a move by Nigeria to dominate that organization, the prognosis for continued spillover is very good. The prospects for OCAM and CARICOM, as earlier discussed, are definitely poor. Both seem to have chosen spillback, OCAM by virtue of politicization and loss of direction, and CARICOM due to rapid increases in nationalistic economic policies. In their decision to abandon the free trade association, the members of ALADI have also experienced spillback. Indeed, one may question to what extent the functions left to ALADI differentiate that organization from SELA, to which all ALADI member-states belong. Due to the limited goals of SELA and its relatively brief existence, SELA's performance has been inconclusive and might be termed encapsulation. There has been a great deal of discussion in the Latin American Council concerning regional integration, but virtually no movement. Finally, the CACM and EAC are not functioning organizations and therefore have no state of integration. However, the structures and basic agreements remain, and no one in those respective member-nations has ruled out the future possibility of rejuvenating those once promising integrative ventures.

Notes

1. Europa Publications, *The Europa Year Book 1980: A World Survey*, vol. I (London: Europa, 1980), pp. 176–177.

2. Six of these states, Ivory Coast, Mali, Mauritania, Niger, Senegal, and Upper Volta, formed the West African Economic Community (CEAO) in 1974. Its functions are the same as those of ECOWAS.

3. See B. W. Mutharika, "A Case Study of Regionalism in Africa," in UNITAR, *Regionalism and the New International Economic Order* (New York: Pergamon Press, 1981).

4. Europa Publications, *Europa Year Book 1980*.

5. See Richard F. Staar, "Economic Integration," in his *The Communist Regimes in Eastern Europe* (Stanford, Calif.: Hoover Institution, 1971); and Paul Marer, "Prospects for Integration in the Council for Mutual Economic Assistance (CMEA)," *International Organization* 30:4 (Autumn 1976).

6. Joint projects included the Peace Electric Power Distribution System, the CMEA Bank, the Intermetall Steel Commission, and the pooling of railroad freight cars.

7. Cameroon, Chad, Congo, Gabon, Madagascar, Mauritania, and Zaire were once members but have withdrawn.

8. See Edward S. Milenky, "Latin America's Multilateral Diplomacy: Integration, Disintegration, and Interdependence," *International Affairs* 53:1 (January 1977), pp. 82–83.

9. See Harold K. Jacobson and Dusan Sidjanski, "Regional Patterns of Economic Cooperation," in Werner J. Feld and Gavin Boyd (Eds.), *Comparative Regional Systems* (New York: Pergamon Press, 1980), pp. 70–73; Joan Edelman Spero, *The Politics of International Economic Relations* (2nd ed.) (New York: St. Martin's Press, 1981), pp. 86–87.

10. Cf. Robert D. Bond, "Regionalism in Latin America," *International Organization* 32:2 (Summer 1978).

11. See, for example, Organization for Economic Cooperation and Development, *Development Cooperation: 1981 Review* (Paris: OECD Secretariat, 1982).

12. Mason Willrich and Melvin A. Conant, "The International Energy Agency: An Interpretation and Assessment," *American Journal of International Law* 71:2 (April 1977), pp. 199–223.

13. *Panama Convention Establishing the Latin American Economic System* (Port of Spain, Trinidad: SELA Permanent Secretariat, n.d.), pp. 1–17.

7
OPEC and Other
Commodity "Cartels"

The shock to the world economy that occurred in October–November 1973 made OPEC an instantly recognized entity throughout the globe. Prior to that time, OPEC was known only to a relatively small number of government and business officials; it received scant attention in academic courses in international relations. When the quadrupling of oil prices and the oil embargo were announced, OPEC's instant renown engendered a concomitant degree of misunderstanding about that economic IGO. As is often the case even now, the mass media in the developed nations—particularly the United States—labeled the organization a "cartel" and encouraged the misperception that OPEC was responsible for the Yom Kippur war–related oil embargo. Neither of these characterizations is correct.

Can one say that OPEC is a cartel? Although the term has been applied generally to the twentieth-century petroleum industry, its technical meaning pertains to a monopoly of private corporations created to control markets and prices so as to ensure greater profits than expected from the forces of supply and demand. Different from the true definition of a cartel, OPEC consists of a large number of governments rather than a small group of corporations, and its techniques and methods of coordination have been erratic. In addition, many exporters of petroleum and natural gas—notably, Canada, Mexico, the People's Republic of China, Oman, Norway, and the Netherlands—remain outside the organization and are the world's largest producers, as are the United States and the Soviet Union (though they are not significant exporters). Finally, OPEC must operate through intermediaries, namely, the multinational oil corporations.[1]

The perception that OPEC is a political organization responsible for the 1973 oil embargo is equally misleading. Many OPEC states (e.g., Iran, Venezuela, and Nigeria) did not participate in that short-lived effort. In fact, the attempt to cause the industrialized nations to alter their foreign policies (for the most part, to withdraw support from Israel) was not the work of OPEC but that of the Organization of Arab Petroleum Exporting Countries (OAPEC), a political "suborganization" to be discussed later.[2]

The focus of this chapter will be the "two OPECs," pre-1974 and post-1973, in addition to brief discussions of those commodity IGOs that would emulate OPEC's economic successes.

The Organization of Petroleum Exporting Countries

The events that led to the creation of OPEC began when, in 1952, the Arab League formed a committee of oil experts and drafted plans for an Arab Petroleum Organization, an Arab Pipeline Corporation, an Arab Tanker Corporation, and a research institute. In the following year, Iraq and Saudi Arabia agreed to hold periodic consultations on petroleum-related matters. Little occurred, however, until the late 1950s, when the Arab oil-producing countries and Venezuela began attempts to negotiate participation ratios with the oil companies. Most of those ratios were, for oil company and host nation respectively, 75–78 percent and 25–22 percent. In some instances, the oil companies' percent approached 90 percent, on which only a royalty for land extension was paid. In those negotiations, the nations were attempting to get participation ratios of 60/40 and 50/50. The major oil companies responded with a system of "play with offer and demand," reducing production and revenues for those states demanding more participation and allocating more production quotas to the more compliant countries. Early in 1959, three consecutive oil price reductions (by West Texas Petroleum, Venezuelan Shell, and British Petroleum) caused the affected nations to send official notes of protest to the U.S. and British governments. The lack of response triggered the calling of the First Arab Petroleum Congress in Cairo in April 1959.[3] The meeting led to the formation one year later of OPEC by Iran, Iraq, Kuwait, Saudi Arabia, and Venezuela. Later, the organization was extended by the accessions of Algeria, Ecuador, Gabon, Indonesia, Libya, Nigeria, Qatar, and the United Arab Emirates.[4]

Initially, the purposes of the organization created in Baghdad in September 1960 were to safeguard the common interests and coordinate the petroleum policies of its member-states, and to halt and reverse the downward trend in the prices dictated by the international oil companies. In 1968, OPEC asserted the following in the Declaration of Petroleum Policy: (1) the permanent and inalienable sovereignty of the producing nations over their natural resources; (2) the doctrine of changing circumstances, in which the early long-term concession agreements could be altered unilaterally when they ceased to meet the interests of the producing states; and (3) a participation by the host governments in the equity of the international oil companies.[5]

Without having achieved any substantial success since 1964 (when the oil companies agreed to uniform royalty rates), OPEC used a confrontation in 1970 between Libya and the oil companies to begin support of the efforts of individual member-states to achieve greater control over their own resources. The OPEC states refused to permit the oil companies to offset the loss of Libyan oil by increasing production in other states. This new stance was more effective due to rapidly rising world demand and a fall in non-OPEC production, principally in the United States. Consequently, the Gulf members of OPEC, under the personal direction of the shah of Iran, concluded in February 1971 the first (the Teheran Agreement) of a series of agreements between those states and a group of sixteen oil companies. This was followed by concessions by the oil companies to Libya in 1971 and to all OPEC states in agreements negotiated in Geneva in 1972 and 1973.

The six Gulf states met during the 1973 Arab-Israeli war to set the price of Saudi Arabian light crude at $5.12 per barrel, an increase of 70 percent in price. Encouraged by the panic conditions that caused spot prices to exceed $17.00 per barrel, OPEC again raised the price in December to $11.65 per barrel of benchmark crude for all OPEC states. With these events, OPEC realized its major goal: the unilateral setting of prices for the crude oil its member-states exported and a greatly lessened role for the international oil companies. This changed fundamentally the pricing issue from an oil-companies/OPEC-states confrontation that the oil companies dominated to a producer-government/consumer-government confrontation that is overtly political in nature. It is this development that has characterized OPEC since 1974.[6]

Structure and Process

The three central institutions of OPEC are the Conference, the Board of Governors, and the Secretariat. These institutions were initially located in Geneva, but were moved to Vienna in 1965. Under agreement with the Austrian government, the institutions and representatives of OPEC are afforded diplomatic status. (See Figure 7.1.)

The Conference is the supreme authority of OPEC. It is composed of delegations from each member-state headed by an individual of ministerial rank, usually the minister of oil, mines, and energy. The Conference meets twice each year, usually once in Vienna and once in the capital of a member-state (according to Article 13 of the OPEC Charter). It may be called into extraordinary session. Although the Charter specifies that all members must be represented at each Conference

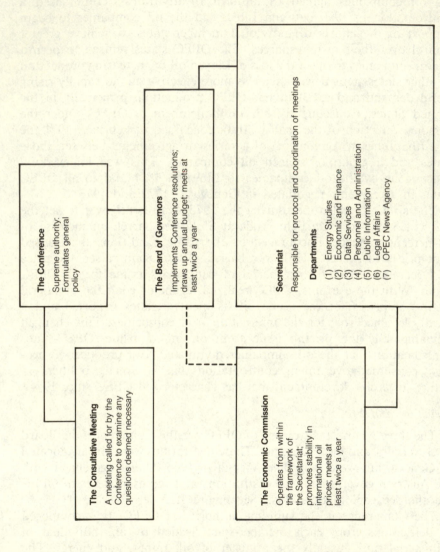

The Conference

Supreme authority; Formulates general policy

The Consultative Meeting

A meeting called for by the Conference to examine any questions deemed necessary

The Board of Governors

Implements Conference resolutions; draws up annual budget; meets at least twice a year

The Economic Commission

Operates from within the framework of the Secretariat; promotes stability in international oil prices; meets at least twice a year

Secretariat

Responsible for protocol and coordination of meetings

Departments

(1) Energy Studies
(2) Economic and Finance
(3) Data Services
(4) Personnel and Administration
(5) Public Information
(6) Legal Affairs
(7) OPEC News Agency

Figure 7.1   The Organizational Structure of OPEC

meeting, it also provides for a quorum of three-fourths of the member-states' representatives to be present to conduct the meeting.

According to Article 15 of the OPEC Charter, the responsibilities of the Conference are to formulate general policy and means of implementation, consider membership applications,[7] approve the appointment of members of the Board of Governors, issue directives to and approve reports from the Board of Governors, approve revisions to the statutes, and consider any matter not specifically allocated to any other arm of the organization.

The decisionmaking process takes place entirely within the Conference. Except for those relating to procedural matters, all decisions require a unanimous vote from all full members. Consequently, the representatives to the Conference work for consensus and compromise before any votes are taken. When this has proven unattainable, the practice has been to declare a series of postponements. All resolutions of the Conference are binding on the member-states (in theory) and become effective thirty days following the meetings unless a time period is otherwise specified or the Secretary-General is notified to the contrary by the member-states before the time period expires.

The Board of Governors is composed of individuals nominated by the member-states and confirmed by the Conference for two-year terms. The Board of Governors directs the management of the organization, draws up the annual budget for Conference approval, submits reports commissioned by the Conference or those originating from the Secretariat, nominates an auditor for one-year terms in office, and prepares the Conference agenda. The Board of Governors meets three times per year, two of those meetings a few days before Conference meetings. Meetings of the Board of Governors require a quorum of two-thirds. Decisions are taken by simple majority, with each governor having one vote.

The Secretariat is the administrative organ, but it has features usually found in executive bodies of other IGOs. The Secretary-General is empowered to represent the organization in other international fora, and heads five functional departments: administration (includes budget, accounts, and discipline); economic (conducts studies and serves as a watchdog on the petroleum industry); legal (reviews and studies judicial developments in the international oil industry); information (includes press, publications, library, and archives); and technical (reviews and studies technological developments in the oil industry). There are, in addition, a statistical unit and the Economics Commission. The Secretary-General serves for three years (a period that may be extended), and must be a national of one of the member-states.[8]

Fund for International Development

The OPEC Fund for International Development was created first as the OPEC Special Fund following the Algiers Conference meeting in March 1975. Initially designed to provide concessional financing to developing countries, the Fund now disburses OPEC official development assistance and has its own ministerial council and governing board. As of 1981, the Fund had distributed approximately $4 billion, mostly in the form of grants.[9]

State of Integration

OPEC is the best example of an organization in which there appears to be little correlation between the success of the organization and integrative progress. Federalists have criticized OPEC for its lack of effective central leadership and institutions necessary to promote policy integration. Functionalists and neofunctionalists have concluded that OPEC's coordination facilities and administrative and policymaking apparati are failures. Further, spillover has been blocked by the member-states; integration in OPEC has been purposefully prognosticated.[10] Nevertheless, when compared to its organizational goals and experience in the 1960s, the successes of the post-1973 OPEC have been phenomenal. In terms of return for the resources of OPEC's member-states, OPEC increased prices by 10 percent in 1976 and 5 percent in 1977, and permitted additional increases and options for individual members to add surcharges in 1979–1980. It may be argued, however, that more of these successes have been created externally (i.e., by international market demand) than by direct action by OPEC.

Clearly there are problems among the member-states. They are diverse in geography, culture, economics, and politics, with little in common other than maintaining optimal terms for the production and sale of oil. The "radical" states (Iraq, Algeria, Libya, Iran, Venezuela, and Nigeria) favor higher prices, nationalization, and indexation of prices to inflation in the developed nations. Although they differ greatly in ideology, political systems, and ties (or lack of them) with the First World, they typically have fairly large populations, limited oil reserves, and ambitious plans for rapid economic development. The "conservative" states (Saudi Arabia, Kuwait, and the United Arab Emirates) are traditional societies with low absorptive capacity for petrodollars and, like Iran, with a concern with the social consequences of rapid modernization.[11]

OPEC's progress has slowed or, perhaps, stalled in the early 1980s due to other difficulties. World demand for oil has lessened as conservation measures and other sources of energy have become effective. The member-states found that it was far easier to agree to raising prices than it was to agree to a plan for reducing production. Various bilateral deals with consumer nations and differing relationships with the international oil companies have tended to fragment OPEC's single-purpose solidarity.[12] Indeed, nothing has caused more concern to the organization than the Iran-Iraq war, a conflict that has disrupted Conference meetings and neutralized both states' oil-exporting power. OPEC's future may be much the same as its recent past: it may cause its own disintegration, or continue to succeed due primarily to conditions outside and beyond the organization.

Related Organizations

Organization of Arab Petroleum Exporting Countries

The Organization of Arab Petroleum Exporting Countries (OAPEC) was created in 1968 after the Arab-Israeli Six-Day war of 1967. It was formed by seven OPEC members: Algeria, Iraq, and Libya (the "radicals"); and Saudi Arabia, Kuwait, Qatar, and the United Arab Emirates (the "conservatives"). Three non-OPEC states were also original members: Bahrain, Syria, and Egypt (the last no longer participates). Unlike OPEC, OAPEC has stressed the political uses of oil. Indeed, it was OAPEC that declared the oil embargo in 1973 against those states that would not condemn Israel (and carried it out only against the Netherlands and the United States). OAPEC's stated purposes are quite vague; its Charter mentions only that it would do nothing contrary to the interests of OPEC. Its central organs are more developed and integrated than are those of OPEC. Decisions are taken by the Council of Ministers by a three-fourths vote, but resolutions must be ratified by all member-states before going into effect. The Secretariat and Board are located in Kuwait City, Kuwait.[13]

Assistencia Reciproca Petrolera
Estatal Latinoamerica (ARPEL)

ARPEL was created in Montevideo, Uruguay, in 1965. Its member-states are Argentina, Bolivia, Brazil, Colombia, Chile, Ecuador, Mexico, Peru, Uruguay, and Venezuela. ARPEL is not a commodity organization. Only three of the member-states are petroleum exporters: Mexico, Ecuador, and Venezuela, of which only the latter two are members of OPEC. ARPEL has confined its activities to the sharing of technological data on such matters as drilling and refining of oil, manufacture of petrochemicals, and the like.

Those Who Would Be Like OPEC

There are a number of economic IGO "producers' groups" that resemble OPEC in two important ways: they are international organizations whose members are the governments of nation-states, and they are organizations that seek only to improve the prices the members receive for a common exported commodity. Perceptions of these producer groups have ranged from their representing "insignificant efforts" to their being "major cartel threats." At the time of this writing, none of the groups have great potential for emulating OPEC's success record, as none can expect the world demand for their commodity on the scale and to the degree that existed for oil in the 1970s. Some have agricultural commodities that cannot be "left in the ground" to appreciate in value or be stored, at least not without prohibitive costs. Those that export mineral ores cannot afford to withhold exports in hopes of increasing demand (and therefore prices), due to inabilities to forgo incomes and sources of foreign exchange. Curiously, many of the latter group are in this situation because the cost of oil imports is so high. Nonetheless, the possibility that one or more of these groups may succeed—as has OPEC—does exist. The following is a brief survey of examples of these producers' groups.

Conseil Intergouvernemental des Pays Exportateurs du Cuivre

The Intergovernmental Council of Copper Exporting Countries (CIPEC) was founded in 1967. Its present headquarters is located in Neuilly-sur-Seine, France. The five full members—Chile, Indonesia, Peru, Zaire, and Zambia—account for nearly 70 percent of the copper exports in the world. Associate members are Australia, Mauritania, Papua New Guinea, and Yugoslavia. CIPEC was not successful in the 1970s due to a combination of factors. First, it does not possess the means to manipulate copper prices on its own. Although it accounts for a majority of the world exports of copper, the United States is nearly self-sufficient in this metal, and Canada is also a major supplier. Second, the price of copper has been depressed, falling over 50 percent in 1974 alone. In addition, other metals are beginning to replace copper at an increasing rate, and that may be the greatest weapon against any possible cartel action. Finally, any ideological harmony that existed among the member-states was shattered by the 1973 coup and dramatic change of government in Chile. CIPEC may yet accomplish something approaching OPEC's achievements, but the organization will need, at the minimum, a great deal of outside financing.[14]

International Bauxite Association

The International Bauxite Association (IBA) was founded in Kingston, Jamaica, in 1974 to harmonize policies for exports, ensure fair prices, and coordinate valuation taxation in relations with the international aluminum companies. IBA is composed of the governments of Australia, the Dominican Republic, Ghana, Guinea, Guyana, Haiti, Indonesia, Jamaica, Sierra Leone, Surinam, and Yugoslavia. During the mid-1970s, the former Jamaican prime minister, Michael Manley, led the effort on behalf of the IBA states to increase bauxite royalties and taxes by a seven-fold increase. Manley was relatively successful with ALCOA, Reynolds, Kaiser, and others, but the success was limited to Jamaica and Manley's leftist government has been replaced by a conservative one. Prospects for IBA to emulate OPEC are not good. Australia, the world's largest producer of alumina, does not seem inclined to permit the transformation of IBA into a producers' cartel. Further, any significant price increases in bauxite would probably spur methods to extract alumina from low-grade clay in the United States and elsewhere. The IBA has discussed efforts to build aluminum smelters to enable the member-states to export aluminum and aluminum products rather than just the ore, but capital and tremendous energy costs have hindered those efforts.

Association of Iron Exporting Countries

The iron-exporters' group was founded in Geneva in 1975 by Algeria, Australia, Chile, India, Mauritania, Peru, Sweden, and Venezuela. Brazil and Canada attended the first meeting but declined membership. Although Algeria and India, the first to call for the organization's creation, wanted an OPEC-like organization for the iron-exporting nations, Australia and Sweden have maintained that the organization should concern itself with the interests of both consumers and producers. Iron ore is distributed around the world and is still plentiful in North America and Europe. The prospects that this organization will ever control prices of exported iron ore are very slim indeed.

Union des Paises Exportadores de Banano

The Association of Banana Exporting Countries (UPEB) was established in 1974. It is composed of Colombia, Costa Rica, Guatemala, Honduras, Nicaragua, and Panama. Ecuador left the organization in 1971. Like most of the agricultural commodity groups, UPEB is an example of an organization that cannot withhold its product from the market to drive up prices. These Latin American states have been adversely affected by competition from African growers, who enjoy preferential treatment in Europe. UPEB enjoyed some success in the early 1970s in raising the "per box tax," but had to back away almost at once due to slumping sales relative to production. In the early 1980s, the member-states have been far more concerned with internal political disruption than with regional economic cooperation and have given scant attention to working toward the goals of UPEB.

Who Might Emulate OPEC?

Several months after OPEC quadrupled the price of oil, the U.S. Council on International Economic Policy published a special report concerning the possibility that any producers' group might affect the U.S. economy in the same manner that OPEC had.[15] The Council concluded that such a prospect was highly unlikely. The argument was that any such effort would require a solidly supported embargo of a given commodity on the consuming nations. The United States has, by virtue of the National Security Act of 1947, strategic stockpiles of critical materials ranging from two to five years supply. With some of these materials, the United States could offer to sell large quantities on the international market and drastically drive down prices. In addition, the technology is or will be developed to utilize new sources of materials and/or substitution of materials. Finally, the economic and ideological cleavages among producer states make cartel actions extremely difficult to operationalize. What the report does not emphasize is the relatively high vulnerability of Western Europe and Japan to producer cartel actions. The Council on International Economic Policy (CIEP) report forecasts little cause for alarm for the United States, but it does not appreciate either the costs incurred should the United States find it must share its stockpiles with the rest of the developed nations or the concomitant effect on world prices and the world economy. The increasing economically interdependent nature of the First World's economy and the world's economy makes the potential for an OPEC-like organization in many essential commodities an ever-present reality. The First World consumers may have weathered OPEC's storm and learned important lessons.[16] The European Community has been able to hold together, and an oil-sharing scheme managed by the IEA has been established (but never tested!). Whether the lessons will suffice in the face of "other OPECs" remains to be seen.

Notes

1. See Bobrow and Kudrle's analysis utilizing five perspectives on resource cartels: theory of cartels, theory of depletable resources, coalition theory, internal

politics approaches, and theory of collective action. Davis B. Bobrow and Robert T. Kudrle, "Theory, Policy, and Resource Cartels," *Journal of Conflict Resolution* 20:1 (March 1976), pp. 3–56.

2. Ian Smart, "Oil, the Super-Powers and the Middle East," *International Affairs* 53:1 (January 1977), pp. 18–19.

3. For background, see Mana Saeed Al-Otaiba, *OPEC and the Petroleum Industry* (New York: Halsted Press, 1975); and J. B. Kelly, *Arabia, the Gulf, and the West* (New York: Basic Books, 1980).

4. The United Arab Emirates was originally a member as Abu Dhabi.

5. See Alvin J. Cottrell (Ed.), *The Persian Gulf States* (Baltimore: Johns Hopkins University Press, 1980).

6. Ibid.

7. Qualifications for membership are as follows: a state must be a net exporter of petroleum in "substantial quantities," and its petroleum interests must be fundamentally similar to those of the OPEC member-states. States are admitted by a three-fourths majority vote, provided that the five original members vote for membership.

8. Zuhayr Mikdashi, "Cooperation Among Oil Exporting Countries with Special Reference to Arab Countries: A Political Economy Analysis," *International Organization* 28:1 (Winter 1974), pp. 6–8.

9. Nan Nguema, "Twenty-one Years of OPEC," *OPEC Bulletin,* October 1981.

10. Ernst Haas, *The Obsolescence of Regional Integration Theory* (Berkeley, Calif.: Institute of International Peace, 1975).

11. Paul Jabber, "Conflict and Cooperation in OPEC: Prospects for the Next Decade," *International Organization* 32:2 (Summer 1978).

12. Mikdashi, "Cooperation," pp. 12–19.

13. See Karen A. Mingst, "Regional Sectorial Economic Integration: The Case of OAPEC," *Journal of Common Market Studies* 16 (December 1977), pp. 95–113; and Hossein Askari and John Thomas Cummings, "The Future of Economic Integration Within the Arab World," *International Journal of Middle East Studies* 8 (1977), pp. 289–315.

14. See Karen A. Mingst, "Cooperation or Illusion: An Examination of the Intergovernmental Council of Copper Exporting Countries," *International Organization* 30:2 (Spring 1976).

15. Council on International Economic Policy, *Special Report: Critical Imported Materials* (Washington, D.C.: Government Printing Office, 1974). This report analyzes nineteen strategic materials, excluding fuels and agriculture.

16. Ivor Richard, "Diplomacy in an Interdependent World," *Academy of Political Science Proceedings* 32:4 (1977), pp. 9–10.

Part 3

Security Alliances

8

The North Atlantic
Treaty Organization

The North Atlantic Alliance, or North Atlantic Treaty Organization (NATO), was created in April 1949 "to safeguard the freedom, common heritage and civilization of the [member-states'] peoples, . . . to promote stability and well-being in the North Atlantic area, . . . for collective defense and for the preservation of peace and security."[1] Beyond these stated purposes, the major motivations for the creation of NATO were Soviet actions in Europe (or, more to the point, perceptions by the founding member-states of those actions) from 1945 to 1948. NATO was to become the first link in what George Kennan had labeled "the policy of containment of Soviet expansionist intentions by the United States and its allies."[2] By the end of the 1970s, NATO was charged with the pursuit of dual "complementary" aims of deterrence and détente.[3]

NATO is a supraregional[4] security alliance that is structurally inter-governmental and not supernational: the member-states do not surrender any degree of sovereignty as a condition of membership. Due to its purposes and membership, it is one of the most important IGO nonstate actors in world politics, yet one of the least (formally) integrated. The member countries are Belgium, Canada, Denmark, France, Federal Republic of Germany, Greece, Iceland, Italy, Luxembourg, Netherlands, Norway, Portugal, Turkey, United Kingdom, and United States. NATO is a collective-defense alliance permitted by Article 51 of the United Nations Charter. During the 1970s and early 1980s, it has served as a primary international forum in East-West relations.

History and Background

The events that motivated the creation of NATO began immediately after World War II. The end of the war in Europe brought on a massive demobilization process by the Western allies. From 1945 to 1946, combat troops on the continent of Europe decreased from 3,100,000 to 391,000 for the United States, 1,321,000 to 488,000 for Great Britain, and 299,000 to 0 for Canada. Concomitantly, the Soviet Union maintained 4,000,000 troops and a war industry fed by German reparations. Soviet expansion during the war into Estonia, Latvia, and Lithuania and parts of Poland, Rumania, Czechoslovakia, Finland, and Germany was enhanced by the imposition of "front governments" that were soon replaced by Soviet-sponsored Communist party governments in Eastern Europe. Soviet actions from 1945 to 1948 were perceived as threats to the security of Western Europe and the United States.[5] These actions included their activities in Northern Iran, Greece, Turkey, Manchuria, North Korea, Malaysia, Burma, and the Philippines. The Soviet's creation of the Cominform in 1947 and the Berlin Blockade (1948–1949) magnified the perception of threat in the West.

On March 17, 1948, the Benelux countries, France, and the United Kingdom signed a fifty-year agreement of economic, social, and cultural collaboration and collective security known as the Brussels Treaty. In September, the defense ministers of the Brussels Treaty Powers decided to create the Western Union Defense Organization (WEU).[6] In December of the same year, while the Berlin Airlift was well under way, negotiations began in Washington, D.C., among the Brussels Treaty states, Canada, and the United States to draft a North Atlantic Treaty. This treaty was signed on April 4, 1949, and joined Denmark, Iceland, Italy, Norway, and Portugal.

The North Atlantic Treaty entered into force on August 24, 1949. During its first full year of operation, French Prime Minister M. René Pleven submitted a plan for a European unified army to include contingents from Germany. In addition, the Consultative Council of the Brussels Treaty decided to merge the military organization of the WEU into NATO. Negotiations to create a European Army began in early 1951. In July of that year, the Paris Conference (the formal title of the negotiations) recommended the creation of a European Army. Seven months later, Greece and Turkey became the thirteenth and fourteenth members of NATO.

The year 1954 was a crucial one in the development of NATO. Surprisingly, the Soviet Union asked to join NATO, but the bid was rejected by the United States, Britain, and France. On August 29, the French National Assembly refused to permit French ratification of the Paris Treaty designed to create the European Defense Community (EDC) that had been signed in 1952 by Belgium, France, Italy, Luxembourg, the Netherlands, and the Federal Republic of Germany (member-states of the ECSC). This action effectively ended for several years all talk of creating a European army.[7] However, the Federal Republic of Germany was invited to join NATO in October 1954 and acceded to active membership on May 5, 1955 (an event followed nine days later by the creation of the Warsaw Treaty Organization).[8]

In the ministerial meetings of the North Atlantic Council in December 1955 and May 1956, the NATO member-states agreed to equip their forces with nuclear weapons, to strengthen air defense through closer cooperation, and to extend cooperation to nonmilitary fields. In the December 1956 meeting, the Council approved recommendations from Italy, Norway, and Canada to create several nonmilitary cooperation programs in Italy and agreed on a mechanism for peaceful settlement of disputes among NATO member-states. Meeting at the summit level in December of the following year, the Council moved to increase cooperation in political, economic, and scientific fields.

The next major event in NATO's development occurred after the Soviet Union began building the Berlin Wall in 1961. The Council decided to increase diplomatic efforts to find new "bases for negotiation" with the Soviet Union; it also decided to create the first NATO mobile task force. In December 1962, U.S. President John Kennedy and British Prime Minister Harold Macmillan agreed to contribute part of their strategic nuclear forces to NATO.

The first "disintegrative" event in NATO was major one. On March 10, 1966, French President Charles de Gaulle announced France's withdrawal from NATO's military organization and ordered all NATO forces and its military headquarters out of France. In the following year, all components of NATO headquarters were moved to Brussels except for the military headquarters, namely, the Supreme Headquarters Allied Powers Europe (SHAPE) that was situated near Mons, Belgium. In December 1967, the long dispute between the United States and the European states that would later (1968) form NATO's "Eurogroup" was resolved. The disagreement as to whether NATO should rely primarily on nuclear as opposed to conventional forces was ended with the adoption of the new strategic concept of "flexible response."

The decade of the 1970s began for NATO with a U.S. pledge to maintain and improve forces in Europe without reductions, except within the framework of reciprocal East-West agreements. In 1972, the NATO member-states began preparations for the Conference on Security and Cooperation in Europe (CSCE) and Mutual and Balanced Force Reductions in Central Europe (MBFRCE). Both conferences between NATO and Warsaw Treaty Organization (WTO) states began in 1973. The CSCE was concluded in August 1975, but the MBFRCE is still ongoing (with no appreciable progress). Following the coup d'etat and Turkish intervention in Cyprus, Greece withdrew its forces from the integrated military command structure of NATO on August 14, 1974.

From 1976 through 1980, the Council and Defense Planning Committee (DPC) moved toward an emphasis on coordinated long-range military planning. A proposal by the Warsaw Pact to renounce first use of nuclear weapons and to restrict NATO membership was rejected. A Tactical Nuclear Forces (TNF) program was adopted. Decisions were taken on theater nuclear force modernization to upgrade and increase Pershing missile emplacements. In the spring of 1980, the emphasis on the dual goals of deterrence and detente shifted toward the former following the Soviet invasion of Afghanistan. The shift was greater when, in 1982, the Soviet Union was accused of complicity in the declaration of military rule in Poland.

Structure

The institutional structure of NATO is relatively highly developed for a non-supranational organization of states. Basically, there are two organizations in NATO: one civilian and one military. The civil structure consists of the highest authority, namely, the North Atlantic Council and the Defense Planning Committee, twenty functionally assigned standing committees, and the General-Secretariat. The military structure is headed by the Military Committee and includes the Canada-U.S. Regional Planning Group and the three NATO commands: SACEUR, SACLANT, and CINCHAN. All but the last four institutions mentioned are located in Brussels, Belgium. (See Figures 8.1 and 8.2.)

The North Atlantic Council

The North Atlantic Council is the policymaking organ of NATO. It meets twice yearly at the ministerial level and can, though rarely, meet at the summit level. Normally, it meets once each week at the ambassadorial level (consisting of permanent representatives to NATO in Brussels). The Council represents the only international forum in which North American and West European nations meet only among themselves with such frequency; the meetings serve a routine function of what might otherwise require over 100 separate bilateral meetings. The Council serves as the major forum for political coordination and policy discussions. It also directs the work of the many functional committees. The most important of these is the Defense Planning Committee (DPC), composed of all the permanent representatives to NATO except France. The DPC concerns itself solely with defense matters and may, on occasion, meet at the ministerial level. Another major committee is the Nuclear Planning Group, in which twelve of the fifteen member-states participate. Still other permanent committees include the Political; military; Economic; Defense Review; Security; Senior Civil Emergency

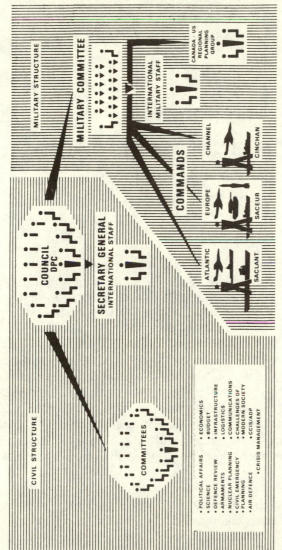

Figure 8.1 Civil and Military Structure

Source: NATO Information Service, *NATO Handbook,* August 1980. p. 30. Reprinted with permission.

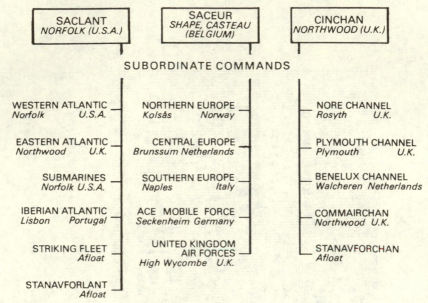

Figure 8.2   Major NATO Commanders

Source: NATO Information Service, *NATO Handbook,* August 1980, p. 54. Reprinted with permission.

Planning; NATO Joint Communications Electronics; Infrastructure; Science; Information and Cultural Relations; Civilian Budget; Military Budget; Infrastructure Payments and Progress; European Airspace Coordination; Operations and Exercises; Challenges of Modern Society; and Command, Control, Information and Automatic Data Processing committees, as well as the Conference of National Armaments Directors. The Council has created several ad hoc steering or specialized committees, such as the Central European Pipeline System (CEPS), NATO Integrated Communications System (NICS), Multirole Combat Aircraft, and SP70 Self-Propelled Howitzer committees.[9] (See Figures 8.3 and 8.4.)

The General-Secretariat

The NATO Secretary-General has been called the "chief executive" of NATO. He serves as chairman of the Council, the DPC, the Nuclear Defense Affairs Committee, and the Nuclear Planning Group. He also directs a large multinational staff and all administrative support to NATO in Brussels. The Secretary-General is personally responsible for promoting and directing consultation within the Alliance. He is empowered to use his good offices when disputes arise between or among the member-states and, with their consent, to initiate inquiries, mediation,

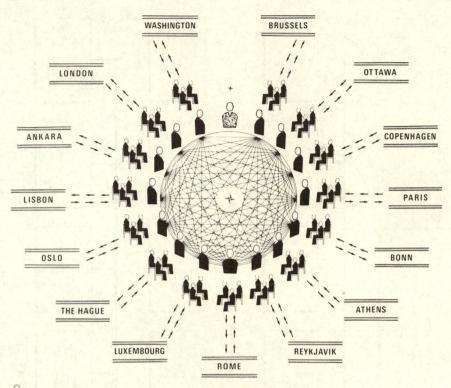

NORTH ATLANTIC COUNCIL

Permanent
Representative

National
Delegation

Chairman and
Secretary General

National
Government

The North Atlantic Council provides a unique forum for confidential and constant intergovernmental consultation on all topics as well as providing the highest level of decision making machinery within NATO. There is no supranational element in the Organization and all the fifteen sovereign member countries have an equal right to express their views round the Council table. Political consultation ranges over the whole field of foreign affairs and is not limited to NATO's geographical area. The only topics excluded are those relating to the purely internal affairs of member countries. Each national delegation is headed by a Permanent Representative with the rank of Ambassador supported by staffs which vary in size. All act on instructions from their capitals. Thus the Council provides a unique type of 'Diplomatic Workshop' under the Chairmanship of the Secretary General. To attain such a high degree of constant consultation between the fifteen by the customary method of bilateral diplomatic exchanges would be quite impracticable – in fact each meeting of the Council represents the equivalent of over 100 bilateral exchanges as shown by the lines in the diagram above.

Figure 8.3   North Atlantic Council

Source: NATO Information Service, *NATO Fact and Figures,* 1978, p. 94. Reprinted with permission.

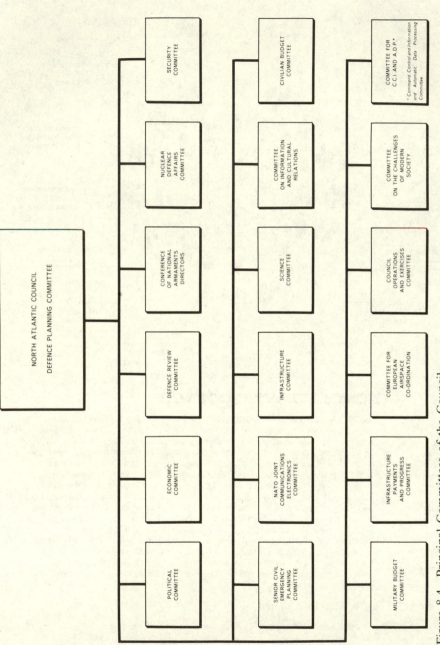

Figure 8.4 Principal Committees of the Council

Source: NATO Information Service, *NATO Facts and Figures,* 1978, p. 206. Reprinted with permission.

conciliation, or arbitration procedures. The International Staffs consist of five major divisions that are each further subdivided into several directorates. The divisions break down as follows: Political Affairs (four directorates); Defense Planning and Policy (three directorates); Defense Support (four directorates); Infrastructure, Logistics, and Council Operations (three directorates); and Scientific Affairs. In addition to the Office of the Secretary-General are the Office of Management, the Office of Financial Controller, and the Board of Auditors.[10] (See Figure 8.5.)

The Military Committee

The Military Committee, the highest military organ in NATO, is responsible for providing recommendations and guidance on military matters to the Council and the DPC. Composed of the Chiefs of Staff of all member-countries except France and Iceland (the latter having no military forces), the Military Committee normally meets three times per year. In order to permit the Committee to function without interruption, each Chief of Staff appoints a permanent military representative. Presidency of the Military Committee rotates annually in alphabetical order of the member-states. However, the chairman is elected by the Committee for a period of two to three years. The chairman attends ministerial meetings of the Council as a right. The Military Committee supervises the activities of twelve allied military agencies that specialize in various areas of communications, data systems, weapon systems research and development, and standardization.[11] (See Figure 8.6.)

The NATO Commands

The three NATO commands—Allied Command Europe (ACE), Allied Command Atlantic (ACLANT), and Channel Command (CINCHAN)— are composed of national forces committed to NATO in peacetime and wartime, as well as forces committed to NATO by the member-states during actual conflict. The NATO commands are responsible for the development of defense plans for their respective geographical regions, for the determination of force requirements, and for the conduct of exercises of forces within their commands. Plans for the defense of the North American region are developed by Canada–United States Regional Planning Group. This organ makes recommendations to the Military Committee but does not supervise joint forces or exercises.

Allied Command Europe has its headquarters at SHAPE in Mons, Belgium. Responsible for the area from the North Cape to the Mediterranean (excluding Britain and Portugal) and from the Atlantic to the eastern border of Turkey, ACE is divided into five commands: Allied Forces Northern Europe (AFNORTH), Allied Forces Central Europe (AFCENT), Allied Forces Southern Europe (AFSOUTH), and U.K. Air

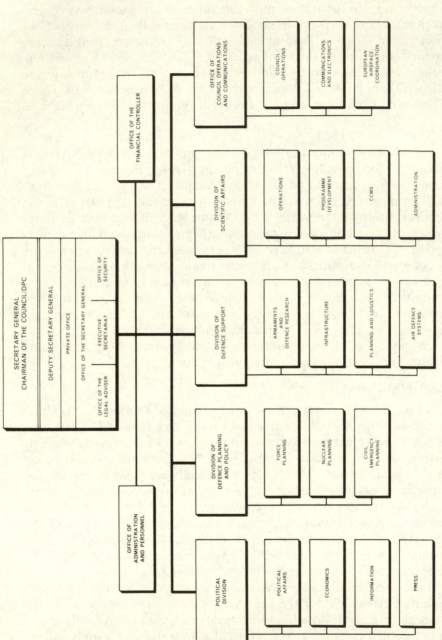

Figure 8.5 NATO International Staff

Source: NATO Information Service, *NATO Facts and Figures,* 1978. p. 208. Reprinted with permission.

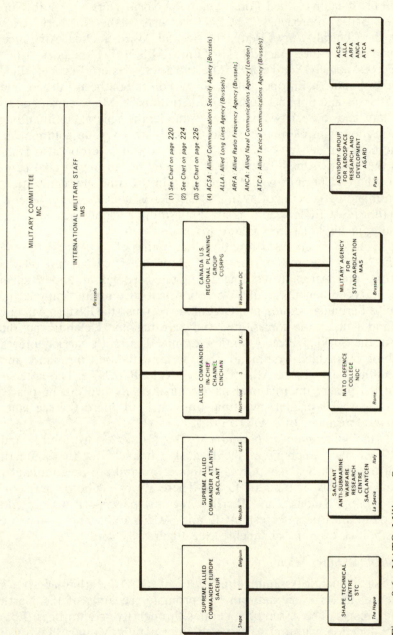

Figure 8.6 NATO Military Structure

Source: NATO Information Service, *NATO Facts and Figures,* 1978. p. 216. Reprinted with permission.

Forces Command, and the Allied Command Europe Mobile Force. AFNORTH contains Allied Forces, namely, North Norway, South Norway, and Baltic Approaches. AFCENT consists of the Northern Army Group, the Central Army Group, the Second Allied Tactical Air Force, and the Fourth Allied Tactical Air Force. AFSOUTH includes Allied Land Forces, namely, Southern Europe and South-Eastern Europe; Allied Air Forces Southern Europe; Allied Naval Forces Southern Europe; and Naval Striking and Support Forces Southern Europe. Major commanders in ACE are said to wear two hats. For example, the general commanding U.S. Army forces in Germany is also Central Army Group commander, and the Commander-in-Chief of U.S. Air Forces in Europe also commands the Fourth Allied Tactical Air Force (although operational command of the NATO units would occur only in wartime). By convention, the commanding general of ACE (SACEUR) is a U.S. Army general. In wartime, SACEUR would control all military land, sea, and air operations in his area. (See Figure 8.7.)

ACLANT covers about 12 million square miles of the Atlantic Ocean from the North Pole to the Tropic of Cancer and from North America to Europe and Africa (excluding the United Kingdom and English Channel). Its components are the Western Atlantic Command (submarine forces plus Bermuda, Azores, and Greenland regions), the Eastern Atlantic Command (submarine forces, maritime air regions, Iceland, and the Faeroes), the Striking Fleet Atlantic Command (aircraft carrier forces), the Submarines Allied Command, the Iberian Atlantic Command, and the Standing Naval Force Atlantic (STANAVFORLANT). The latter is the first permanent international naval squadron formed during peacetime. SACLANT's primary wartime mission is to guard the sea lanes for the reinforcement of NATO Europe.

The Allied Command Channel (ACCHAN) serves to control and protect merchant shipping in the English Channel and the southern areas of the North Sea. The forces in this command are predominantly naval but include maritime air forces. There are five subordinate commands (Nore, Plymouth, and Benelux regions, plus maritime air and mine countermeasures forces). ACE and ACCHAN share air-defense responsibilities over the channel.[12] (See Figures 8.8 and 8.9.)

The North Atlantic Assembly

The North Atlantic Assembly (until 1966, the NATO Parliamentarian's Conference) meets every autumn to "promote the aims of the North Atlantic Treaty." The Assembly operates through five committees (Economic; Education, Cultural Affairs and Information; Military; Political; Scientific and Technical) and consists of 172 legislators from the fifteen member-states' parliaments. The Assembly serves to promote stronger

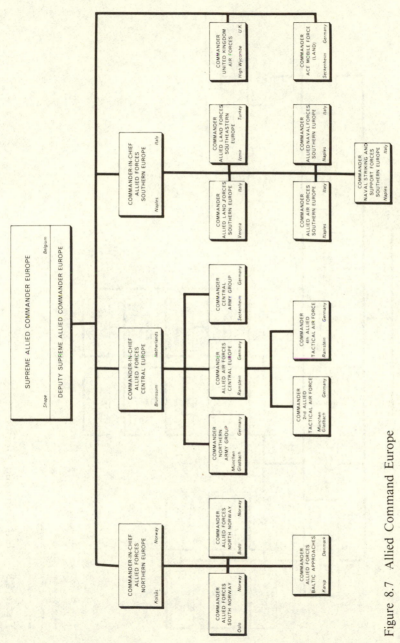

Figure 8.7 Allied Command Europe

Source: NATO Information Service, *NATO Facts and Figures*, 1978, p. 220. Reprinted with permission.

118

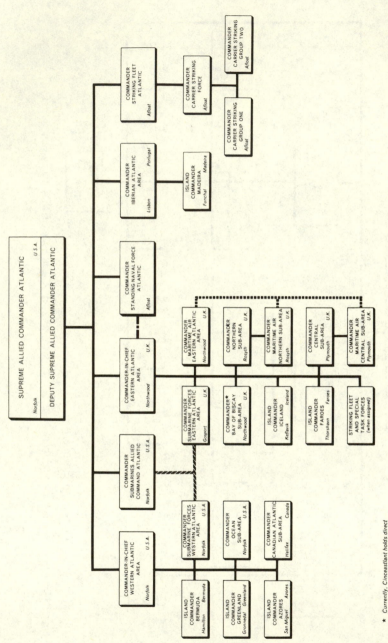

Figure 8.8 Allied Command Atlantic

Source: NATO Information Service, *NATO Facts and Figures,* 1978. p. 224. Reprinted with permission.

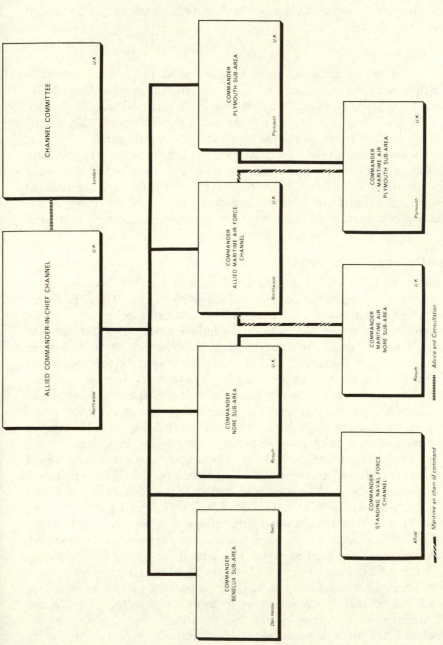

Figure 8.9 Allied Command Channel

Source: NATO Information Service, *NATO Facts and Figures*, 1978, p. 226. Reprinted with permission.

ties between the NATO countries' lawmakers. Recommendations of the Assembly are presented to the North Atlantic Council by the Secretary-General.

The Eurogroup

The Eurogroup is an informal association of the defense ministers of Belgium, Denmark, Germany, Greece, Italy, Luxembourg, the Netherlands, Norway, Portugal, Turkey, and the United Kingdom. Created in 1968, the Eurogroup attempts to achieve closer European cooperation within NATO.[13] It has served to foster security interdependence among the members through the European Defense Improvement Program and the Independent European Program Group (the latter includes France). Most of its efforts have been directed toward the achievement of multilateral ventures in research and development of weapon systems, communications, logistics support, training projects, and procurement.[14]

The Decisionmaking Process

Since NATO was not designed to be, and has not become, a supranational organization, decisionmaking at the Council and principal committee levels has been a process of attempts to achieve "common consent." As none of the nations surrender sovereignty through the North Atlantic Treaty, there are no grounds for applying the technique of majority rule. Furthermore, the states do not strive for unanimity, since that in itself would imply some higher authority over the member-states. The attempt to decide by consensus is a time-consuming operation. Decisions are generally taken with a least-common-denominator character. However, once the Council has taken a decision, it is binding on all member-states unless later expressly changed by the Council.

Wartime decisionmaking in the NATO military commands is designed to be quite different. In the event of an attack on any NATO member-state from outside the Alliance, those national forces so designated would be under the command of SACEUR, SACLANT, and CINCHAN, and a NATO hierarchical command structure would be instituted immediately. To date, such a contingency has never been tested (fortunately). Moreover, there are legal reasons as to why it might not be completely successful. According to Article 5 of the North Atlantic Treaty, each party (member-state) pledges to consider an attack on one as an attack on all, but to take "such action as it deems necessary . . . to restore and maintain the security of the North Atlantic area."[15] Any of the member-states, then, may decide only to consult on the matter or to put their forces on an increased readiness condition despite orders emanating from the NATO commanders. This situation, in which a unilateral decision must be made as to which action is necessary, often occurs during NATO exercises. Since the emergency communications networks are bilevel (one NATO, one national) for all forces, the Americans have found themselves practicing an all-out war while the British or Dutch at the same or nearby installation "aren't playing" (and/or vice-versa).

State of Integration

An evaluation of the state of integration of NATO depends upon one's perspective and level of analysis. Differing conclusions might be reached if one views the civilian and military organizations separately, the central institutions alone, or the original aims of the Treaty. In terms of Schmitter's actor strategies (see Chapter 3), the central institutions have been characterized by encapsulation, operating within the member-state's collective zone of indifference. The nonparticipation decisions of France and Greece may be considered symptoms of disintegration. Although NATO is intended to be a nonsupranational organization designed only to serve as a collective security alliance, there have been several cases of spillover. Political consultation has increased from Korea to Camp David and Afghanistan. Economic cooperation has been facilitated through the Committee of Economic Advisors' consultations on leading economic indicators, East-West trade, and the like. NATO infrastructure integration has been enhanced through interdependent programs in airfields and air traffic control, transportation and supply systems, communications and radar warning systems (NATO Air Defense and Ground Environment, or NADGE), fuel pipelines, and weapons and fuel storage. Scientific cooperation has included operations research, nuclear weapons technology research, weather and computer science research, and NATO fellowships, grants, and university exchange programs. Other areas include civil-defense planning (fuel, food and agriculture, transportation, and medicine) and environmental concerns (following President Nixon's initiative in 1969).

Unfortunately, the successes and failures of integrative efforts in NATO cannot be explained by any of the current international integration theories. Indeed, none of those theories was developed to explain integration in NATO or in any other regional security alliance. Although Deutsch's "security community" and the ideas of other "pluralists" might at first glance appear to be suitable explanations, Deutsch's concept concerns the preventing of conflict among members of a "community of nations," not mutual defense against a real or perceived external threat. Furthermore, the pluralists' indicators (variables) of social behavior—international communications, trade and flows of finance, labor mobility, tourism, and the like—are scarcely relevant to political and military integration in NATO.[16] A prominent neofunctionalist, J. S. Nye, has argued that military and political matters are too controversial to foster integration, and that the growth of military and political regional organizations depends on shocks from the environment and hegemonic leadership (for which there can be no systematic theory).[17]

"Integration theorists" have either expressed disappointment in or ignored integration in NATO. Article II of the North Atlantic Treaty promised economic collaboration, harmonization of economic and social policy, promotion of stability, and understanding of one another's institutions—all beyond military planning and the rationalization of technical and administrative infrastructure. That NATO did not become the "Atlantic Community" and that those additional functions were made the competence of the European Community (if only for Western Europe) perhaps explain the pluralists' loss of interest in NATO.[18] The functionalists, meanwhile, found that military integration in NATO did not qualify as "steps toward positive integration."[19] In his thorough study of "functionalism and spillover" in NATO, Francis Beer concluded:

> While structures and tasks in each area changed and became increasingly differentiated, binding institutional procedures remained weak and there was limited task expansion. NATO authority remained mostly indirect and of limited effectiveness; there was little authoritative decision-making on matters of major importance to the participants. Legitimacy did not grow to the extent that actors were willing to support sizeable joint activity except when it was directly in their own interest.[20]

The neofunctionalists discuss integration in NATO and the Warsaw Pact as the work of the dominant, nuclear superpower partner. Federalists have consistently stressed the role of external threats to European security, but neglect to explain why such threats require more than the establishment of a military alliance.[21] In summary, theories of international political integration are not well suited to the study of integration in NATO.

The nonutility of international integration theories does not prevent the identification of some of the more obvious barriers to integration in NATO. Inframember rivalries and disputes have been numerous: France's long-standing accusation of U.S. hegemony in the Alliance; Greece and Turkey over Cyprus and other disputed islands; the United Kingdom and Iceland during the "Cod War." Arguments over which general strategies should be emphasized began in the early 1960s: flexible response versus tactical nuclear weapons reliance in particular. Decisions to increase nuclear missile placements and to deploy the neutron bomb have divided the member-states and led to increased protest activity in Europe. In fact, the Treaty may constitute the greatest barrier to integration. By limiting the geographic area of concern and by precluding the establishment of supranational institutions and regulatory and enforcement mechanisms, the Treaty provisions reinforce the full sovereignty of each member, making any real policy or institutional integration unlikely.

Perhaps nothing better illustrates current barriers to integration in NATO than the efforts to achieve weapons standardization in the Alliance.[22] Increasingly in this area, the imperative of enhancing collaborative security (e.g., through the adoption of one standard weapon system) has been frustrated by growing economic competition in arms production among many of the member-states. Even the seemingly obvious and easily attainable goals of spare parts and components have fallen victim to parochial interests among business and labor leaders (protection of sales and profits, employment, and research-and-development activities), the ability of national government departments and agencies to delay or "stonewall" programs, Third Country transfer restrictions or market dependence, and defense industries' concern over the transfer of technology.[23]

Despite the many barriers, however, NATO has met its primary objectives in over thirty years of existence. It remains one of the most important international actors in the world today, perhaps no less so than to the organization considered next, the Warsaw Treaty Organization.

Notes

1. *NATO Handbook* (Brussels: NATO Information Service, 1980), p. 13.

2. George F. Kennan, "The Sources of Soviet Conduct," *Foreign Affairs* 25 (July 1947), pp. 566–582.

3. See, for example, Alexander M. Haig, "NATO and Western Security," *Vickers Lecture Series* (Lawrence: University of Kansas, 1979).

4. Although the geographical area of concern is regional, it extends beyond the North Atlantic to the Mediterranean Sea. NATO membership covers two continents, three when most of Turkey is considered.

5. The perceptions were often inaccurate. See, for example, the discussion of mutual responses to threat in Henry T. Nash, *American Foreign Policy: Changing Perspectives on National Security* (Homewood, Ill.: Dorsey Press, 1978), pp. 5–33.

6. The WEU is further discussed in Chapter 9.

7. For background on the European Defense Community (EDC), see Roger Morgan, *West European Politics Since 1945* (New York: Capricorn Books, 1972), pp. 136–142.

8. See Chapter 9.

9. *NATO: Facts About the North Atlantic Treaty Organization* (Brussels: NATO Information Service, 1980).

10. Ibid.

11. Ibid.

12. *NATO Handbook,* pp. 34–37; 55–56.

13. It was also formed to counter U.S. dominance in the Alliance, particularly in the areas of strategic doctrine and arms production.

14. Werner J. Feld, "Western Europe," in Werner J. Feld and Gavin Boyd (Eds.), *Comparative Regional Systems* (New York: Pergamon Press, 1980), pp. 126–129.

15. See Article 5 of the North Atlantic Treaty.

16. Charles Pentland, *International Theory and European Integration* (New York: Free Press, 1973), pp. 198–199.

17. J. S. Nye, *Peace in Parts: Integration and Conflict in Regional Organization* (Boston: Little, Brown and Co., 1971), p 22.

18. Pentland, *International Theory,* p. 53.

19. This "criticism" has been applied also to the Warsaw Pact and other military and security regional organizations, as well as to international business and finance organizations.

20. Francis A. Beer, *Integration and Disintegration in NATO: Processes of Alliance Cohesion and Prospects for Atlantic Community* (Columbus: Ohio State University Press, 1969), p. 239.

21. Pentland, *International Theory,* pp. 156 and 229.

22. Phillip Taylor, "Weapons Standardization in NATO: Collaborative Security or Economic Competition," *International Organization* 36:1 (Winter 1982), pp. 95–112.

23. Ibid.

9
The Warsaw Pact and Other Alliances

The Warsaw Treaty Organization (WTO, or Warsaw Pact) is a political-military alliance consisting of the Soviet Union, Bulgaria, Czechoslovakia, the German Democratic Republic (DDR), Hungary, Poland, and Rumania. The political basis of the alliance is founded on the Treaty of Friendship, Cooperation, and Mutual Assistance signed in Warsaw on May 14, 1955. Significantly, this Treaty was completed nine days after West Germany joined NATO and one day before the Austrian State Treaty was signed. Although it provides the legal basis for the political functions of the WTO, the operations of the military alliance are based on several bilateral status-of-forces agreements between the Soviet Union and each of the WTO states.

The stated purposes of the Treaty of Friendship, Cooperation, and Mutual Assistance are to promote the maintenance of peace, to safeguard the security of individual members from the West, to strengthen economic and cultural ties between the members (with the aim of forming a socialist commonwealth), and to work toward a general European treaty concerning collective security. It has been argued, however, that the direct reasons for the creation of the WTO were the establishment of an East-bloc military alliance in response to West German membership in NATO, to create a Soviet bargaining tool to be used in East-West relations, to provide a formal bond linking East Europe to the Soviet Union,[1] and to provide a legal basis for continued presence of Soviet troops in Poland and the DDR (to replace that lost through the Austrian State Treaty).[2]

In addition to the collective-security factor, the WTO has several political functions. It has served to communicate Soviet views on a number of issues critical to Soviet foreign policy: the "two-Germanys" question, nuclear weapons placement in Europe, and mutual and balanced force reductions. It has also served as a bargaining chip in Soviet diplomatic relations with members of NATO (e.g., SS-20 installations in East Europe and the timing of military maneuvers and exercises).[3] Intra-Pact functions include conflict resolution and "indirect" Soviet control (e.g., Hungary in 1956, Czechoslovakia in 1968, and Poland in 1981–1982).

The status-of-forces bilateral treaty system provides for the maintenance of Soviet forces in East Europe and the legal basis for the military alliance. Each individual treaty establishes the following:

1. Movement of Soviet forces in the host country.
2. The jurisdiction over Soviet forces, individual soldiers, members of Soviet military families, and civilian employees while on the territory of the host country.
3. Soviet control and use of military installations on the territory of the host country.
4. Jurisdiction of local authorities in civil and criminal matters arising out of, or in conjunction with, the presence of Soviet troops.
5. Matters subject to the exclusive jurisdiction of Soviet authorities.
6. Settlement of mutual claims.[4]

History and Development

The first step toward the creation of the WTO was taken at the Safeguarding of Peace and Collective Security Conference held in Moscow in November–December 1954. The declaration published at the Conference indicated that if the NATO states were to ratify the Paris Agreement (to permit West Germany membership in NATO), the countries represented at the Moscow Conference would meet again to "adopt measures for safeguarding their security."[5] The communiqué did not deter ratification of the Paris Treaty, and the WTO was established in May 1955.

The development of the WTO has taken place in three distinct stages. The first stage arose from Stalin's death and the resultant power struggle in the USSR up to 1960. Initially, the organization was of little importance to the signatories other than as legitimization of increasing numbers of Soviet troops in Eastern Europe. The Polish and Hungarian uprisings were protests in part against the larger number of Soviet troops assigned under the aegis of the WTO. Two days after Hungary withdrew from the Warsaw Pact, the Soviets invaded with "WTO authority" to preserve the alliance. However, in 1958 Soviet troops were withdrawn from Rumania, an event that signaled the beginning of Rumania's maverick stance in Soviet-Rumanian relations. The Soviets further reduced forces in Hungary and proposed negotiations for a nonaggression pact with NATO.

The beginning of the second stage was the Soviets' attempt to give the WTO more substance. Following the Sino-Soviet rift and Albania's condemnation of the German Peace Treaty and subsequent withdrawal from WTO participation, Khrushchev opted to increase the role of the East Europeans in sharing the financial burden of troop maintenance. In addition, increased tension over Berlin motivated Soviet attempts to bolster the WTO. In 1961, the Soviet Union began to stress closer military cooperation and increased force levels in the Pact. During Khrushchev's last four years in office, the Soviets conducted nine joint maneuvers in the WTO.

The third stage, marked by the ascent of Brezhnev and Kosygin, saw an effort to operationalize their predecessors' stillborn initiatives. Since 1964, an exponential growth has occurred in the number of joint maneuvers, and intensive steps have been taken to increase force levels and to standardize weapons and doctrine. Soviet advocacy of increased integration was confounded by rising East European nationalism and a showdown with Rumania that forced a return to the status quo ante. The Soviet invasion of Czechoslovakia in 1968 exacerbated that difficulty and, paradoxically, increased the Soviet Union's dependence on the WTO. Again, the Soviets attempted to cloak a unilateral action (with very minor subsequent involvement by Bulgaria, the DDR, Hungary, and Poland) with the mantle of WTO collective action. Rumania condemned the action, and Albania used it as an excuse to withdraw formally from the alliance.[6]

There was a general relaxation of Soviet control after the Czechoslovakian crisis. New institutions were created in 1969 and 1976 (discussed in the following section on "structure"). However, the Soviet Union renewed their efforts to bolster the WTO throughout the 1970s. Large-scale joint exercises included the "Brother-in-Arms" (DDR), "Shield 76" (Poland), "Alliance 77" (Hungary and Czechoslovakia), and "Alliance 78" (Rumania). The intensive militarization and increased Soviet military control suggest the Soviet value on the WTO as a (defensive) counterweight to NATO. However, the increased conventional and nuclear forces and the doctrine of "defense through offensive action in attacker's territory" has given the WTO a substantial offensive quality in the early 1980s.[7]

Structure

As in NATO, the organization of the WTO is a combination of military and civilian organizational structures. Unlike the NATO Treaty, however, the Treaty of Friendship, Cooperation, and Mutual Security does not constitute an institutional structure. Rather, it has established

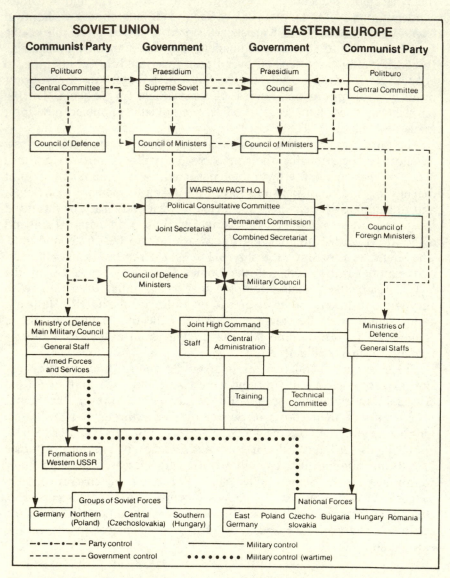

Figure 9.1   The Warsaw Pact

Source: International Institute for Strategic Studies, *The Military Balance, 1982–83* (London: International Institute for Strategic Studies, 1982), p. 19. Reprinted with permission.

only a Unified Command (Article 5) and the Political Consultative Committee (PCC) (Article 6). Subsequent institutions, in turn, have been established by the PCC. (See Figure 9.1.)

The Civilian Organization

The civilian institutions within the WTO consist of the Political Consultative Committee (the WTO's highest authority) and the Committee of Defense Ministers, the Committee of Foreign Ministers, the Military Council, the Permanent Commission, and the Combined Secretariat. The PCC consists of delegations of the member-states led by the party first secretary, head of state, and foreign minister of each nation. The venue rotates among the member-states, and chairmanship of the PCC is held by each nation in turn. The committee was intended to meet not less than twice each year. However, since 1972 meetings have taken place in alternate years. The military organization is represented through the attendance at meetings by the commander-in-chief of the Warsaw Pact Joint Armed Forces.[8]

The Committee of Defense Ministers and the Military Council were established in 1969 by the PCC as part of a reorganization of the Pact's military structure. The creation of these organizations explains, in part, the decreased frequency of PCC meetings. The Committee of Defense Ministers is a permanent organ that meets annually. As in the PCC, each member-state provides the Chairman venue in turn. The meetings center on an annual report from the Commander-in-Chief of the Joint Armed Forces. The Military Committee is a consultative body of national Chiefs of Staff or deputy ministers of defense who have the status of Deputy-Commanders-in-Chief of the Joint Armed Forces. The Council normally meets twice each year under the chairmanship of the Pact's Commander-in-Chief. The autumn meeting is combined with the General Conference of National Force Commanders.[9]

The first auxiliary organs created by the PCC (in 1956) were the Combined Secretariat and the Permanent Commission. The Secretariat is, in effect, the executive agency of the WTO. Significantly, this body is chaired by the Chief of Staff of the Combined Armed Forces (who is always a Soviet general). The Combined Secretariat controls the technical interests of the alliance (e.g., armaments, logistics, and research and development) and prepares the agenda for PCC meetings. The Permanent Commission is of lesser importance (e.g., it has not always been chaired by a Soviet official). The Commission is responsible for making foreign-policy recommendations to the PCC and the Secretariat.

At a 1976 meeting of the PCC, the Committee of Foreign Ministers was created to "improve the mechanism of political cooperation."[10] The Committee consults periodically on foreign policy and advises the PCC on matters it deems relevant, but it is not authorized to take binding decisions. Its first meeting was held in Moscow in 1977. Subsequent meetings have taken place yearly in each member-state in turn.

The Military Organization

The military operations and activities of the WTO are under the command and control of the Combined Supreme Command (CSC). Although established in January 1956, its stated purpose of military planning and coordination was fulfilled by a special branch of the Soviet General Staff until 1969. Since that time, the CSC and its staff perform those functions, but the organization is dominated by Soviet general officers. The CSC is led by the Supreme Commander of the Combined Forces, again always a Soviet General. This individual also holds the office of Soviet first deputy minister of defense. The CSC had been located in Moscow, but was moved in 1972 to Lvov, USSR.[11] The CSC has met irregularly, and conferences of the general officers of the Warsaw Pact nations have been convened to address specific military issues. Still, operations plans and military exercises are managed continually by the Soviet Commander. There are six groups of armed forces under the CSC's direct supervision: Group of Soviet Forces, (in Germany), Soviet Northern Group of Forces (in Poland), Soviet Central Group of Forces (in Czechoslovakia), Soviet Southern Group of Forces (in Hungary), Soviet Forces in Western Russia, and all forces of the National People's Army of East Germany. In contrast to the East German forces, the other five groups are subordinate to the CSC only during periods of external threat and only for such time until the threat is removed. The composition of Warsaw Pact forces is illustrated in Table 9.1.

The Decisionmaking Process

Each member-state of the Warsaw Pact has, by Article 6 of the Treaty, one vote in the highest formal organ, the Political Consultative Committee (PCC). Yet all decisions and resolutions taken there are adopted by consensus. No nation may block the consensus, but any member who does not agree with a PCC decision is permitted to abstain from its implementation.[12] The PCC is charged with making the determination as to when a crisis meets the criteria for executing the provisions of the Treaty. However, the decision to invade Czechoslovakia in 1968 was not considered by the PCC, even though it was carried out under WTO auspices. If this event is still indicative of decisionmaking in the WTO, many of the functions (perhaps those most important) are handled through bilateral or multilateral agreements between the USSR and the East European states or are simply unilateral Soviet actions legitimized

TABLE 9.1.   Principal Regional Forces in the Warsaw Pact Countries

Country/Service	Regular Forces	Reserves	Main Armaments	Other
U.S.S.R. (pop. 265,500,000)				
Army	1,825,000		50,000 tks. 63,000 AFV 20,000 arty. guns	Strategic nuclear forces: ICBM 1398 IRBM 220 MRBM 380 SLBM 1003 acft. 850
Navy	443,000			
Air Force	475,000	5,000,000 to 25,000,000 (all services)	189 atk. subs. 68 msl. subs. 709 maj. ships 775 cbt. acft.	
Marines	12,000		4,350 cbt. acft. 9,000 AA arty. 10,000 SAMs 93 amph. ships	
Total	2,475,000	25,000,000		
ALL OTHER WARSAW PACT COUNTRIES (pop. 109,700,000)				
Army	775,000	750,000	14,870 tks. 20,315 AFVs 7,285 arty. guns	
Navy	59,000	45,000	8 subs. 229 maj. ships	
Air Force	265,000	100,000	2,205 cbt. acft. 348 SAMs 5 SAM regts. 36 SAM bns. 60 SAM btrys. 5 AD regts.	
		1,251,000 (all services)		Paramilitary forces: 2,153,500
Total	1,099,000	4,299,500		

Source: Amos A. Jordan and William J. Taylor, Jr., American National Security (Baltimore: Johns Hopkins University Press, 1982), p. 477. Reprinted with permission.

by the WTO. Given the domination by Soviet officers, military decisionmaking in the WTO is less ambiguous than that in any other alliance (e.g., NATO). However, the Soviet Union does appear to be constrained by a lack of both support and consensus in the WTO. That the Soviet Union did not do in Poland in 1981 what it did in Hungary and Czechoslovakia indicates that the Soviets pay a price when they force their will upon their satellite countries.

State of Integration

There are many similarities between the WTO and NATO. Neither is a true supranational entity, nor was either intended to be one (by treaty). Both are military-security alliances designed to deter and/or repel aggression one to another. Both have separate but interlocking civilian and military structures. As with NATO, an evaluation of integration in the WTO depends upon the level of analysis and the perspective of the evaluator. Such analyses are often made by comparison—that is, the state of integration of one relative to the other.[13]

Technically, the WTO is more integrated than is the Atlantic Alliance. This is true primarily with regard to Soviet dominance of the Pact. Although the United States continues to dominate NATO, Soviet control is clearly (and formally) far greater in the WTO. (If the United States has used a pencil, the Soviets employ a cattle prod.) In general, the Soviet Union has tried consistently to integrate its policies in East Europe and not to integrate the East European Pact states into its policymaking.[14]

The WTO civilian organization exhibits less international integration than does the civilian organization in NATO. In terms of Schmitter's actor strategies, significant spillaround has characterized this organization, thus increasing the scope of WTO authority. However, what little increase in authority that has been permitted the central institutions remains under Soviet control. The reforms of 1969 and 1976 that led to the creation of new organs under the PCC was little more than symbolic democratization of the civilian organization. To date, these reforms have not demonstrated any substantive concessions made by the Soviet Union.

The military structure is effectively more integrated than that of NATO. WTO forces are commanded by Soviet general officers. Non-Soviet officers (usually assigned as deputy commanders of WTO forces) are trained in the USSR. Standardization in ideology and doctrine is maintained by party control. All officers in the grade of colonel and above must be Communist party members. WTO forces are most integrated through weapons standardization and logistics.

Military integration in training and weaponry has been managed by the Central Administration for Training and the Central Administration for Standardization of Weapons and Equipment, both suborgans of the Military Council. COMECON has been integrated effectively into defense-related matters (a feat that appears unlikely for NATO and the EC, for example). COMECON's Defense Industry Commission assists in the coordination of small arms manufacture in Czechoslovakia, Poland, and the DDR, and in the deployment of Soviet heavier armaments by WTO forces. COMECON has been used also to manage the building of auto expressways from the USSR to East Europe to facilitate rapid mobilization of forces, weapons, and equipment to the West. Certainly there is less doubt as to the efficiency of central military command in time of war than exists for the NATO military structure.

Other Security Organizations, Present and Past

There are several security organizations and military alliances in existence, but none approach the importance of NATO and the WTO. Two that did, CENTO and SEATO, no longer exist but deserve mention here for their historical import. Two smaller organizations, the Western European Union and ANZUS, will also be discussed briefly in this section. Security arrangements that form part of or a basis of other IGOs (e.g., the Rio Pact of the OAS and the Arab League's Treaty of Joint Defense and Economic Cooperation) will be covered in subsequent chapters.

Central Treaty Organization

The Central Treaty Organization (CENTO) was created by the Baghdad Pact in February 1955 by the United Kingdom, Pakistan, Iran, Turkey, and Iraq. The United States had pushed for the creation of CENTO as part of its containment policy but maintained only observer status throughout the life of the organization. Iraq withdrew formally in 1959 after a leftist government assumed power in that nation. The organization was dissolved on September 26, 1979, following the Iranian revolution. However, it had ceased to function effectively before that time due to lack of continued interest by Turkey and Pakistan.

The Baghdad Pact (originally concluded between Turkey and Pakistan) provided for cooperation in security and defense matters and the establishment of a Military Council, and contained a pledge to refrain from mutual interference in domestic matters as well as a promise by the signatories to enter other international organizations only if they were compatible with the Treaty. As CENTO developed and the original security arrangements faltered, it created institutions to promote economic development and scientific and technical cooperation.

CENTO's institutional structure included the Council of Ministers (policymaking body); the Deputy Council of Ministers (executive body), consisting of ambassadors accredited to Turkey; the Secretariat; the Scientific Council; the Economic Committee; and the Military Committee. (The latter served only a consultative function, having no command structure or assigned forces.) Decisions taken in the Council of Ministers required unanimity; however, the divergent security interests of the member-states made the achievement of a general consensus difficult. In fact, no significant decisions were taken during its existence.[15] (See Figure 9.2.)

Perhaps the only strength of CENTO was the stability in the region afforded by the military power built by the shah of Iran. CENTO's greatest weaknesses were "the chinks in the armor" caused by India's

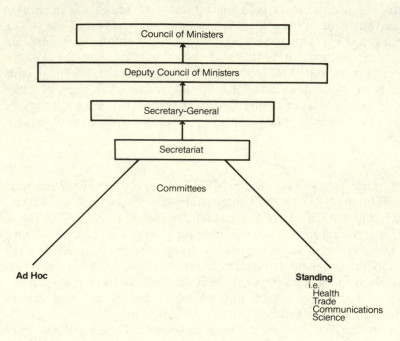

CENTO

Council of Ministers

Deputy Council of Ministers

Secretary-General

Secretariat

Committees

Ad Hoc

Standing
i.e.
Health
Trade
Communications
Science

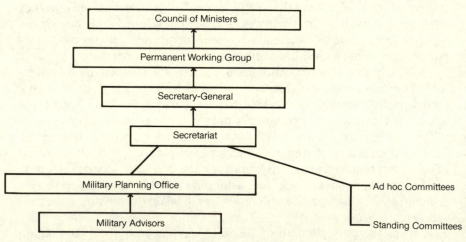

SEATO

Council of Ministers

Permanent Working Group

Secretary-General

Secretariat

Military Planning Office

Military Advisors

Ad hoc Committees

Standing Committees

Figure 9.2   The Structure of CENTO and SEATO

refusal to join and by the United States' decision not to join the alliance.[16] CENTO did manage to irritate the Soviets (if that was an aim of the organization) and to alienate much of the Arab World. Many Arab nations (Egypt, in particular) viewed an association with imperialist Britain and the neoimperialist United States as anathema.[17]

South East Asia Treaty Organization

The South East Asia Treaty Organization (SEATO) was created on September 8, 1954, with the signing of the South East Asia Collective Defense Treaty at Manila. The signatories were the United States, Britain, France, Australia, New Zealand, Pakistan, the Philippines, and Thailand. Only the last two states were true Southeast Asian nations. Conspicuous by their absence were the "militant neutrals" of the 1950s—India and Indonesia—as well as Ceylon, Burma, and the newly created states of Laos, Cambodia, and the "free territory of Vietnam." The organization was dissolved on June 30, 1977, when all the member-states abrogated the Treaty.

Structurally, SEATO resembled NATO except that it had no standing military forces or integrated command structure. The provisions of the Treaty bound the members to settle disputes peacefully (and in accordance with the UN Charter), to maintain the capacity to resist armed attack and subversion,[18] to strengthen free institutions, to view an armed attack anywhere in the geographic region[19] as endangering the peace and security of all, and, in the event of such attack, to consult on appropriate measures provided that actions taken in a member-state's territory had that nation's consent. The central institutions were the Council (which met annually at the ministerial level), the Council of Permanent Representatives and Permanent Working Group (executive bodies), the Secretariat, and the Military Planning Office and associated military committees. SEATO headquarters were in Bangkok, Thailand.[20] (See Figure 9.2.)

SEATO was created during the aftermath of the Korean conflict, after the "fall of China" and immediately following the French defeat at Dien Bien Phu and the Geneva Settlement (1954). The Eisenhower administration had been talking (for the first time) about "falling dominoes" and envisioned SEATO as the third link in the containment fence around communism. SEATO is best remembered (and most maligned) for U.S. involvement (and that of others) in Vietnam. The Treaty was designed to deter Ho Chi Minh (and those like him), but that deterrence depended on a gross underestimiation of Ho's staying power and fierce nationalism, and of the SEATO member-states' reluctance to stake national interests on a political stance based on uncertain legal and nationalistic underpinnings.[21] SEATO's demise was sealed by the failure of the United

States in Vietnam. The U.S. effort failed because it represented a unidimensional (military) solution to the multidimensional problems of Southeast Asian stability.

ANZUS Pact

ANZUS (named for Australia, New Zealand, United States—the Pact's only members) was created in 1952. Its stated purpose is to meet an armed attack on any of the member-states in the Pacific area in accordance with the "constitutional processes" of each member. The vaguely worded treaty establishes no military integration arrangement or permanent headquarters or staff. The only institution is the ANZUS Council, which usually meets in Washington, D.C., Canberra, or Wellington. The meetings are attended by the three nations' foreign ministers or their deputies; high-ranking military officers meet at the same time but separate from the Council.

Although ostensibly a military-security organization, ANZUS has served only as a vehicle for political consultation. Items discussed in its meetings range from the Soviet naval build-up in the Indian Ocean and the political situations in Vietnam, Laos, and Kampuchea, to discussions on the plight of refugees (e.g., the Vietnamese "boat people").[22] The organization has some importance to the three member-states, but it is unlikely to become an important nonstate actor in world politics.

Western European Union

The Western European Union (WEU) was created by the Paris Agreements and four additional protocols signed on October 23, 1954, by the current member-states: Belgium, France, West Germany, Italy, Luxembourg, the Netherlands, and the United Kingdom. The purposes of the organization are to coordinate the defenses of the members, to encourage European integration (through political collaboration), and to facilitate cooperation in economic, social, and cultural matters. The WEU originated in connection with the rejection by the French National Assembly of the European Defense Community Treaty. Since that treaty was designed in part to manage the rearmament of West Germany and its integration into the Western European system, and since the Brussels Treaty had been superseded by the creation of NATO, the Western European states modified the Brussels Treaty to create an organization that would perform part of the functions intended for the EDC.

The organizational structure of the WEU includes the Council, the Assembly, and three technical/administrative organs: the Agency for Control of Armaments, the Standing Committee for Armaments, and the Secretariat. The Council is a diplomatic conference of ministers (meeting annually) and permanent representatives (meeting weekly in

London). Most of its resolutions must be adopted by unanimous vote, although some areas (e.g., arms control) can be made binding on all member-states following a two-thirds or simple-majority vote in the Council. In order to avoid overlapping competences with NATO, the Council has limited itself in military matters to the level of troops of the member-states, the stationing of British troops on the continent, and the activities of the Agency for Control of Armaments and the Standing Committee for Armaments.[23] The Assembly, which meets twice each year, has a consultative role but has not limited the substantive issues it may address. It may consider any political, social, or cultural matter related to European integration. It can also discuss matters concerning the defense of Western Europe and was, until 1978, the only international parliamentary organ in Europe to do so.[24]

The Agency for the Control of Armaments was intended to control the quality and quantity of German armaments, but its functions have become symbolic through a series of modifications to the Treaty's Protocol III. The Standing Committee on Armaments attempts to foster greater efficiency and standardization of European weapons and equipment, in concert with NATO's standardization efforts. The Secretariat has a purely administrative role. All WEU institutions are located in London except the Assembly, which meets in Paris.

Most of the original functions of the WEU have been absorbed by NATO and the EC. Prior to Britain's entry into the European Community, economic review meetings (which were abandoned in 1973) served as a bridge between Britain and the EC. The WEU still performs a similar function between France and NATO. It also served successfully as a political framework for re-arming West Germany and supervised the 1955 referendum on the SAAR. Today, however, it functions only as a forum for political consultations. Recent issues discussed in its meetings include East-West relations, the size of member-states' military forces, political changes in Spain and Portugal, aviation and nuclear energy in Western Europe, and events in Southern Africa.[25]

Notes

1. Andrzej Korbonski, "The Warsaw Pact," *International Conciliation* 573 (May 1969), pp. 5–73.

2. Richard F. Staar, *The Communist Regimes in Eastern Europe* (Stanford, Calif.: Hoover Institution, 1971), p. 215.

3. Richard Dana, "The Warsaw Treaty Organization: A Brief Description," *Defense and Foreign Affairs Handbook* (Washington, D.C.: Government Printing Office, 1980), p. 711.

4. Staar, *Communist Regimes*, p. 216.

5. Dana, "Warsaw Treaty Organization."

6. Ibid., p. 719.

7. For background, see Friedrich Wiener and William J. Lewis, *The Warsaw Pact Armies* (Vienna: Carl Veberreuter Publishers, 1977).

8. Keesing Publication, *Treaties and Alliances of the World* (New York: Charles Scribner's Sons, 1978), p. 121.

9. Ibid.

10. The creation of the Committee of Foreign Ministers may be seen as a Soviet concession to East European demands for a greater role in policymaking and as a personal victory for Rumania's Ceausescu, who wanted to dilute the military function by strengthening the WTO's political functions.

11. The move was designed to give the impression of placing the CSC at the geographical center of the Pact. However, CSC headquarters remain in the USSR.

12. Korbonski, "Warsaw Pact," p. 21.

13. See, for example, *The Atlantic Alliance and the Warsaw Pact: A Comparative Study* (Brussels: NATO Information Service, 1980).

14. Cf. Robin Alison Remington, *The Warsaw Pact: Case Studies in Communist Conflict Resolution* (Cambridge, Mass.: MIT Press, 1971).

15. Europa Publications, *Europa Handbook of the World* (London: Europa, 1976).

16. James P. Piscatori and R. K. Ramazani, "The Middle East," in Werner J. Feld and Gavin Boyd, (Eds.), *Comparative Regional Systems* (New York: Pergamon Press, 1980), p. 293.

17. Louis J. Halle, *The Cold War as History* (New York: Harper and Row, 1971).

18. "Subversion" is not mentioned in the North Atlantic Treaty.

19. The Treaty area extended south of 21 degrees 30′ north latitude to the general area of Southeast Asia and Southwest Pacific (Taiwan was intentionally omitted from the area).

20. For background, see George M. Kahin and John W. Lewis, *The United States in Vietnam* (rev. ed.) (New York: Dial Press, 1969); and Stanley R. Larsen and James L. Collins, *Allied Participation in Vietnam* (Washington, D.C.: Government Printing Office, 1975).

21. Russell H. Fifield, *Americans in South East Asia* (New York: Crowell, 1973).

22. "ANZUS Council Meets," *State Department Bulletin*, April 1980, pp. 53–58.

23. A. H. Robertson, "The Creation of the Western European Union," *European Yearbook* 2 (1979), pp. 126–129.

24. Western European Assembly Documents, *Twenty-fourth Annual Report of the Council* (Doc. 801, Chapter III, 1979).

25. Ibid.

Part 4

Political International
Governmental Organizations

10
The Organization of
American States

The Organization of American States (OAS) is a multipurpose regional international governmental organization. Like all such organizations, its functions are political, economic, judicial, cultural, and social. However, the OAS is primarily a political organization; its emphasis has been political consultation with regard to regional stability and security and on conflict resolution (more a diplomatic than military function). The legal bases for the organization are the Charter of the Organization of American States (1948), as reorganized by the Protocol of Amendment of 1967; the Inter-American Treaty for Peaceful Settlement of Disputes (1948); and the Inter-American Treaty of Reciprocal Assistance (or Rio Pact of 1947).

The stated purposes of the OAS are to promote peace, justice, and solidarity, and to strengthen collaboration among the member-states in order to defend their individual sovereignty, integrity, and independence. The OAS is a regional organization constituted under the provisions of Article 51 of the United Nations Charter.[1] Its stated goals are to strengthen the peace and security of North and South America; to prevent possible causes of interstate difficulties and ensure the pacific settlement of disputes arising among the member-states; to organize "solidarity action" in the event of outside aggression; to seek the solution of political, juridical, and economic problems arising among them; and to promote mutual economic, social, and cultural development through cooperative action.[2] Its Treaty affirms the principles of sovereignty and territorial integrity: "No state or group of states has the right to intervene in any way, directly or indirectly, for any reason whatever, in the internal or external affairs of any other state."[3] The Treaty also contains reaffirmations of the principles of human rights, economic cooperation, democracy (as the approach and proper political basis of governments), and adherence to international law.[4]

The OAS Charter articulates a set of rules for the member-states and catalogues what appears to be an impressive list of interstate relations. However, the member-states are permitted to determine what amount (if any) of sovereignty they are willing to relinquish in the name of inter-American solidarity and "good neighbor" or regional cooperation. The Charter also provides any reluctant member with the necessary escape clauses to ensure latitude of action for questions of both high and low politics. Such freedom of action includes the right to invoke adverse domestic legislation, for example, in reference to economic and cultural cooperation.[5]

The OAS Charter was ratified initially by twenty-one North, Central, and South American nations. Current membership stands at twenty-eight. Other than small states or nonindependent areas in the Caribbean, the only nations in the hemisphere not members of the OAS are Canada and Guyana.[6] Many nonhemispheric states have observer status in the OAS, including those that are members of the Inter-American Development Bank: Belgium, Denmark, Great Britain, Israel, Japan, Spain, Switzerland, West Germany, and Yugoslavia.

History and Development

The development of "Pan-Americanism" leading to the creation of the OAS can be traced to the First Congress of American States and the Treaty of Perpetual Union League and Confederation signed by Colombia, Central America, Peru, and Mexico in 1826. The second effort was the creation of the International Union of American Republics in 1890. The name of that organization was changed in 1910 to the Union of American Republics and, again in 1923, to the Union of Republics of the American Continent. Its principal organ, the Commercial Bureau, was located in Washington, D.C., and renamed the Pan-American Union. The functions of the Union were strictly limited to collection and distribution of commercial information. A decision was taken in 1928 to prohibit the central institutions from exercising any political functions. The reason concerned an issue that threatened to destroy the Union, namely, the United States' refusal to accept formally the principle of nonintervention in the hemisphere. By 1936, however, the United States had reversed its position. It accepted the principle of nonintervention as an "unqualifed legal principle,"[7] abandoned the Roosevelt Corollary, and pressed for a hemispheric defense plan. World War II strengthened that resolve and motivated the Act of Chapultepec and the Rio Pact.[8]

The Act of Chapultepec was the result of the Inter-American Conference on Problems of War and Peace in Mexico City; its purpose was to establish a system of continental security for the American states. However, the first permanent collective defense treaty for the Western Hemisphere was signed in 1947. The Inter-American Treaty of Reciprocal

Assistance (or Rio Pact) is a joint security arrangement that binds the member-states to consider any act of armed aggression within the security zone (whether internal or external) as a threat to hemispheric peace and, hence, as an attack on all. The states are required only to consult following such aggressions; however, joint sanctions may be carried out against "aggressor states" within the zone. The Treaty has been invoked sixteen times; all cases involved intramember disputes in the Caribbean area. Sanctions were applied on four occasions: in the Dominican Republic in 1960 and in Cuba in 1962, 1964, and 1967.[9] The successful conclusion of the Rio Pact facilitated the creation of the OAS one year later.

Both the Charter of the Organization of American States and the Inter-American Treaty for the Peaceful Settlement of Disputes were signed in Bogotá, Colombia, in April 1948. The latter treaty provides the legal framework and mechanisms for conflict resolution (arbitration is prescribed), but the system envisioned is relatively uncoordinated and none of the provisions is compulsory.

An ideological concern pervaded the search for the causes of conflict in the area in the early 1950s. This led to the adoption of the Declaration of Solidarity for the Preservation of the Political Integrity of the American States against the Intervention of International Communism (1954). Fidel Castro's seizure of power in Cuba confirmed latent fears of aggressive Communist expansion in the hemisphere and motivated the Declaration of San Jose (which condemned intervention or the threat of intervention by an extra-continental power in the affairs of any American state) in 1960 and the Resolution of Punte del Este (which declared principles of communism incompatible with the principles of the Inter-American Systems) in 1962.[10]

The first economic cooperation venture occurred in 1957 through the Economic Declaration of Buenos Aires. In response to the deterioration of the terms of trade for raw material exporters, the declaration prescribed only a panacea by which industrialization in Latin America was encouraged in an effort to achieve import substitution. However, a major step in economic cooperation occurred in 1959 through the creation of the Inter-American Development Bank (IDB). Designed to finance economic and social development projects in Latin America, the IDB finances hard loans (those with interest rates close to commercial banking markets) and soft loans (those with low interest rates for infrastructure or other "non-profit-related" projects) through the Fund for Special Operations. The IDB serves to provide technical assistance to the member-countries and manages the Pre-investment Fund for Latin American Integration for projects designed to promote and accelerate Latin American integration.[11]

During the Cuban Missile Crisis of 1962, the OAS Council supported U.S. efforts to remove missile bases in Cuba, and the OAS foreign ministers suspended Cuba from participation in the OAS. Sanctions against Cuba were approved in 1964 by a vote of 15 to 4 (those opposed were Bolivia, Chile, Mexico, and Uruguay). In the following year, the Inter-American Peace Force was created in response to the Dominican crisis. It was dissolved in 1966 when U.S. troops withdrew from the Dominican Republic.

A major structural reorganization of the OAS was achieved in 1970 when the Protocol of Buenos Aires entered into force. The General Assembly was established as the highest authority, replacing the Inter-American Conferences and the three Councils (see the section on "structure" in this chapter). In 1972, Canada joined the IDB. This event was significant for two reasons. First, Canada had disdained OAS membership, claiming initially that its duty to the Commonwealth prevented it from joining the OAS and, after 1960, stating its desire to maintain diplomatic and trade relations with Cuba. The more probable reason, however, was its unwillingness to join an organization dominated by the United States.[12] Second, Canada's entry into the IDB paved the way for the membership of nonhemispheric nations. By 1976, six Western European states, Japan, Israel, and Yugoslavia were IDB members.[13]

During the 1970s, several important resolutions were passed in the General Assembly. Special studies were commissioned concerning control of multinational enterprises, energy problems, and food production in 1974. The member-states were permitted to normalize relations with Cuba in 1975 (although an effort to return Cuba's participatory status in the OAS was thwarted by the United States). Several human rights resolutions and the proclaimed Decade of Women (1976–1985) were concluded in 1976. Additional human rights resolutions and a condemnation of terrorism were opposed in 1977. In 1979, the Inter-American Court of Human Rights was created.

Structure

The major organs of the OAS are the General Assembly; the Permanent Council; the Meeting of Consultation (consisting of Ministers of Foreign Affairs); the Inter-American Economic and Social Council; the Inter-American Council for Education, Science, and Culture; the Inter-American Commission on Human Rights; and the General Secretariat. The OAS organizational structure also includes six specialized organizations, four special agencies/commissions, and several ad hoc specialized conferences. (See Figure 10.1.)

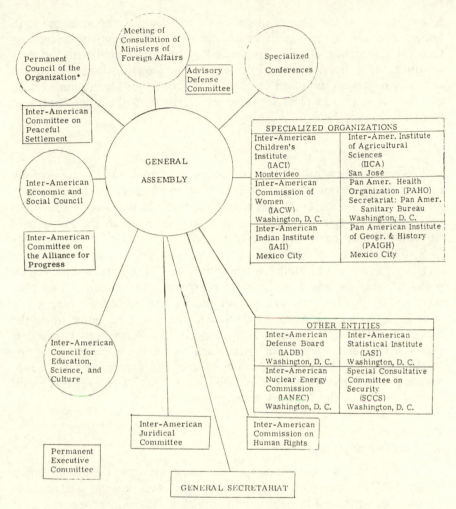

Figure 10.1   The Organization of American States

Source: James R. Rose, *An Inter-American Peace Force Within the Framework of the Organization of American States* (Metuchen, N.J.: Scarecrow Press, 1970), pp. 322–323. Reprinted with permission.

The General Assembly

As the supreme organ of the OAS, the General Assembly has powers to determine the general policies of the organizations and the structure and functions of all OAS institutions, and to consider any matter related to coexistence of the American states. In addition, it approves the OAS budget and the admission of new members, and elects the Secretary-General. Consisting of delegates headed by one accredited with the rank of ambassador from each member-state, the General Assembly meets annually in the capital of an OAS member-country. (The annual change of venue is symbolic; prior to 1970, all meetings of the Inter-American Conference were held in Washington, D.C.)

The Permanent Council

The principal political tasks of the Permanent Council are twofold: to act as a provisional organ of consultation in cases of armed attack on any member-state, and to serve as a mediator in the pacific settlement of disputes between or among member-states. However, the Permanent Council does not have the power of initiative. It cannot act until parties to a dispute request assistance, nor until violence has erupted or the territorial integrity of a state has been violated.[14] The Permanent Council performs the routine functions of preparing for General Assembly meetings by drafting resolutions and setting the agenda. In emergency situations, it may serve as a provisional consultative body until the Meeting of Foreign Ministers is convened. The Permanent Council is composed of one ambassador from each member-state. The positions of chairman and vice-chairman are held by each member-state's representative in turn for a period of three months. The Permanent Council is responsible to the General Assembly.

The Meeting of Consultation of Ministers of Foreign Affairs

The Meeting of Consultation is the most important political organ of the OAS. It convenes when matters pertinent to the Charter are considered urgent (at the request of any member-state). However, it is the Permanent Council that decides (by absolute-majority vote) on the merits of any such request. The specific function of the Meeting of Consultation is to meet when a situation requires invoking the provisions of the Inter-American Treaty of Reciprocal Assistance (Rio Pact). It then decides the collective measures required to oppose attack and selects punitive measures as needed relative to acts of any aggressor-nation(s).[15] Any measure to be taken requires a two-thirds vote of the foreign ministers (those directly involved in the conflict are not permitted to vote). Decisions of the Meeting of Consultation are binding on all OAS member-states. However, no member-state is required to use armed force if it has not agreed to it. The nonpermanent Defense Advisory Committee is subordinate to the Meeting of Consultation. Composed of high-ranking military officers from each of the member-states, it advises on military and technical matters.[16]

The Inter-American Economic and Social Council

The purpose of this body is to meet at least once each year to coordinate OAS-sponsored economic and social developmental activities, to evaluate the progress of those states receiving program assistance, and to promote Latin American economic integration. Membership is drawn from government, business, labor, and professional groups in all of the member-states.[17]

The Inter-American Council
for Education, Science, and Culture

This body replaced the Inter-American Cultural Council in 1970. Structured in the same manner as the Economic and Social Council, it meets annually to consider and propose to the General Assembly scientific, educational, and cultural cooperation programs.

The Inter-American Commission on Human Rights

The Human Rights Commission is composed of seven jurists elected by the General Assembly for terms of four years. It meets twice annually but may be called into special sessions. A special agreement (the Costa Rica Convention) regulates the structure and activities of this body.

The Inter-American Juridical Committee

The Juridical Committee is a product of a merger of the Inter-American Council of Jurists and the pre-1970 Inter-American Juridical Committee. It functions as a consultative body to other OAS institutions and promotes the progressive development and codification of international law. The Juridical Committee is composed of eleven jurists elected by the General Assembly for staggered terms of four years.[18]

The General-Secretariat

The General-Secretariat is the permanent central administrative organ of the OAS. Its functions are to provide general administrative support to all OAS institutions, to prepare and monitor the OAS budget, and to serve as the custodian of the OAS archives. The Secretary-General is elected by the General Assembly to a five-year term. His or her successor may not be from the same nation. The Secretariat is located in Washington, D.C.

Specialized Organs

There are six specialized organizations: the Inter-American Institute of Agricultural Sciences, the Pan-American Health Organization, the Inter-American Commission of Women, the Inter-American Children's Institute, the Pan-American Institute of Geography and History, and the Inter-American Indian Institute. The five specialized agencies/commissions are the Inter-American Defense Board, the Inter-American Statistical Institute, the Inter-American Nuclear Energy Commission, the Administrative Tribunal, and the Inter-American Emergency Aid Fund. Also included in the category of specialized organs are numerous ad hoc conferences composed of technical experts on matters commissioned by other bodies of the OAS.

State of Integration

The OAS is a multipurpose regional IGO. As such, its state or states of integration should be evaluated in terms of each of its major purposes or functions. The central political function of the OAS is conflict resolution among the member-states. Its security function is embodied in the Rio Pact and the several related bilateral treaties. Its economic function includes many trade and development conferences/programs but is most salient in the area of Inter-American Development Bank activities. Cultural, scientific, and educational programs involving program coordination and technical cooperation/exchange have been numerous and successful but are not significantly important to an evaluation of the OAS as a world actor. This analysis, then, will emphasize the degree of political, security, and economic cooperation achieved under the aegis of the OAS.

From the establishment of the Bogotá Treaty in 1948 (OAS Charter) until 1969, the OAS has acted in concert to attempt to settle peacefully eleven intramember violent disputes. These disputes involved exile invasions (Costa Rica–Nicaragua, 1948; Guatemala-Honduras, 1954; Costa Rica–Nicaragua, 1955; Panama-Cuba, 1959; and Nicaragua–Costa Rica, 1959), a border dispute (Honduras-Nicaragua, 1957), an attempted assassination (Venezuela–Dominican Republic, 1960), forcible entry into an embassy (Dominican Republic–Haiti, 1963), riots in the Canal Zone (Panama–United States, 1964), a coup d'etat (Dominican Republic), and the "soccer wars" of 1969 (Honduras–El Salvador). Although OAS efforts brought about a settlement in only three of the eleven cases, it did manage to help isolate ten cases, to end the fighting in six, and to abate the violence in eight. In their study, Haas and Nye found that for the same time period the OAS's average weighted success in conflict resolution was more than double that of the Organization of African Unity's conflict-resolution efforts, and nearly quadruple that of the Arab League.[19]

One of the most significant developments in OAS conflict resolution has been the "Try OAS First" issue. The OAS is the only regional organization that has attempted to force its member-states to exhaust OAS remedies before taking a dispute to the UN Security Council. The effort began in 1954 when Guatemala was attacked (with U.S. support) by Honduras and Nicaragua. The issue was raised again by Cuba in 1960, Haiti in 1963, and Panama in 1964. The Try OAS First principle was abandoned in the late 1960s. The OAS failed to achieve complete control over disputes among its member-states, but, at the same time, the UN Security Council lost the capacity to regulate or curtail OAS regional enforcement operations.[20]

One of the most important aspects (and, perhaps, the most successful from the perspective of the Latin American states) of OAS conflict resolution has been the long-term effort to reduce or eliminate U.S. intervention in Latin American affairs. Until the late 1970s, the United States seemed to accept fully the principle of nonintervention and to be satisfied with OAS-sponsored multilateral efforts. However, the successful leftist insurgencies in Nicaragua, Guatemala, and El Salvador in the early 1980s may have reversed that trend. Increasingly, the United States has been frustrated by the refusal of OAS member-states to take action on what it perceives to be Cuban-Soviet "exportation of communism."

The security function of the OAS has been one of its consistently salient features. Indeed, the OAS in its present form evolved in part from a mutual concern for collective security following World War II. At the same time as the U.S. preoccupation has been the containment/prevention of the spread of communism throughout the hemisphere, the Latin American states have exhibited decreasing concern over that issue. Prior to 1982, the Rio Treaty had been invoked sixteen times, but all such instances involved intramember-state disputes. In April 1982, Argentina attempted to invoke the Rio Treaty against Britain in its dispute over the sovereignty of the Falkland Islands. The United States was placed in a "no-win" position, attempting to mediate the dispute between a NATO ally and an OAS partner while being forced to decide its position on the sovereignty question before considering its obligations under the Rio Treaty. The episode may seriously damage the future viability of collective security in the OAS. The Latin American states have demonstrated a determination to maintain effective responsive security cooperation through periodic restructuring measures. The United States' disenchantment may signal a significant retrenchment, however.

It is in the area of economic cooperation that the United States most dominates the OAS. Although the Latin American states would prefer a far greater emphasis on development assistance through the OAS, little of substance has occurred in this area since the creation of the IDB and President Kennedy's Alliance for Progress in the early 1960s. During the 1970s, U.S. aid to Latin America was decreased substantially. In 1978, the United States announced a significant decrease in its quota contribution to the IDB. It also began to shift from multilateral OAS economic projects to bilateral trade and aid arrangements.[21] President Reagan's proposal in March 1982 of a "Marshall Plan" for Caribbean nations was welcomed by the Latin American states, but it would have enhanced U.S.–Latin American relations had the proposal been contained in an OAS economic-cooperation program.

In general, it may be argued that the OAS Inter-American system is neither structurally nor volitionally a "process of integration." Although its scope of cooperation has certainly increased, its level of authority as a distinct entity independent from the policymaking of the separate member-states is practically nil. Yet, as Duffy and Feld have argued, there is nothing intrinsically wrong with a system that is coordinated by the member-states rather than being managed by supranational institutions, provided that the member-states have the political will to act in concert. According to Duffy and Feld's "national-interest model," policy integration can occur in the absence of any significant institutional integration. The model posits four operational concepts: (1) that of geographical continuity, a historical pattern of political interaction, and a set of social norms; (2) that the international organization is one of many means by which the member-states can attempt to maximize long-range benefits through negotiated settlement rather than supranational technocratic decisionmaking; (3) that nationalism is the main centrifugal force affecting the organization, thus guaranteeing "national and coherent decisionmaking"; and (4) that national interest as the sum of foreign-policy goals and domestic objectives forms the basis of the system.[22] These factors appear to fit the inter-American system. Indeed, what the Thomases argued twenty years ago is still valid: that in contrast to traditional international law wherein resolutions of conferences become "law" only after treaties are signed and ratified, many Inter-American resolutions became immediately binding on the member-states.[23] William Manger's observation made more than ten years ago is also equally relevant today:

> The current mood is not toward more internationalism but toward more nationalism, not to a strengthening of international organization but to a

lessening of the authority of international agencies and a reaffirmation of national individuality and sovereignty.[24]

The Organization of American States is an important world actor, but its present importance and its future viability depend on a continuing negotiated consensus of its member-states, not on a legally prescribed schedule of gradual yielding of sovereignty to supranational institutions. In a very real sense, this factor is both a source of the OAS's viability and a reason for optimism concerning its future.

Notes

1. See Article I of the OAS Charter. See Keesing Publication, *Treaties and Alliances of the World* (New York: Charles Scribner's Sons, 1968), p. 145.
2. Article IV of the Charter.
3. Article XIII of the Charter.
4. Article V of the Charter.
5. From Articles XXXII and XLIX of the Charter.
6. Guyana has been denied membership due to a long-standing border dispute with Venezuela, although it does have observer status. See G. Pope Atkins, *Latin America in the International Political System* (New York: Free Press, 1977), p. 321.
7. The United States has not accepted a strict (Latin American) interpretation of "intervention." It has intervened in Argentina (1945), Guatemala (1954), Cuba (1961), the Dominican Republic (1965), Chile (1970–1973), and El Salvador (1981–1982).
8. Atkins, *Latin America,* pp. 325–329.
9. The Rio Pact is augmented by five bilateral treaties: U.S.-Brazil, U.S.-Chile, U.S.-Colombia, U.S.-Peru, and U.S.-Uruguay.
10. The first Punte del Este Conference in 1961 began the Alliance for Progress, which entailed massive U.S. economic assistance to Latin America as a means to stop the spread of communism. See Jerome Slater, *The OAS and United States Foreign Policy* (Columbus: Ohio State University Press, 1967).
11. See R. Peter DeWitt, Jr., *The Inter-American Development Bank and Political Influence* (New York: Praeger Publishers, 1977).
12. Atkins, *Latin America,* p. 322.
13. Ibid., p. 345.
14. *OAS Official Documents,* OAS/Ser. K.XIII, Doc. 113 (Washington, D.C.: OAS Secretariat, 1979), p. 6.
15. Article III of the Inter-American Treaty of Reciprocal Assistance provides a catalog of the punitive measures available: recall of diplomats, breaking of diplomatic or consular relations, complete or partial interruption of economic relations, interruption of international transportation and communications, and the use of armed force.
16. Keesing, *Treaties,* p. 148.

17. Atkins, *Latin America,* p. 319.

18. Ibid., pp. 317–318.

19. Joseph S. Nye, *Peace in Parts* (Boston: Little, Brown and Co., 1971), pp. 135–172.

20. Inis L. Claude, Jr., "The OAS, The UN, and the United States," in Richard A. Falk and Saul H. Mendlovitz (Eds.), *Regional Politics and World Order* (San Francisco: W. H. Freeman and Co., 1973), pp. 277–297.

21. Francis Gannon, "Should the Americas Reorganize the OAS?" *Vital Speeches Magazine* (December 15, 1979), p. 141.

22. Charles A. Duffy and Werner J. Feld, "Whither Regional Integration Theory?" in Werner J. Feld and Gavin Boyd (Eds.), *Comparative Regional Systems* (New York: Pergamon Press, 1980), pp. 497–521.

23. Ann Van Wynen Thomas and A. J. Thomas, Jr., "The Rule-Making System of the OAS," in Paul A. Tharp, Jr. (Ed.), *Regional International Organizations: Structures and Functions* (New York: St. Martin's Press, 1971), pp. 109–140.

24. William Manger, "Reform of the OAS," in Tharp, *Regional International Organizations,* p. 150.

11

The Organization of
African Unity

The Organization of African Unity (OAU) is a political regional intergovernmental organization. Founded in May 1963, the OAU is composed of fifty African nations, including all the independent states on the African continent except the Republic of South Africa (including its "trust," Namibia, and the unrecognized "homeland" states). Like the OAS, the OAU is a multipurpose organization, but its political functions far overshadow any economic, social, or cultural efforts in the organization. Briefly, its political functions are to support movements to end colonial and white-minority governments in Africa; to provide intra-African conflict resolution; to unite in support of common positions in the United Nations, North-South Conferences, and other international fora (e.g., the Lomé Convention with the EC); and to support the ideological concept of Pan-Africanism.

The stated purposes of the OAU are set forth in Article II of its Charter:

1. to promote the unity and solidarity of the African states;
2. to coordinate and intensify their cooperation and efforts to achieve a better life for the peoples of Africa;
3. to eradicate all forms of colonialism from Africa; and
4. to promote international cooperation, having due regard to the Charter of the United Nations and the Universal Declaration of Human Rights.[1]

In pursuit of these purposes, the members of the OAU pledged themselves in Article III of the Charter to adhere to the following principles:

1. the sovereign equality of all member-states;
2. noninterference in the internal affairs of states;

3. respect for the sovereignty and territorial integrity of each state and for its inalienable right to independent existence;
4. peaceful settlement of disputes by negotiation, mediation, conciliation, or arbitration;
5. unreserved condemnation, in all its forms, of political assassination as well as of subversive activities on the part of neighboring states or any other state;
6. absolute dedication to the total emancipation of the African territories that are still dependent; and
7. affirmation of a policy of nonalignment with regard to blocs.[2]

History and Development

Many scholars trace the developments leading to creation of the OAU to the series of international meetings known as the Pan-African Congress. The first such meeting took place in the United States in 1900, attended by prominent blacks from the United States, Britain, and the West Indies. The second meeting, held in Paris in 1919, was dominated by blacks from France and the United States. As with the first Congress, the purpose of the second was to "popularize" the concept of Pan-Africanism and to discuss means of improving colonial governments in Africa. Following two other less successful meetings, the fifth Congress held in Manchester in 1945 was the first to feature significant African representation. The delegates to the fifth Congress rejected colonialism in any form and advocated immediate independence for the peoples of Africa.

Although there were several attempts by the Pan-African Congress to create a regional organization, it was the proliferation of newly independent states in Africa in the late 1950s and early 1960s that gave impetus to regional integration. These states were physically and economically small, and many constituted geographical borders that had no ideological or demographic significance. In response to these difficulties, many African leaders turned to each other, having been left afloat with inadequate preparation or assistance from their former metropoles. The first major step toward the creation of the OAU was taken at the initial All Africa People's Conference held in Accra, Ghana, in December 1958. After meeting again in June 1960 in Ethiopia, this group (known as the Casablanca group)[3] adopted the Casablanca Charter on January 7, 1961, which called for a joint military command and an African common market. The leaders of the Casablanca-group nations advocated the socialist development of all Africa, centered on the creation of a strong central international authority.

In May 1961, Liberian President William Tubman invited to a conference nineteen other independent African (mostly Francophone) states[4] opposed to the Casablanca group's socialist ideology. This group, known as the Monrovia group, met again in Lagos, Nigeria, to draft a charter for an organization of inter-African and Malagasy states. Differing strongly with the Casablanca group's perceived "revolutionary and radical" prescriptions for African continental problems, the Monrovia group favored gradual, evolutionary methods.[5] Despite their ideological differences, however, both groups saw the need to create a continental organization as tantamount.

Ethiopian Emperor Haile Selassie provided the means for a reconciliation of the interests of the two groups in May 1963. At his invitation, thirty African foreign ministers met in Addis Ababa to prepare an agenda for a summit meeting of African heads of state and government. The mood at Addis Ababa was amazingly conducive to compromise. Following discussions concerning defense, decolonialization, various economic and social cooperation measures, and apartheid and racial discrimination, the foreign ministers drafted a charter for the OAU similar to the Monrovia group's design (probably because the binding force of the Casablanca group had disappeared with the resolution of the Algerian crisis). One week later, the heads of state and government of the thirty African states signed the OAU Charter after just two and one-half days of discussion.[6]

The first meeting of the Council of Ministers was held in August 1963, and of the Assembly of Heads of State and Government, in 1964. The Permanent Secretariat was established in Addis Ababa that same year. The Committee of Five (later, the Committee of Nine, or the Liberation Committee) was created in 1965 to assist nationalist movements. In 1967, the first successful OAU-sponsored conflict resolution action, a border dispute between Kenya and Somalia, was accomplished. During 1968–1969, the OAU passed several resolutions in support of the Nigerian government concerning the Biafran conflict. These actions were consistent with the OAU's principles of respect for the sovereignty and territorial integrity of the member-states. They also reflected a fear on the part of many leaders that civil wars and separatist movements might prove to be readily contagious.

The activities of the OAU in the decade of the 1970s generated far more heat than light. In 1973, the Liberation Committee issued the Accra Declaration on African Liberation, which stated that only armed struggle would achieve decolonialization in Africa, and the Assembly issued the African Declaration on Cooperation, Development, and Economic Interdependence. Attempts to resolve disputes between Somalia and Ethiopia as well as between Tanzania and Uganda were unsuccessful.

Following Angolan independence, the OAU agreed to recognize the government of the Popular Movement for the Liberation of Angola (MPLA) and admitted Angola, its forty-seventh member. The following year, however, Morocco suspended participation in the OAU, protesting the decision to admit the delegate of the Sahrawi Arab Democratic Republic. When, in 1978, the Comoros delegates were expelled as "representatives of mercenaries," the Assembly became polarized over the question of foreign influence in Africa. The 1979 Assembly meeting featured a walkout by the leaders of the Arab League states, resulting from Egyptian President Sadat's defense of the Camp David peace agreement. With the resolution of the Rhodesian problem and the creation of the state of Zimbabwe in 1980, one of the OAU's principal goals was achieved: Zimbabwe became the OAU's fiftieth member.[7]

Structure

The major institutions created by the OAU Charter are the Assembly of Heads of State and Government, the Council of Ministers, the Arbitration Commission (Commission of Mediation, Conciliation, and Arbitration), the Liberation Committee, and the General-Secretariat. Also included are several specialized commissions, the most important of which are the Economic and Social Commission; the Educational, Cultural, Scientific, and Health Commission; and the Defense Commission. The Scientific, Technical, and Research Commission, the Inter-African Research Fund, and the African Development Bank are associated organs of the OAU. (See Figure 11.1.)

The Assembly of Heads of State and Government

The Assembly is the supreme organ and policymaking body of the OAU. Delegates to the Assembly are the member-states' chief executives; hence, each Assembly meeting is a summit-level conference. The Assembly meets annually in a different African capital each year. By custom, the Assembly chairman for the meeting and throughout the ensuing year is the leader of the nation that hosts the meeting. By approval of two-thirds of the member-states, the Assembly can meet in extraordinary session. That the Assembly is the highest authority of the OAU reflects clearly the principle of absolute sovereignty of the member-states. This principle is indicative of strong nationalism and the "strong ruler–small ruling elite" characteristic of most African nations.[8]

The Council of Ministers

The second most important OAU body is the Council of Ministers. Consisting of the foreign ministers (or their representatives) of the

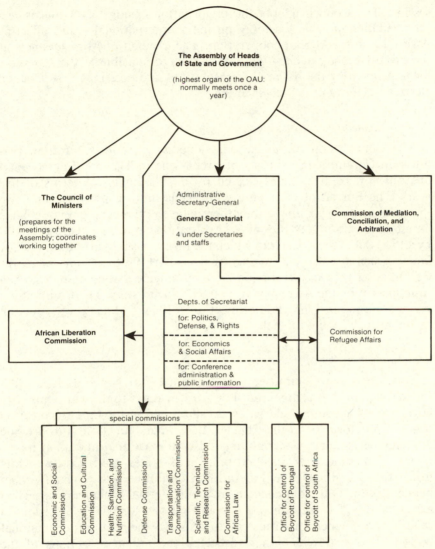

Figure 11.1   Structure of the Organization of African Unity

member-states, it normally meets twice each year (once preceding each Assembly meeting and once each February). The most important function of the Council is to make Assembly meetings possible by preparing an acceptable agenda. Since the number of extraordinary Assembly meetings has increased to over one-half the number of annual meetings, the Council has taken on the role of a crisis committee to attempt to formulate common OAU positions prior to each extraordinary Assembly session. The Council adopts the organization's budget and makes recommendations to the Assembly on major international issues affecting Africa and intra-African cooperation. The Council of Ministers acts as the executive body of the OAU and is thus responsible to the Assembly for implementing the Assembly's resolutions and decisions. The Council elects its chairman at each meeting.[9]

The Arbitration Commission

The Commission of Mediation, Conciliation, and Arbitration (Arbitration Commission) consists of twenty-one individuals from twenty-one different member-states elected by the Assembly for terms of five years. The Bureau of the Commission consists of a president and two vice-presidents (who, unlike the other eighteen members, are not eligible for reelection). The activities of the Arbitration Commission are governed by a Protocol to the Charter to which the member-states are automatically bound when they accede to the Charter. The Protocol empowers the Commission to take jurisdiction over intramember-state disputes when so requested by the Assembly or Council of Ministers. The Commission was established in 1965, did not meet until 1968, and has yet to function as intended by the Protocol.

The Liberation Committee

The Liberation Committee (or "Committee of Nine" as it is often called, referring to the nine front-line African states to the white-minority governments in southern Africa) was established in 1964, but its creation was not provided for in the Charter. Its primary function is to provide and channel financial and military aid to the national liberation movements in nonindependent territories and states governed by white minorities. Originally, the Liberation Committee was virtually independent of the OAU, but concern by moderate OAU members regarding accountability for their financial contributions forced the decision to require the Council of Ministers to approve the Committee's annual budget. This requirement has restricted the unilateral actions of the OAU's more radical members, who make up the Liberation Committee. The Committee serves as the most important contact to the OAU for African liberation movements. Although the Assembly is often divided over support for rival liberation groups in a given nation or territory, recognition of a single group by the Liberation Committee is usually followed by OAU recognition and then by UN recognition. The resultant flow of financial and technical resources to a given single group has had the desirable though unintended effect of reducing the number of rival splinter groups.[10]

The General-Secretariat

The General-Secretariat, located in Addis Ababa, provides administrative support to all other OAU organs. Its principal departments are Political, Legal, Economic and Social, Educational and Cultural, Press and Information, Protocol, and Administrative. The Secretariat is headed by an Administrative Secretary-General, who is elected to a four-year term by the Assembly. The title has more than symbolic import. As the leaders of the original OAU states did not want a "political" leader of the Secretariat like that of the United Nations, the Charter strictly limits the Secretariat to administrative functions and requires "neutrality and impartiality."[11]

Specialized Commissions

Initially, there were seven special commissions organized in 1963 as part of the OAU structure. However, in 1968 the number was reduced to three when the Education and Cultural Matters, Health/Sanitation/Nutrition, and Scientific and Technical Research Commissions were merged into the Education, Science, and Cultural Commission. In addition, the Economic and Social Affairs and Transport and Communications Commissions became the Economic and Social Commission. The Defense Commission remained, but the Jurists Commission was abolished. The three specialized commissions currently in effect are composed of ministers of the member-states, who are either selected by virture of their portfolio or designated as such by their member-states. The commissions are responsible to the Assembly and rank in importance from the most political to the low-level technical matters considered.

The Decisionmaking Process

All decisions and resolutions of the OAU are taken in the Assembly of Heads of State and Government. Each member-state has one vote, and substantive decisions require a two-thirds majority of the OAU members. Questions of procedure are decided by a simple majority, as is any determination of whether a particular question is substantive or procedural. Two-thirds of the membership constitutes a quorum at Assembly meetings. Generally, the same rules apply to the Council of Ministers. However, the only "independent" decisional powers given the Council are to approve the budget submitted by the Administrative Secretary-General and to determine its own rules of procedure. The Council does prepare the agenda and resolutions for the Assembly, but it does not have the power of initiative. There are no provisions for formal consultations with other bodies of the OAU; indeed, there is little evidence that such consultation takes place. For example, the commissions seem to have little impact on OAU policymaking. They meet irregularly and have not had the funds or expertise to develop their proposals beyond general designs for increased future cooperation.

State of Integration

Scholarly attempts to analyze integration in the OAU seem either to profess very pessimistic conclusions[12] or to argue that integration theories developed for the study of European integration cannot apply to "unique African variables."[13] Clearly, when one considers the degree of emphasis on national sovereignty and policy independence exhibited in the Charter (even more than is true for the OAS), the lack of integration in the OAU is not surprising. The organization could have been created as a far more integrated (supranational) body. To the advocates of Pan-Africanism in 1963 (principally Ghana's President Kwame Nkrumah), the Charter was probably something of a failure. Far from constructing a federal arrangement qua Pan-Africanism, the OAU Charter is a reaffirmation of nationalism and sovereignty won over many years of struggle. An evaluation of the OAU's first twenty years with respect to its stated purposes and functions, however, provides little basis for a positive assessment.

Attempts by the OAU to promote African unity, coordinate cooperation for a better life, eradicate colonialism, and promote international cooperation "with due regard for the UN Charter and the Universal Declaration on Human Rights"[14] have had little effect. What success has occurred, as in decolonialization and majority rule in Zimbabwe, could have happened or did happen in spite of the OAU's existence. The reasons underlying the OAU's ineffectiveness are many and varied, but the main source of difficulty has been and continues to be the extreme nationalism of the African states and their consistent refusal to yield any sovereignty to OAU-managed cooperation ventures. OAU institutions have floundered due to a lack of technical expertise, political support, and adequate funding. (For instance, many of the member-states refuse to pay or have fallen far behind in their annual assessed contributions.) The numerous attempts to resolve intramember conflict have been unsuccessful. The Arbitration Commission has yet to function properly. When third-party pacific settlement has occurred, it was the result, more often than not, of an ad hoc initiative by one or more of the leaders of the African states. On more than one occasion, the announcement during an Assembly meeting of the outbreak of violent conflict on the continent has sent the delegates packing (for fear that the same thing might happen to them in their absence), rather than engendering a constructive discussion of the problem.[15] In addition, the principle of nonintervention (as interpreted by OAU members) has paralyzed the OAU on matters such as refugees and human rights. Refugee problems have been relegated to the affected states or to other international organizations. In spite of the flagrant violations of human rights that occurred in Africa during the 1970s (Idi Amin Dada, to name one such perpetrator), only in July of 1979 was any resolution on human rights passed in the OAU.[16]

Perhaps the functional area most in need of incorporation and integration in the OAU is economic development. The OAU has a specialized body to serve this need (the Economic and Social Commission), but its activities have been meager and are overshadowed by regional arrangements (like ECOWAS), the ACP organization of the Lomé Convention with the EC, and the UN Economic Commission for Africa (UNECA). The African Development Bank was created in 1964, but its actual origin predates the OAU by three years and it is not an integral part of the OAU system (as is the Inter-American Development Bank in the OAS). To date, the OAU has not succeeded in tapping the potential economic assistance of its oil-rich Arab member-states (and Nigeria) or that of other OPEC members.[17] A proposal to create an African Economic Community was made and ignored in November 1976. However, some positive steps were taken through the "Lagos Plan of Action," which was adopted at the first OAU economic summit early in 1980.

Given the dismal picture just painted, what are the accomplishments of the OAU (or, perhaps more to the point, what are the reasons for its continued existence)? First, the OAU has served to stabilize politically much of Africa. Although failing to find an ideological basis as a substitute for Pan-Africanism, it has established a widely accepted set of rules for intermember relations. The principles of sovereign equality, nonintervention in internal affairs, respect for former colonial boundaries, and restraint from subversive activities embodied in Article III of the Charter, though not always observed, have given African states a political center for increased political and diplomatic cooperation. The formation of a set of common values among African elites has engendered a degree of stability that would not have been possible without the OAU. The OAU's recognition of the legitimate boundaries of each member-state did not prevent numerous border disputes, but it did deter attempts to redraw the map of Africa based on hundreds of conflicting claims. Second, the OAU provides the largest African international forum for the discussion of problems and the formation of "African opinion." It has increased the level of communication among its member-states. That the states feel compelled to justify their actions to the OAU says much for the recognized legitimacy and influence of the organization. Third, the OAU has facilitated a great deal of African influence in international relations. The Assembly has been employed as a caucus for the formation of common positions in the UN General Assembly and other international fora. In its role as an influential pressure group, the OAU has kept faith with its commitment to nonalignment, avoiding involvement in conflicts among the superpowers.

The prospects for further integration in the OAU are minimal, given the probable continuation of the status quo. In terms of Schmitter's "actor strategies," the OAU institutions have been encapsulated, a condition that is likely to persist. Any attempt to increase the authority of the organization will meet strong opposition in the nationalistic member-states. Other than the Assembly, the only OAU bodies with any authority either have not been used (e.g., the Arbitration Commission) or have had limits placed on their freedom of action (e.g., the Liberation Committee). Generally, spillback has occurred as the specialized commissions have been reduced and combined.[18] The proposal to achieve an African common market and the OAU peacekeeping force sent to Chad in 1981 may be construed as possible spillaround strategies, but these efforts must be continued if they are to have any significance. Without the adoption of a substantial economic function, and unless the polarization of the Arab-Black states and the moderate-progressive "camps" begun in 1979 can be resolved, the OAU will be limited, at best, to its present low level of integration.

Notes

1. Zdenek Cervenka, *The Organization of African Unity and Its Charter* (London: Hurst and Co., 1969), pp. 232–233.

2. Ibid.

3. Ghana, Guinea, Mali, Morocco, Libya, Egypt, and the Provisional Government of Algeria.

4. Those in attendance were Cameroon, Central African Republic, Chad, Congo, Dahomey, Ethiopia, Gabon, Ivory Coast, Liberia, Madagascar, Mauritania, Niger, Nigeria, Senegal, Sierra Leone, Somalia, Togo, Tunisia, and Upper Volta.

5. For example, the Casablanca group advocated the removal of colonial powers from Africa through the use of military force, and the Monrovia group favored a slower decolonialization process through diplomacy; the Casablanca leaders wanted a federal African organization of states, whereas those in the Monrovia group advocated something less than a confederal arrangement.

6. Leslie Rubin and Brian Weinstein, *Introduction to African Politics* (New York: Praeger Publishers, 1974), pp. 225–230.

7. Europa Publications, *The Europa Year Book, 1980,* vol. I (London: Europa, 1980), pp. 248–255.

8. See Helen Kitchen, *Africa: From Mystery to Maze* (Lexington, Mass.: Lexington Books, 1976).

9. *African Year Book and Who's Who, 1977* (London: Africa Journal Limited, 1977).

10. Franz Ansprenger, *Die Befreiungspolitik der Organisation fur Afrikanische Einheit* (Munich, 1975), p. 49.

11. B. David Meyers, "The OAU's Administrative Secretary General," *International Organization* 30:3 (Summer 1976), pp. 508–509.

12. See Arthur Hazlewood, *African Integration and Disintegration* (London: Oxford University Press, 1967); and Ansprenger, *Die Befreiungspolitik.*

13. See Chimelu Chime, *Integration and Politics Among African States* (Uppsala: Scandinavian Institute of African Studies, 1977); and Ali Mazrui, *Africa's International Relations* (Boulder, Colo.: Westview Press, 1977).

14. See Article II of the OAU Charter.

15. See Adda B. Bozeman, *Conflict in Africa* (Princeton, N.J.: Princeton University Press, 1976).

16. Warren Weinstein, "Human Rights in Africa: A Long-Awaited Voice," *Current History* 78 (March 1980), p. 455.

17. See Victor Le Vine and Timothy Luke, *The Arab-African Connection: Political and Economic Realities* (Boulder, Colo.: Westview Press, 1979).

18. Chime, *Integration and Politics,* p. 377.

12

Other Political IGOs

There are several multipurpose or political international governmental organizations in existence. None rivals the OAS or OAU in scope and importance. However, no survey of political IGOs would be complete without discussions of the Council of Europe and the Commonwealth. This chapter covers these later organizations, as well as brief analyses of the Council of Entente, the Organization of Central American States, and the South Pacific Forum.

The Council of Europe

The Council of Europe was created by the Statute of the Council of Europe, which was signed in London on May 5, 1949, by representatives of the governments of Belgium, Denmark, France, Ireland, Italy, Luxembourg, the Netherlands, Norway, Sweden, and the United Kingdom. The current membership of the organization consists of twenty-one Western European nations. (See Table 12.1.) The stated aims of the Council of Europe are to achieve greater unity among the member-states by safeguarding the ideals and principles of their common heritage and facilitating economic and social progress; to promote individual freedoms, political liberty, and closer political ties among European states; and to uphold the principles of parliamentary democracy, the rule of law, and human rights.[1] At present, the activities of the Council of Europe cover a wide range of social, cultural, and technical (scientific cooperation) matters; political consultation; and, by far the organizations' most important endeavor, human rights. The only area excluded from the organization's competence is that of national defense.[2]

History and Development

The idea for the creation of the Council of Europe was based on political concerns for post–World War II Germany, economic and military dependence on the United States, and ideological concerns about Soviet expansionism. Specifically, it grew out of Winston Churchill's repeated

TABLE 12.1.   Council of Europe Membership

	Membership Year	MEMBERSHIP IN OTHER ORGANIZATIONS			Members Parl. Assembly
		OECD	NATO	EEC	
Austria	1956	*			6
Belgium	1949	*	*	*	7
Cyprus	1961				3
Denmark	1949	*	*	*	5
France	1949	*	(*)	*	18
Germany F.R.	1951	*	*	*	18
Greece	1949	*	*	*	7
Iceland	1950	*	*		3
Ireland	1949	*	*	*	4
Italy	1949	*	*	*	18
Liechtenstein	1978				2
Luxembourg	1949	*	*	*	3
Malta	1965				3
Netherlands	1949	*	*	*	7
Norway	1949	*	*		5
Portugal	1979	*	*		7
Spain	1978	*			12
Sweden	1949	*			6
Switzerland	1963	*			6
Turkey	1949	*	*		12
United Kingdom	1949	*	*	*	18

calls for a "United States of Europe" and the merger of the United Europe Movement (Britain), the European Union of Federalists (the Netherlands), the European League of Economic Cooperation (France), and the Council for a United Europe (France). These organizations formed the International Committee of the Movements for European Unity in December 1947 and held the first Congress of Europe at the Hague in May 1948. Two months following the Hague Congress, French Foreign Minister M. Bidault proposed to the Consultative Committee of the Brussels Treaty the creation of a European parliamentary assembly. Although the Belgians supported the French proposal, other nations (principally Britain) favored the formation of a European Council of Ministers to discuss all matters of common interest except defense and economic matters (the competences of the newly created NATO and Organization of European Economic Cooperation, respectively). The discussions led first to the appointment of a Conference of Ambassadors in London, to which the Brussels Treaty states invited Denmark, Ireland,

Italy, Norway, and Sweden, and subsequently to completion of the Statute of the Council of Europe.[3]

There were several attempts in the 1950s to make the Council of Europe a political authority with institutions jointly associated with or parallel to the European Community, but this effort failed due to objections by the non-EC states (principally Britain and the Scandinavian countries). A combined Belgian-German-Italian initiative for political unity produced in 1965 only a watered-down resolution to pursue policies that would pave the way to political union. During its first twenty years, the Council of Europe has approved 104 conventions. Of these, 5 related to privileges and immunities of the organization, 7 to human rights, 10 to social matters, 12 to public health, 7 to cultural matters, 3 to patents, 5 to television, 3 to public international law, 28 to other legal subjects, 14 to penal law, and 3 to the "movement of persons" (immigration, naturalization, and so on).

The work of the Council involves several other functional areas as well. Economic concerns include consumer protection and truth-in-advertising. Social affairs are covered by, among others, the European Code of Social Security and the European Convention on Social Security. In the field of health, the Council has worked toward the harmonization of medical techniques and equipment. The major theme in cultural affairs has been permanent education and cultural development. Still other programs are directed to conservation of natural resources, legal cooperation, regional planning, and public administration.[4]

The most important function of the Council of Europe today is protection of human rights. The European Convention on Human Rights and its five protocols came into force in 1953. One of the protocols permits the citizens of those states who have ratified it to appeal directly to the European Commission on Human Rights and the European Court of Human Rights. Successful cases in which the Court has forced compliance by a member-state include the penal code in Austria, bilingualism in Belgium, and freedom of the press in the United Kingdom. A complaint brought by the Scandinavian countries in 1967 against the suspension of political freedoms and parliamentary government by the Papadopolous regime forced the forfeiture of Greece's membership until a democratic government had been reinstated.[5]

Structure

The major organs of the Council of Europe are the Committee of Ministers, the Minister's Deputies, the Parliamentary Assembly, the Secretariat, the Commission on Human Rights, and the European Court of Human Rights. The Commission of Ministers consists of the foreign ministers from all the member-states. Its functions are to conclude conventions or agreements and to draft common policies for adoption by the governments of the member-states.[6] The Committee meets twice each year, once in Strasbourg and once in Paris immediately preceding the OECD meeting. Decisions to refer recommendations to governments, meet in secrecy, or amend the statute require a unanimous vote. Admission of new members requires a two-thirds majority.[7] (See Figure 12.1.)

The Minister's Deputies consist of the senior diplomat of each member-state, who is accredited as the permanent representative to the Council. Created in 1952, the Minister's Deputies are the executive organ, performing the routine work of the Council at monthly meetings. However, decisions taken by the Deputies have the same force as those adopted by the Committee of Ministers.

The Parliamentary Assembly consists of 170 members chosen by their respective national parliaments (allocations of seats are indicated in Table 12.1). As in the European Parliament, members are seated by European political party groups (Christian Democrats, Socialists, Liberals, Joint Group of Democrats, Independents [Conservatives], and Communists). The Assembly meets annually in Strasbourg (the venue of all Council institutions) and usually convenes four subsession meetings per year. Each session elects a president and eight vice-presidents (collectively referred to as the Bureau). There are also twelve permanent committees and a Standing Committee responsible for setting the Assembly's agenda. In 1950, a joint committee consisting of eight members of the Committee of Ministers and eight members of the Assembly was created to act as a liaison between these two bodies. An "annual colloquy" established in 1961 serves as an expanded version of the joint committee.

The Secretariat consists of nine functional departments and the Secretary-General. The Secretary-General is elected by the Assembly from a list of candidates provided by the Committee of Ministers. Responsible to both the Assembly and Committee of Ministers, the Secretary-General is limited to a purely administrative role. However, he may place items on the agenda of the Committee of Ministers.[8] He may also conduct investigations into the extent to which any member-state's domestic law complies with the European Convention on Human Rights.[9]

The Commission on Human Rights consists of a president, two vice-presidents, and fifteen members. The Commission accepts complaints from member-states or individuals concerning alleged violations of the Convention. It serves to determine the substance of such complaints and to mediate between the parties to find a "friendly settlement." Failing this, the Commission may refer the matter to the Committee

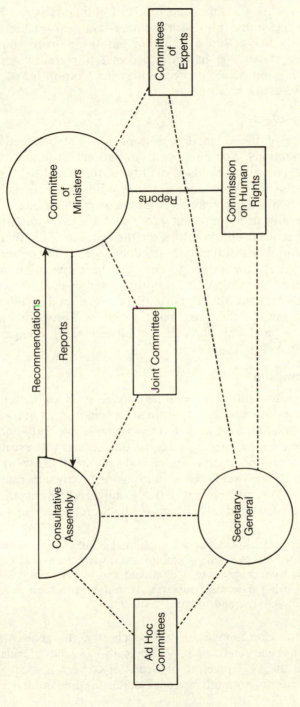

Figure 12.1 Council of Europe

of Ministers and/or the European Court of Human Rights. The Court, consisting of one judge from each member-state (except Liechtenstein), determines whether or not a violation has taken place (but only for those eighteen states who have made declaration under Article 46 of the convention) and passes its decision to the Committee of Ministers, which supervises its execution.[10]

State of Integration

The Statute of the Council of Europe was not designed to satisfy federalist aspirations. The intentional limitations on authority imposed by the Statute go only so far as to qualify for the pluralists' "community of state engaged in a process of sensitive adjustment to each other."[11] In terms of Schmitter's actor-strategies model, the Council has been engaged generally in a consistent process of spillaround. Although the statute has restricted opportunities for the build-up of authority, it has left to the central institutions the freedom to expand the scope of the organization (excepting security matters). The Convention on Human Rights, however, does represent significant spillover. The Commission and Court of Human Rights are supranational bodies administering supranational law. In this area, the Council of Europe member-states have agreed to yield important sectors of national sovereignty.

The Commonwealth

The Commonwealth is a voluntary association of nation-states (it has no formal international agreement or charter as its legal basis) including Britain and most of its former colonies. The forty-one member-states and three special members[12] constitute several interesting dichotomies: rich and very poor, large (India) and very small (Tuvalu), capitalist and socialist, the world's oldest and newest governmental systems, members of NATO and members of the Nonaligned Movement. According to a former official of the Commonwealth Secretariat,

> The Commonwealth defies definition, and is difficult to categorize. It has been dismissed as a relic of empire and disparaged as a talking shop. Some critics have pronounced it moribund and others have predicted its demise. Yet it has more than survived. It continues to grow in numbers, to expand in activity, and to gain in strength.[13]

Although the Commonwealth has no charter, the goals of the organization have been enunciated—specifically, in the "Declaration of Principles" at the 1971 meeting of Heads of Government in Singapore. These goals are to promote national understanding and world peace, representative institutions, personal freedoms and the democratic process, free trade, and the progressive removal of wealth disparity; to eliminate colonial domination, racial oppression, poverty, injustice, and coercion; and to serve as an example of a multinational approach to maintaining peace.[14]

History and Development

The origins of the Commonwealth can be traced to the late 1800s, when the newly independent states of Canada, Australia, New Zealand, and South Africa (the Dominions) joined with Britain to form the British Commonwealth (the name did not come into popular usage until several years later). With the growth of nationalism and sovereign independence, the Dominions decisively rejected a proposal for an imperial federation, and the Imperial War Cabinet of 1917–1918 did not outlast World War I. The Balfour Report of 1926 affirmed the sovereign equality and "free association" status of the Dominions, which the British Parliament formalized in the 1931 Statute of Westminster.[15] By that time, the Irish Free State and Newfoundland had joined the "British Club."

The admission of India and Pakistan into the Commonwealth upon their attainment of independence in 1947 marked a turning point in the evolution of the organization. The admission of Asian members to the Anglo club was only part of the transformation. When India became a republic in 1949, the other states were confronted with the decision to accept its republican status. After long and heated discussions, "allegiance to the crown" as a condition for membership was replaced by acceptance of the crown as "a symbol of free association" and the Head of the Commonwealth.[16] This occurrence opened the way for the entry of former British colonies in Africa, the Caribbean, the Mediterranean, and the Pacific, most of which were gaining independence in the late 1950s and early 1960s.

The Commonwealth became an association based on consultation, discussion, and ad hoc cooperation. It provides a forum on which the leaders of approximately one-quarter of the world's population can meet regularly to discuss Commonwealth and global concerns with a "candor unknown elsewhere."[17] The major on-going programs created by the heads of government include the Commonwealth Scholarship and Fellowship Plan (1965), and the Commonwealth Information Programme (1971), the Commonwealth Fund for Technical Cooperation (1971), the Book Development Programme (1971), the Commonwealth Youth Programme (1973), and the Commonwealth Programme of Applied Studies in Government (1975).[18]

Structure

The institutional structure of the Commonwealth is scant, but what does exist is significant given the absence of an organization charter. The supreme authority, consisting of the Meetings of Heads of Government, convenes every two years in the capital of one of the member-states. No voting occurs in these meetings, and decisions are taken by consensus. By tradition, the heads of government meet in an informal environment without benefit of entourage (aides), notes, or a formal record of the proceedings. Prepared speeches are expressly forbidden.[19] This feature accounts in part for the degree of candor in the meetings mentioned earlier. Senior cabinet secretaries or permanent secretaries to the heads of government meet regularly every year to provide continuity between Meetings. (See Figure 12.2.)

Meetings at the ministerial level are conducted with some regularity. Since 1959, the Commonwealth finance ministers have met in the week prior to the annual International Monetary Fund and World Bank meetings. Ministers of education, health, and law meet separately approximately every three years.

The only permanent institution in the Commonwealth is the Secretariat, which was established in 1965. The enacting memorandum of the Heads of Government made it clear that the Secretariat should be modest and excluded from any executive functions. The Secretary-General serves a five-year term and supervises eleven functional divisions (administration, education, food, information, international affairs, law, applied sciences, economic affairs, youth, export market development, and advisors to the Secretary-General. The Secretariat supports the many ad hoc study groups created by the heads of government. Recently, most of these have addressed the North-South debate and the New International Economic Order.[20]

State of Integration

"An institution so uniquely and sublimely preposterous can surely never die. The British Commonwealth is the degenerate heir of the British Empire, an heir whose least affliction is a kind of political delirium tremens."[21] This characterization by the right-wing British commentator, "Peter Simple," is probably unfair, particularly in application to the Commonwealth of the 1980s. The bitter arguments of the past two decades over Britain's handling of Rhodesia and its relations with the Republic of South Africa (especially those concerning arms sales) are largely over. The other issue that threatened the Commonwealth's continued existence was Britain's entry into the EC, but this appears to have been settled for most of developing Commonwealth

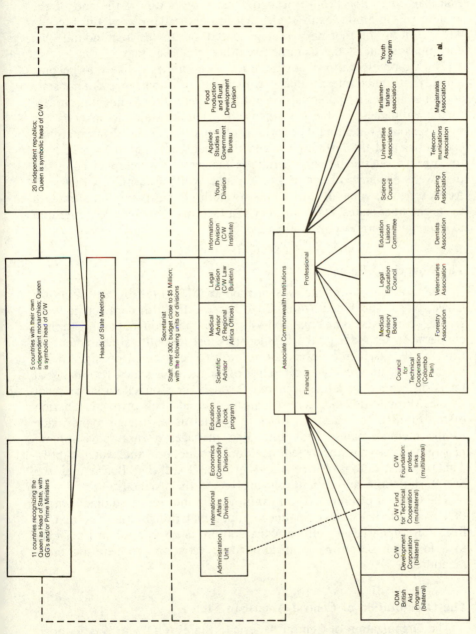

Figure 12.2 Organization of the Commonwealth

states by their inclusion into the Lomé Conventions. Two notable examples of spillback have occurred recently, however: the end of the System of Commonwealth Preferences and the demise of the Sterling Area (a form of monetary system based on the British pound that encompassed all of the Commonwealth except Canada).

The Commonwealth is not intended to be nor is it likely to become a highly integrated international organization. Its importance as a nonstate actor lies not in its potential for policy or institutional integration, but in the willingness of the leaders of the member-states to take on the most serious contemporary world problems, particularly international economies and the NIEO. However, the heads of government will have to improve on the broad generalities concerning developing countries that were products of the 1979 Commonwealth Summit in Lusaka.[22] At present, the value of the Commonwealth lies in its unique attraction to its member-states' leaders rather than in any demonstrated potential to become an important world actor.

The Council of Entente

The Council of Entente was formed in May 1959 by Benin, Ivory Coast, Niger, and Upper Volta. Togo became the fifth member in 1966. Initially conceived as an organ for political cooperation first and economic cooperation secondarily, the Council has lost its political character and transformed itself into an economic body. The Council consists of the heads of state and economic ministers of the member-states. Its functional focus on economies alone occurred through the Council's management of the Mutual Aid and Loan Guarantee Fund. The primary function of the Fund is to finance changes in the terms of foreign loans made to the member-states. The Fund also manages a rural development program involving stockbreeding, food production, and water supply. The two institutions of the Fund are the Executive Board and the Secretariat. Both are directly responsible to the Council.[23]

The Council of Entente is an example of a multipurpose organization that has experienced a pronounced functional transformation—that is, from an emphasis on political consultation as envisioned in its Treaty to a focus on becoming a single-purpose economic cooperation organization.

The Organization of Central American States

The Organization of Central American States (ODECA) was founded by the 1951 Charter of San Salvador among Costa Rica, El Salvador, Guatemala, Honduras, and Nicaragua. The current ODECA Charter was a result of renegotiations in 1965. The stated purposes of the organization are to strengthen Central American unity; to establish mutual consultations; to ensure peaceful settlement of disputes; to harmonize solutions to common problems; and to promote economic, social, and cultural development. The structure of the organization consists of the Meeting of Heads of Government and the Conference of Foreign Ministers (both are policymaking bodies), the Executive Council, the Legislative Council, the Central American Court of Justice, the Economic Council, and the Central American Bureau (i.e., the General-Secretariat).[24]

The single function that has dominated ODECA activities in the 1970s has been mediation of intramember disputes. The border dispute between Honduras and El Salvador that began in 1970 was resolved finally in 1976 when a cease-fire supervision unit was placed at the border. The ODECA Heads of Government supported Guatemala's claim to sovereignty over Belize in 1975, but without result. Since 1979, the ODECA has been torn and rendered virtually ineffective by regime changes and civil strife in all states except Costa Rica.

The South Pacific Forum

The South Pacific Forum is a gathering of the heads of government of twelve independent states in the South Pacific (Australia, New Zealand, and a few Third World nations). Begun in 1971, the Forum meets annually, or when requested to do so by one of the participants. The South Pacific Forum has no charter or formal international agreement establishing the legal basis, rules, activities, or any institutions for the body. Decisions taken at meetings are by consensus only. In April 1973, the Forum did establish a formal IGO, the South Pacific Bureau for Economic Cooperation (SPEC). The Committee, Secretariat, Association of South Pacific Airlines, and South Pacific Forum Fisheries Agency of SPEC are responsible to the South Pacific Forum in matters of intra-area trade, transport, communications, and economic development. The Forum itself may discuss a wide range of issues, including political matters of common concern.[25]

Notes

1. Article 1 of the Statute of the Council of Europe.
2. Ibid.
3. See Gerald J. Mangone, *A Short History of International Organization* (New York: McGraw-Hill, 1954).
4. Council of Europe, *Forum* 2/81 (Strasbourg: Secretariat, 1981).

5. From interviews in Bonn and Strasbourg, February 1982. See also A. B. McNulty, "Stock-Taking on the European Commission on Human Rights" (Council of Europe Document DH [68] 7, 1968).

6. Articles 14 and 15 of the Statute.

7. Article 20 of the Statute.

8. Article 36 of the Statute.

9. Article 51 of the European Convention on Human Rights.

10. See Moses Moskowitz, *International Concern with Human Rights* (Dobbs Ferry, N.Y.: Oceana Publications, 1974).

11. Charles Pentland, *International Theory and European Integration* (New York: Free Press, 1973), p. 29.

12. Four nations have withdrawn from membership: Newfoundland (when it became a province of Canada in 1949), Ireland (1949), the Union of South Africa (over the issue of apartheid in 1961), and Pakistan (over recognition of Bangladesh in 1972). The special members are Nauru, St. Vincent and the Grenadines, and Tuvalu. They participate in functional activities but not in the Meetings of the Heads of Government.

13. Charles Gunawardena, "Perspective: Serving a Wider Commonwealth," in Shridath Ramphal (Ed.), *One World to Share: Selected Speeches of the Commonwealth Secretary-General* (London: Hutchinson Denham, 1979).

14. Ibid., Appendix A.

15. Andrew Walker, *The Commonwealth: A New Look* (New York: Pergamon Press, 1978).

16. Ramphal, *One World,* Appendix B.

17. Canadian Prime Minister Pierre Trudeau, quoted in Walker, *The Commonwealth.*

18. Europa Publications, *The Europa Year Book 1980: A World Survey,* vol. I (London: Europa, 1980), pp. 149–161.

19. From an interview with the Cypriot ambassador to West Germany, December 1981.

20. Europa, *Year Book 1980,* pp. 149–161.

21. "Peter Simple," *Daily Telegraph,* July 10, 1976.

22. "Final Communiqué, Commonwealth Heads of Government Meeting, Lusaka, August, 1979" (London Press Service, Verbatim Service 049/79, 9 August 1979), points 52–56.

23. Europa, *Year Book 1980,* p. 163.

24. Ibid., p. 261.

25. Ibid., pp. 272–273.

Part 5

Cultural/Ideological
International Governmental
Organizations

13
The Arab League

Cultural/ideological international governmental organizations are, like political IGOs, multipurpose organizations. The scopes of their respective functions and structures vary from one organization to the next, but they typically include economic and political functions as well as social and cultural concerns. Specifically, cultural/ideological organizations reflect the ethnic, national, religious, kinship, and/or philosophical bonds that the members of these groups wish to preserve or expand through concerted unified efforts. In addition, membership is restricted to those nation-states whose citizens and leaders are predominantly members of one ethnic or religious group (e.g., Arabs, Scandinavians, or Muslims). The Arab League is one such organization. It may have been (and often is) classified as a political/multipurpose organization. Yet, the member-states of the Arab League constitute a regional organization that encompasses all of Northern Africa and much of the Middle East, but exclude Black African states and the very similar (yet non-Arab) states of Iran and Turkey. Clearly, Arab solidarity is far more important in the Arab League than are Pan-Africanism or Pan-Americanism to the OAU and OAS, respectively. One might argue that despite the divisiveness caused by the "Palestinian question," the factors that have held the Arab League together are Israel and the development of a cohesive ideology peculiar to the organization.[1]

The Arab League (formally, the League of Arab States) was created by the Alexandria Protocol of October 7, 1944, and its Pact was signed on March 22, 1945. The legal bases of the League were extended by the Treaty for Joint Defense and Economic Cooperation (1950) and the 1976 interpretation of the Charter Annex on Palestine. The Arab League Pact stated that the purposes of the organization are intended to be functional but not political: to coordinate policy while safeguarding the independence and sovereignty of the member-states; to supervise and execute agreements among the member-states; to foster international concern with the affairs and interests of Arab countries; and to facilitate cooperation in economic, financial, cultural, social, health, legal, and communications matters. The Joint Defense Treaty provides for coordination of military resources and consultation in the event of extraregional attack on the member-states (including attack by Israel). The legal bases of the Arab League make no attempt to create a supranational organization, nor do they envision Arab political unity. Generally, the Arab League was created to promote policy harmony or cooperation and to legitimize the ideal of Arab brotherhood, even though its founders realized that creating the machinery to accomplish these goals was a practical impossibility.

History and Development

The origins of the Arab League can be traced to the nineteenth-century Arab nationalist movements against domination by the Ottoman Empire. Following World War I and the break-up of the Ottoman control of the region, Arab nationalist movements formed as a result of the League of Nations mandate system and against Britain in Iraq and Palestine and France in Syria and Lebanon. Unable to supply Islam as a rallying force for nationalistic movements, Arab intellectuals began to appeal to Arab *gawmiyya,* or "awakening," to motivate both nationalism and anti-imperialism.[2] During World War II, that anti-imperialism began to include efforts to resist the "new imperialism of Zion," as Jewish immigration from Europe to Palestine increased significantly. This realization led to a series of Pan-Arab Conferences that transcended the separate national movements (Syria, for example, was trying to create a united "Greater Syria" to encompass Syria, Jordan, and Iraq). In 1944, Egyptian Prime Minister Nahas held several bilateral meetings with other Arab leaders and secured agreement for a summit meeting in Alexandria. On October 7, 1944, the summit produced the Alexandria Protocol, which in turn led to the signing of the Arab League Pact six months later.[3]

The first ten years in the development of the Arab League were characterized by significant institutionalization and the expansion of functional scope,[4] which culminated in the Cultural Treaty (1946); the Joint Defense and Economic Cooperation Treaty (1950); agreements on extradition, writs of letters of request, and nationality (1952); the Arab Telecommunications Union, the Economic Council Conference of Education Ministers, the Convention of Privileges and Immunities (of the Arab League), and several trade agreements (1953); and the Arab Postal Union and Nationalists Agreement (1954). The second decade of the Arab League saw increasing institutionalization, but functional concerns were dominated by economies. From 1955 to 1959 the League adopted a Common Tariff Nomenclature and an Arab Financial Institution for

Economic Development, and in 1959 it held the First Arab Oil Conference, which led to the creation of OPEC a year later. The achievement of an Arab Economic Unity Agreement in 1962 was marred by the decision of the UAR to cease active participation in the Organization. The dispute was short-lived, however, and the UAR resumed active participation in March 1963. The following year was one of initiating Arab League summits. The first Summit of Arab Kings and Presidents was held in January, the first meeting of the Council of Arab Information/ Ministers was held in March, the first session of the Economic Unity Council was held in August, and the first Conference of Arab Ministers of Communications was held in November.[5]

The Arab League began concerted efforts to speak with one voice in other international fora when, in 1965, an integrated plan to defend Palestine in the United Nations was approved. In the same year, the Arab Common Market was established and, a year later, the Arab League Administrative Court began to function. The following year, 1967, marked the first discussions of the use of oil as a political weapon (specifically, an embargo against the United States and Britain was considered). At the Fifth Summit Conference (1969), the Arab kings and presidents issued a call for mobilization of all Arab States against Israel. However, little of substance occurred in the Arab League between the wars of 1967 and 1973. Again, the only important activity was the establishment of many new organizational functional bodies: the Industrial Development Center and Arab Fund for Economic and Social Development (1968); the Arab Organization for Agricultural Development and the Arab Educational Cultural and Scientific Organization (1970); the Arab Labor Organization (1971); and the Conference on Traffic, Arab Women, and National Development (1972). The Yom Kippur war brought a declaration defining Arab demands for the settlement of the conflict in the Middle East, the quadrupling of the price of oil, and three new institutions to help poor African states: the Arab Loan Fund for Africa, the Arab Bank for Economic Development in Africa, and the Arab Fund for Technical Assistance.[6]

The later 1970s were characterized by a shift of attention to the disputes in the Western Sahara and the conflict in Lebanon, and then to serious internal dissension brought on by Sadat's visit to Israel and subsequent (related) events. The Joint Defense Council met in July 1974 to coordinate political, financial, and military assistance in the defense of Lebanon. In 1976, a mediation mission was sent to Algeria, Morocco, and Mauritania in an effort to settle the dispute over the Western Sahara. Also, an Arab Peacekeeping Force was "sent" to Lebanon (the forces were almost entirely Syrian in composition and were already in place). The first Afro-Arab Summit was held in March 1977; however, discussions on the Western Sahara and Lebanon had ceased by that time, never to be revived.

The initial source of serious internal dissension was Sadat's historic visit to address the Israeli Knesset. With the Tripoli Declaration of December 1977, Algeria, Iraq, Libya, and the People's Democratic Republic of Yemen boycotted League meetings attended by Egypt. Following the Camp David Accords, the Arab League member-states (excluding Egypt) agreed to sever diplomatic and political relations with Egypt, to suspend its membership in the League, to withhold all technical and financial aid, and to cease trading with Egypt. Before these decisions came into force, Egypt announced that it had "frozen" its activities in the League. However, funds for projects already begun under the Arab Fund for Economic and Social Development were continued.[7]

The first meeting of the new decade (November 1980) of the Ministerial Conference was scantly attended. Egypt was "out," and Algeria, Lebanon, Libya, Syria, South Yemen, and the PLO boycotted the meeting due to intramember differences over the Egypt-Israeli peace accords, the Iraqi-Iranian war, and the "rights of Palestinians." Consequently, little was accomplished other than discussions over whether Jordan's King Hussein should be given the role of spokesman for the Palestinians.[8]

Structure

The major central institutions of the Arab League are the Council, the General-Secretariat, the Defense and Economic Cooperation Groups, and fourteen specialized agencies. The League's headquarters were moved from Cairo to Tunis, Tunisia, in 1980. (See Figure 13.1.)

The Council

The Council is the supreme organ of the Arab League. Since 1964, it has met sporadically at the summit level (Conference of Kings and Presidents), but it normally meets twice annually (March and September) at the ministerial level. The Council may meet in extraordinary session at the request of two member-states. The Council presidency rotates among the member-states in turn. The functions of the Council are to pass resolutions (binding on all states that approve them) and nonbinding recommendations; to mediate disputes; to coordinate cooperation with the United Nations and other international organizations; to coordinate defense measures in case of attack or the threat of attack; and to act as an "internal legislature" (approve budgets, appointments, and the like).[9]

There are sixteen committees subordinate to the Council. The most important of these functionally assigned committees are the political

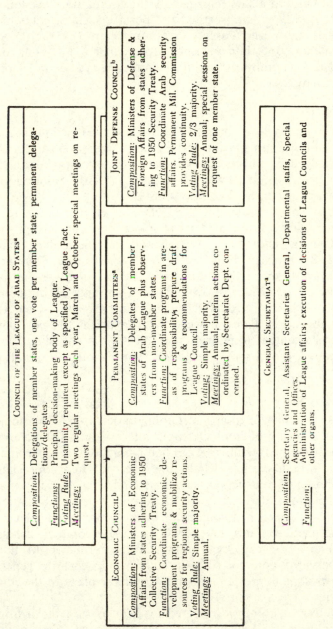

COUNCIL OF THE LEAGUE OF ARAB STATES[a]

Composition: Delegations of member states, one vote per member state; permanent delegations/delegates.
Functions: Principal decision-making body of League.
Voting Rule: Unanimity required except as specified by League Pact.
Meetings: Two regular meetings each year, March and October; special meetings on request.

JOINT DEFENSE COUNCIL[b]

Composition: Ministers of Defense & Foreign Affairs from states adhering to 1950 Security Treaty.
Function: Coordinate Arab security affairs. Permanent Mil. Commission provides continuity.
Voting Rule: 2/3 majority.
Meetings: Annual; special sessions on request of one member state.

ECONOMIC COUNCIL[b]

Composition: Ministers of Economic Affairs from states adhering to 1950 Collective Security Treaty.
Function: Coordinate economic development programs & mobilize resources for regional security actions.
Voting Rule: Simple majority.
Meetings: Annual.

PERMANENT COMMITTEES[a]

Composition: Delegates of member states of Arab League plus observers from non-member states.
Function: Coordinate programs in areas of responsibility; prepare draft programs & recommendations for League Council.
Voting: Simple majority.
Meetings: Annual; interim actions coordinated by Secretariat Dept. concerned.

GENERAL SECRETARIAT[a]

Composition: Secretary General, Assistant Secretaries General, Departmental staffs, Special Agencies and Offices.
Function: Administration of League affairs; execution of decisions of League Councils and other organs.

[a] Provided by League Pact   [b] Added by Security Treaty of 1950

Figure 13.1 Organizational Structure of the Arab League

Source: Robert W. Macdonald, *The League of Arab States: A Study in the Dynamics of Regional Organization.* Copyright © by Princeton University Press; reprinted by permission of Princeton University Press.

(consisting of foreign ministers), cultural (which supervises the Cultural Department and cultural affiars managed by the Secretariat); economic; communications (land, sea, air, weather, and postal); social; legal (which replaced the Nationality and Passport Committee in 1947); Arab oil experts; information; and human rights (particularly for violations committed by Israel) committees; and the Conference of Liaison Officers (for trade coordination).

The General-Secretariat

The Secretariat acts both as an executive body for Council decisions/ directives and as the administrative and financial support organ for the League. Its thirteen departments are political, economic, legal, cultural, social and labor, petroleum, finance, Palestine, health, information, communications, protocol, and African affairs.

The Secretary-General is appointed by the Council and he, in turn, appoints all other officers in the Secretariat subject to Council approval. The Secretary-General has an active, visible political role in the League. Until Mahmud Riad resigned in 1979, the Arab League Secretary-General had always been an Egyptian. Riad and his predecessors had built an impressive bureaucracy of over 500 civil servants (all but about 60 Egyptian) that was modeled after the EC Commission. When the Secretariat was moved to Tunis, however, the Egyptians did not move with it. The transplanted Secretariat now has a staff of about 150, indicating perhaps a diminished role for the non-Egyptian Secretariat-General.

Defense and Economic Cooperation

The legal basis for the five groups pertaining to defense and economic cooperation is the Treaty of Joint Defense and Economic Cooperation (1950). The Arab Unified Military Command functions to coordinate military policy for the liberation of Palestine. The Arab Economic Unity Council is composed of ministers of economic affairs (or their deputies) and serves the purpose of exchange of ideas and policy coordination. The Joint Defense Council is a conference of both foreign and defense ministers of the member-states designed to supervise common defense efforts. The Military Advisory Organization and the Permanent Military Commission consist of representatives of the nation-state's army general staffs. Their purpose is to create and submit military plans to the Joint Defense Council.

The Arab Deterrent Force was created in 1976 to stop the fighting and to maintain peace in Lebanon. Although the Force is not multinational, the Arab League Summit Conference decreed in October that its financing would be borne by the League's member-states by the following formula: Saudi Arabia, 20 percent; Kuwait, 20 percent; the United Arab Emirates, 15 percent; Qatar, 10 percent; and the remaining seventeen member-states plus the PLO, 35 percent.[10]

Special Institutions

There are six special institutions that were established by and are responsible to the Council. These include the Academy of Arab Music, the Administrative Tribunal, the Arab Authority for Exhibitions (for art and cultural displays in the member-states), the Arab Center for Industrial Development, the Arab Institute of Forestry, and the Special Bureau for Boycotting Israel (and those who trade with Israel). The last two of these are located in Syria.

Specialized Agencies

The fourteen specialized agencies of the Arab League are similar in design and intent to the specialized agencies of the United Nations. All member-states of the League are automatically members of the League's specialized agencies, however. These organs perform functions, respectively, in the following areas: the study of arid regions; educational, cultural, and scientific (ALECSO) services; health; petroleum research; labor; administrative science; agricultural development; technical standardization; postal; broadcasting; telecommunications; civil aviation; remedies for crime; and atomic energy. In addition, the Arab League maintains offices and information centers in fourteen countries (including five in the United States) and has representatives in Kenya, Nigeria, and Senegal.

The Decisionmaking Process

The focal point of the decisionmaking process is the League's supreme authority, the Council. There, all member-states (including the official representatives of Palestine, the PLO) have one vote. Voting on substantive issues proceeds by unanimity; procedural or administrative questions require either simple or two-thirds majority votes for approval. Due to the relatively open and fluid nature of the League's institutional structure and the fact that no one body has sole power of initiative, the Secretariat has played a significant decisionmaking role. As executor as well as administrator, the Secretariat commands a large staff for the gathering of information and conducting of long-term studies. It also controls the Council's agenda and is in a position to influence the scope and nature of issues before the Council. Moreover, the Secretary-General has political power based on his roles of organizational spokesman, conflict mediator (especially prior to 1960), and representative to the United Nations.

Another important actor in the decisionmaking process is the Political Committee. Usually composed of the member-states' foreign ministers and always meeting prior to each council meeting, the Political Committee acts like the COREPER of the EC; that is, it votes recommendations and filters divisive issues before they reach the Council. Measures proposed by the Secretariat and approved by the Political Committee are almost always assured of passage in the Council. Indeed, it is often the same group of individuals who meet informally first, then as the Political Committee, and finally as the Council to vote on their own recommendations.[11]

The institutional development of decisionmaking in the Arab League has, in general, been somewhat slow. This is true for several reasons. The emphasis on individual sovereignty and restricted purposes (i.e., restricted by the Charter) of the League result in least-common-denominator outputs and policy coordination rather than policymaking. In addition, the Islamic imperative to consult, combined with the tribal notion of consensus among elders, is a contributing factor. The decisionmaking process appears to work well for routine matters, but it fails for critical issues and in times of crisis.[12]

State of Integration

An assessment of the state of integration in the Arab League is difficult, particularly when the organization is considered as a whole. As with the political IGOs, the stated purposes of the League Charter become muddled by subsequent decisions and activities, thus making performance evaluations problematic. Schmitter's actor-strategy model, when applied to the Arab League, would lead one to conclude that the League was characterized by spillaround from 1945 until the mid-1970s. Great numbers of economic, social, cultural, and military institutions were created, expanding the scope of the organization without a concomitant increase in decisional authority. Since 1976, fewer institutions and new functions have been initiated, and decisional authority within the League has decreased, principally due to the suspension of Egypt and the several boycotts of Council meetings by the "rejectionist" states (Algeria, Iraq, Libya, South Yemen, and the PLO). The moderate increase in issue areas but decreased decisional authority is what Schmitter labeled muddle-about.

One of the League's most important functions potentially is the settlement of intermember disputes. The Charter provides that "the Council shall mediate in all differences which threaten to lead to war"[13] and that mediation and arbitration can be undertaken following a majority vote in the Council. However, the Arab League's record of accomplishment in this area has been unimpressive. Only one dispute (Syria/Lebanon, 1949) has been submitted to arbitration. Attempts to settle disputes involving Syria/Jordan (1950), UAR/Lebanon (1958), Kuwait/Iraq (1961), Yemen (1962), Lebanon (1976), Western Sahara (1976), and Chad (1980) were unsuccessful. There were cases of successful settlement (Sudan, 1958; Kuwait, 1961; Syria/UAR, 1961; Morocco, 1963; and North and South Yemen, 1973), but these successes were due to the personal involvement of the League's Secretary-General.[14] In a 1969 study comparing the peacekeeping efforts of the OAS, OAU, and the Arab League, J. S. Nye found that for disputes through the early 1960s, the success ratio in the Arab League was far lower than that of the OAS and even lower than that of the OAU. Nye argued that the Arab League had helped to isolate or abate only one of the three cases attempted, and was unable to end the fighting in any of the attempts.[15]

In its economic endeavors, the Arab League has founded numerous banks, funds, and joint ventures. It also attempted to create a common market (Council of Arab Economic Unity) in 1964. However, despite huge sums of petrodollars accumulated in the OAPEC states annually, the banks and funds have not been very well capitalized. Currently there exist only six members of the common market: Egypt (now "suspended"), Syria, Jordan, Sudan, Libya, and Iraq (only the latter two have oil wealth). The common market provisions as to common tariffs, export and import regulations, and coordination of agricultural and industrial policies have yet to be drafted let alone implemented. At present, the Council of Economic Unity consists of four joint companies and ten unions of national industries. Trade between the member-states, as among all Arab League states, reflects the political relationships of the states rather than any concerted effort toward economic integration.[16]

The social and cultural activities of the League are the most integrated and the most successful both because they are the least politically divisive and because they directly represent the ideological imperative of "Arab brotherhood." Related programs include those devoted to educational improvement and exchange, studies on social problems (but with little attempt at harmonization), promotion of youth and sports activities, establishment of libraries and museums, and hundreds of conferences and seminars involving professionals, teachers, and technicians. These activities are based on both the Charter and the Cultural Treaty of 1946.[17]

Collective security and a combined political voice in the United Nations are prominent objectives of the Arab League. However, although the collective-security function is well institutionalized, it does not function against Israel as it was designed to do; indeed, it was scarcely noticed during the 1967 and 1973 wars. More importantly, the Egyptian-Israeli peace treaty and subsequent suspension of Egypt's participation in the League have removed the largest military force of any Arab nation from the collective-security machinery.[18] In its efforts to speak with one voice in the United Nations, the Arab League has been far more successful. The Council considers draft resolutions prior to each General Assembly session and the League members act as an effective voting bloc, particularly on issues involving anticolonialism/anti-neoimperialism, Israel, and the Palestinians (i.e., support for the PLO). The member-states also work closely together as a sub-bloc within Third World groups.

Integration in the Arab League has been restricted by political rivalries among the member-states, divisiveness between the conservative monarchies, and radical dictatorships. However, the greatest barriers are jealously guarded sovereignty and the limited aims of the Charter. Arab leaders often argue that the League should be criticized not for accomplishing too little but for attempting too much. Perhaps the most surprising thing of all about the Arab League today is that it still exists. Despite the rhetoric of Arab solidarity and brotherhood, we might be tempted to surmise that if the state of Israel were to disappear one day, the Arab League would evaporate the next.

Notes

1. See M. Abdel-Kadar Hatem, *Information and the Arab Cause* (London: Longman Group, 1974), pp. 105–172; and Michael C. Hudson, *Arab Politics: The Search for Legitimacy* (New Haven, Conn.: Yale University Press, 1977), pp. 33–55.

2. James P. Piscatory and R. K. Ramazani, "The Middle East," in Werner J. Feld and Gavin Boyd (Eds.), *Comparative Regional Systems* (New York: Pergamon, 1980), p. 279.

3. R. W. Macdonald, *The League of Arab States* (Princeton, N.J.: Princeton University Press, 1965), pp. 9–24.

4. It was also characterized by Egyptian President Nassar's design for the support of national liberation movements and anti-regime activities (by fostering Arab unity through diplomacy, propaganda, and insurgency aid) in Morocco, Tunisia, Libya, Lebanon, Syria, Iraq, Kuwait, Saudi Arabia, and Yemen. See Hudson, *Arab Politics,* pp. 240–241.

5. Europa Publications, *The Middle East and North Africa 1979–80* (London: Europa, 1979), p. 152.

6. Ibid., p. 153.

7. Europa Publications, *The Europa Year Book 1980: A World Survey* vol. I (London: Europa, 1980), pp. 124, 128–129.

8. Arthur S. Banks and William Overstreet (Eds.), *Political Handbook of the World* (New York: McGraw-Hill, 1981), p. 574.

9. Articles 3–6 and 16 of the Charter of the League of Arab States.

10. Europa, *Middle East and North Africa,* p. 150.

11. Macdonald, *The League,* pp. 53–72.

12. Piscatory and Ramazani, "The Middle East," p. 285.

13. Article 5 of the Charter.

14. H. A. Hassouna, *The League of Arab States and Regional Disputes* (Dobbs Ferry, N.Y.: Oceana Publications, 1975), pp. 363–373.

15. J. S. Nye, *Peace in Parts: Integration and Conflict in International Organization* (Boston: Little, Brown and Co., 1971), p. 171.

16. A. G. Musrey, *An Arab Common Market* (New York: Praeger Publishers, 1969), p. 164.

17. Macdonald, *The League,* pp. 171–192.

18. In 1979, Egypt had 395,000 active military forces and 515,000 reserve forces.

14
The Nordic Council and the Islamic Conference

The Nordic Council and the Islamic Conference are cultural/ideological international governmental organizations. Both are organized by memberships and purposes based on common cultural heritages and shared ideological (political) beliefs. The two organizations were created solely for the purpose of consultation; there was no intent for functional integration or supranational decisionmaking in either body. Integration in these IGOs is therefore intentionally minimal. Yet a great deal of integration has occurred, particularly in the older organization, the Nordic Council.

The Nordic Council

The Nordic Council was inaugurated in 1953 following the failure of the Scandinavian Defense Union, which had been created in 1949. The charter members of the Council were Denmark, Iceland, Sweden, and Norway. After achieving assent from the Soviet Union, Finland joined in 1955.[1] The original stated purpose of the organization was simple: to consult on matters of common interest and to produce resolutions calling on the member-governments to pass legislation that would implement the resolutions. The present legal basis of the Council, the Treaty of Cooperation in 1962 (Treaty of Helsinki), empowers the Council of Europe to consider economic, social, cultural, environmental, legal, and communications questions. In addition, the Council has served as an advisory body to the Nordic Council of Ministers since 1971.

History and Development

The first attempts at Nordic cooperation took place in the 1850s following the fragmentation of the region into small political units as well as several conferences and mutual pledges of brotherhood between the kings of Denmark and Sweden. However, the Swedes' refusal to aid the Danes when they were attacked by Prussia in 1864 ended the brief era of alliances and discussions about functional integration. In the late 1800s and early 1900s, several joint conferences and committees (nearly all at the subnational level) were formed to continue varying degrees of functional cooperation. Following World War II and a period devoid of intraregional conflict since 1814, the desire to consolidate the many bodies into one permanent organization was widely articulated in the Scandinavian states. In 1951, the leader of the Danish delegation to the Nordic Interparliamentary Union, Hans Hedtoft, proposed the creation of a Nordic Council of Parliamentarians. A draft proposal was negotiated and approved by all governments except the Finnish government in 1952, and the Nordic Council began its legal existence in January 1953.[2]

In 1961, Denmark and Norway began to develop interests in joining the European Community, whereas Finland, Iceland, and Sweden clearly had no such intentions. This situation led to the signing of the Helsinki Treaty in 1962, a formalization (codification) of the many institutions and functional collaboration that had been achieved within the Council. In 1972, the Nordic Council of Ministers and a joint secretariat for the Council of Parliamentarians were established. Several committees that had operated independently were brought under the Nordic Council umbrella. In addition, three special agencies were created by the Council of Ministers: the Nordic Fund for Industrial Development, the Nordic Cultural Fund, and the Nordic Investment Bank.[3]

Structure

The primary institutions of the Nordic Council are the Council, the Presidium, five standing committees, and two special committees. The Nordic Council of Ministers is a spillover of the Nordic Council but is considered a separate international body. (See Figure 14.1.)

The Council is in fact a parliamentary assembly consisting of seventy-eight delegates elected annually from the parliament of each member-state (sixteen from Denmark, seventeen from Finland, eighteen each from Norway and Sweden, and six from Iceland). Delegates are chosen on a proportional basis reflecting the strength of their parties within the national parliaments (similar to the method employed for the Council of Europe). National government officials are also seated, but they have no voting rights. The Council meets once each year for about a week to adopt recommendations to be sent to the Nordic Council of Ministers.[4]

The Presidium performs the work of the organization between annual meetings of the Council, providing the element of continuity and performing routine functions for the Nordic Council. It is composed of five individuals elected each year by the Council and is presided over

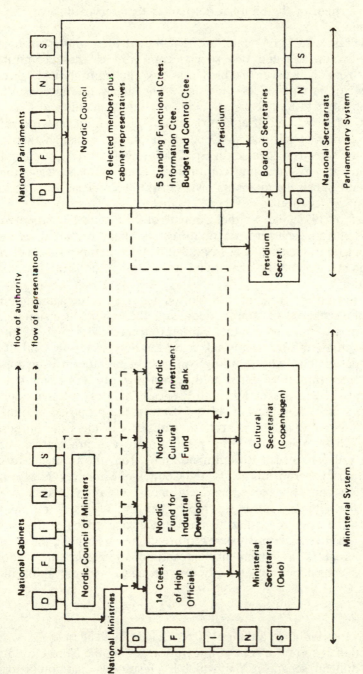

Figure 14.1 Nordic Institutional Structure (1977)

by the chairman of the national delegation that serves that year as the host nation.

The delegates to the Council are distributed to membership on five standing committees and two special committees. These committees meet during and between Council sessions and communicate directly with the Nordic Council of Ministers. The five standing committees are Economic, Cultural, Legal, Social and Environment, and Communications. The two special committees are Information and Budget.[5]

The Nordic Council has no General-Secretariat, although there is a Presidium Secretariat located in Stockholm that serves both the Presidium and the five standing committees. Each national delegation to the Nordic Council maintains its own separate secretariat at its national parliament in its capital.

Created in 1972, the Nordic Council of Ministers is composed of one minister from each government; ministers who attend are determined by the topic(s) to be discussed. In addition, each member-state's cabinet has a minister for Nordic affairs and an official responsible for Nordic Cooperation.[6]

Since the chosen role of the Nordic Council is consultation and cooperation rather than supranationalism, there is no decisionmaking process per se. However, a rather complex structure has evolved. In the Council, initiatives are usually taken by the Secretaries-General of the national delegations. The standing committees employ investigators to consider these initiatives, often holding hearings of civil servants (technocrats) of the various national ministries. The staffs of the standing committees play an important role by drafting the proposed resolutions and recommending amendments. The Council considers the proposals, operating on the unanimity principle (the norms of pragmatism, compromise, and consensus). Recommendations from the Council are sent to the national governments and/or the Council of Ministers. The Council of Ministers can only recommend common legislation to each of the national parliaments, but it is empowered to "legislate" on matters relating to the three funds and to the internal operations of the Nordic Council.[7] The five governments are required to report back to the Council on their progress in implementing resolutions. Because the feedback process is continuous, resolutions are frequently altered to facilitate compliance.[8]

State of Integration

Any evaluation that attempts to correlate the effectiveness of the Nordic Council and the extent of integration among the Nordic countries is at best difficult; separating that which is a result of a common historical source of law and culture or the efforts of the many subnational groups in existence as early as 1872 from the direct accomplishments of the Nordic Council is problematic.[9] What can be said is that the degree of integration among Nordic states is substantial. This is especially true in the areas of harmonizing laws pertaining to citizenship, adoption, children's rights, copyrights and trademarks, installment plans, aviation, environmental control, social security, and the like. Functional groups control or monitor telecommunications, aviation, railways, and highways. The Nordic states have established a passport union, a customs union, and a postal union. Governments coordinate in the fields of public health, cultural affairs, recreation, education, scientific research, and planning and development. Clearly, not all of this government coordination is due to the existence of the Nordic Council. Despite the modest degree of formal structural and policy integration, the Nordic states have accomplished significant levels of harmonization and economic integration through joint ventures, corporate ties, and the evolution of a common labor market.[10]

The Nordic countries practice what has been termed "negative cooperation" in the fields of foreign policy and security. Due to the exigencies of the "Nordic balance," Norwegian and Danish membership in NATO, Swedish neutrality, and "Finlandization," discussions of security and sensitive foreign-policy matters are strenuously avoided within the Nordic Council. Whether the Nordic balance concept is a result of coordinated policies or of a fortuitous pattern of national interests has not been determined. However, intense regular consultation does take place among the five ministers of defense.[11]

Institutional and policy integration in the Nordic Council is relatively nil; yet attitudinal integration by virtue of the strong cultural/ideological ties among the member-states is very high. The Nordic states have created what Karl Deutsch has called a "security community," an area in which interstate war has become unthinkable. The Nordic Council has served to organize and control an integration process that has produced some remarkable accomplishments without the perceived need to create a supranational institutional structure.[12]

The Islamic Conference

The Organization of the Islamic Conference was formally established in May 1971 among forty-one nations and the PLO. Membership spans an area from Northern Africa to Southeast Asia, with most of the member-states located in the Middle and Near East. Egypt's membership was suspended in 1979, as was Afghanistan's in 1980. Iraq is the only Islamic state that is not a member of the Islamic Conference.

The Islamic Conference is a true cultural/ideological organization. Despite important political and economic differences among the member-states, they are bound by the organization's requirement that they respect Islamic laws and principles. The stated aims of the organization are to promote Islamic solidarity; to consolidate cooperation in social, cultural, economic, and scientific areas of common concern; to eradicate racial discrimination and colonialism in all its forms (a direct reference to Israel and those who support her); to support international peace and security; to coordinate efforts to safeguard holy places and support the Palestinians' cause; to safeguard the dignity, independence, and national rights of all Muslim peoples; and to promote cooperation among member-states and other countries.[13]

History and Development

The concept of pan-Islamism (as understood today) dates back to the 1850s, but nothing of substance occurred to create a purely religious conference of Islamic states until 1962. When the power struggle between Egyptian President Nasser and Saudi King Faisal over the control and purposes of the Arab League was won by Nasser, Faisal created the World Islamic League, an organization more to his liking and one whose headquarters was not Cairo but Mecca. The World Islamic League envisioned nothing more than the conduct of annual Islamic summit conferences. However, the first such conference did not take place until after the 1967 Arab-Israeli war and a subsequent improvement in Saudi-Egyptian relations.

A 1969 summit meeting in Rabat, Morocco, and meetings of the Islamic foreign ministers in 1970 in Jeddah and Karachi featured discussions on the status of Jerusalem and the Palestinian problem. These issues raised questions of organizational competence. Subsequently, the Organization of the Islamic Conference was formally established in 1971 and the Charter was ratified at the Foreign Ministers' Conference in March 1972. The International Islamic News Agency was also created in 1972, and the Islamic Development Bank followed in 1974. The Islamic States Broadcasting Organization was initiated in 1975, and the Islamic Solidarity Fund was created in 1977. Efforts to consolidate the Islamic Cultural Centers in non-Muslim countries continued throughout the 1970s. The Islamic Conference has conducted annual summit conferences and Conferences of Foreign Ministers since 1971. The first Islamic Economic Conference was held in 1976.[14]

Structure

There has been little institutionalization in the Organization of the Islamic Conference. The primary political body is the Conference of

197

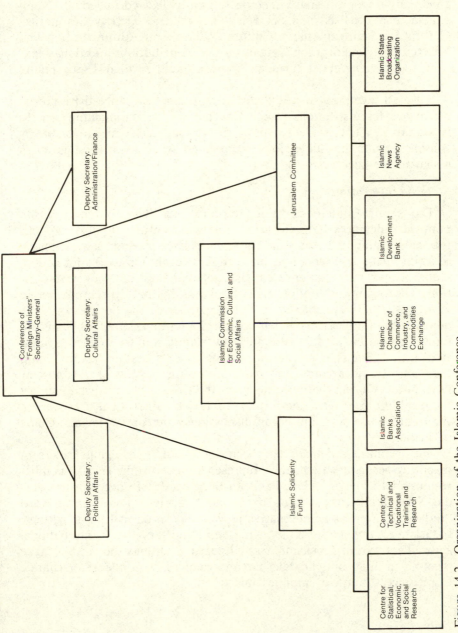

Figure 14.2 Organization of the Islamic Conference

198 *The Nordic Council and the Islamic Conference*

Heads of State; however, the Conference of Foreign Ministers has attained an equally important status. The Secretariat is located in Jeddah, Saudi Arabia, and consists of a Secretary-General and Deputy Secretaries-General for Political Affairs, Cultural Affairs, and Administration and Finance. The Organization is financed by "contributions and donations" from the member-states (principally from Saudi Arabia).[15] (See Figure 14.2.)

Since all meetings are conducted *in camera,* and since there are no provisions for institutions in the Charter, the decisionmaking process is secretive. What is known, however, is that decisions are taken by consensus, and that all nations represented when a decision is taken assent to the decision.[16]

State of Integration

The Islamic Conference is not a supranational IGO, for which reason political differences have thwarted and will continue to thwart institutional integration. The annual conferences have reflected some measure of attitudinal integration, and the resultant resolutions, calls for action, requests, and reaffirmations demonstrate some degree of policy integration. The organization supported the Turks in the Cyprus conflict in 1974, but little was achieved in the remainder of the decade. In 1980, however, the Conference condemned the Soviet invasion of Afghanistan, foreign pressures (the United States) on Islamic countries (Iran), aggression against Somalia, the hostage-taking in Iran as "un-Islamic," and the Camp David accords, and it supported the boycott of the Moscow Olympics.[17] During the following year, the Conference renewed support for the PLO, continued the boycott of Israel, called for a cease-fire in the Iraqi-Iranian war, and began discussions to create an Islamic Court of Justice.[18]

The Islamic Conference has been successful in bringing leaders of disputing heads of state or their representatives to some level of conflict resolution. Examples include Pakistan-Bangladesh, Morocco-Algeria, Jordan-Syria, and (without result) Iran-Iraq.[19] In view of the trend toward "re-Islamization" as an alternative to Westernization in Islamic nations, the Islamic Conference should increase in importance as an international actor. That Syrian President Assad refused to attend the Arab League meeting in 1980 but did take an important part in the 1980 Islamic Conference summit exemplifies this trend.[20]

Notes

1. The Finns secured an unarticulated agreement from the other Scandinavian states that there would be no discussion in the Council of "controversial (i.e.,

anti-Soviet) economic and external policies." F. Wendt, *The Nordic Council and Cooperation in Scandinavia* (Copenhagen: Munksgaard, 1959), p. 105.

2. B. Sundelius, "Nordic Cooperation: A Dynamic Integration Process" (Ph.D. dissertation, University of Denver, 1976), pp. 4–12; and E. Solem, *The Nordic Council and Scandinavian Integration* (New York: Praeger Publishers, 1977), pp. 40–43.

3. B. Sundelius, *Managing Transnationalism in Northern Europe* (Boulder, Colo: Westview Press, 1978), pp. 44–49.

4. Europa Publications, *The Europa Year Book 1980: A World Survey*, vol. I (London: Europa, 1980), pp. 232–233.

5. Arthur S. Banks and William Overstreet (Eds.), *Political Handbook of the World 1981* (New York: McGraw-Hill, 1981), p. 571.

6. Solem, *Nordic Council*, pp. 49–54.

7. B. Sundelius, "Transgovernmental Interactions in the Nordic Region," *Cooperation and Conflict* 12 (1977), pp. 74–80.

8. Solem, *Nordic Council*, pp. 36, 48.

9. Ibid., pp. 87–94.

10. Sundelius, *Managing Transnationalism*, p. 41.

11. Ibid., p. 81.

12. Ibid., p. 114.

13. Europa Publications, *The Middle East and North Africa 1980–81* (London: Europa, 1980), p. 172.

14. Banks and Overstreet, *Political Handbook*, p. 605.

15. Europa, *Middle East*, p. 172.

16. *Washington Post*, January 29, 1980, p. A1.

17. *New York Times*, November 11, 1980, p. 3.

18. *New York Times*, January 25, 1981, p. 13.

19. *New York Times*, February 1, 1981, pp. 11 and IV-4.

20. R. Glasgow, "Der Islam—dynamischer Machtfaktor der modernen Welt," *Die Arabische Welt: Geschichte, Probleme, Prospektiven* (Freiburg: Verlag Ploetz, 1978), pp. 179–183.

Part 6

Integration Among
Nongovernmental Actors

15

Multinational Corporations and International Labor Unions

All of the nonstate actors previously covered in this volume have been international governmental organizations (IGOs). This chapter begins discussions of international nongovernmental organizations (INGOs), of which there are numerous examples: the International Red Cross, the World Council of Churches, Amnesty International, and many others (see Chapter 2). However, two of the most important contemporary issues in international politics, the international economic order and international terrorism, have given certain INGOs substantially greater importance as nonstate actors in international politics. These actors are multinational corporations, international labor groups, and transnational ethnic ("terrorist") groups. Multinational corporations and labor organizations constitute the focus of this chapter. International labor organizations are included in this part of the text as one of many (though largely unsuccessful) efforts to control multinationals. A discussion of transnational ethnic groups begins the ensuing chapter.

Multinational Corporations

Multinational corporations are integrated independent subsidiary networks controlled from the parent nation-state by corporate command headquarters. These entities (hereafter referred to as MNCs) have been labeled multinational enterprises, transnational enterprises or corporations, international businesses, multinational undertakings, and global corporations.[1] Regardless of what label is applied, MNCs are powerful economic actors and, hence, increasingly important political nonstate actors. This is not a new phenomenon, however. The earliest MNCs were established in the last century, and a few have been in existence already for more than one hundred years.

Stated simply, MNCs are businesses (including conglomerates and financial institutions) that have set up factories, assembly plants, warehouses, and sales and service outlets in nations outside the home country (nation of origin). These entities are called subsidiaries, which, although under the direct or substantial indirect control of the "parent" company, are generally considered to be legally separate and distinct businesses. The most widely accepted list of criteria to determine which businesses qualify as MNCs is that of the Harvard School of Business: (1) unlimited life; (2) multiple identity; (3) at least $100 million gross sales per year; (4) operation in six or more countries (but they do not qualify if they only sell or license across borders); and (5) generation of at least 25 percent of income from outside the home or parent country.[2] According to Raymond Vernon, an MNC is "a parent company that controls a large cluster of corporations of various nationalities . . . [that has] access to a common pool of human and financial resources and seems responsive to a common strategy."[3]

Multinational corporations may be classified by type of enterprise, by ownership, and by the degree of autonomy exercised by the subsidiaries. Types of enterprises include extractive (oil, metals), agriculture (fruit, coffee), manufacturing (e.g., automobiles), service (hotels), financial (banks), and conglomerates (such as ITT and the Japanese "zaibatsu" or holding companies). The ownership typology includes wholly owned firms, joint ventures (with or without local capital), and so-called fade-out joint ventures (involving eventual take-over by the host-nation government and/or investors).[4] The degree of autonomy involves what Howard Perlmutter has labeled "ethnocentric" (such that all decisions are made in the parent company), "polycentric" (most decisions are made independently by the subsidiaries), and "geocentric" (involving decisionmaking collaboration between parent company and subsidiaries to produce an "international outlook").[5]

The discussion of what MNCs are may be made clearer by some attention to who they are. By the Harvard definition (and according to one of that school's leading scholars), in 1977 there were 250 MNCs with headquarters in the United States, 150 in Europe, 70 in Japan, and 20 in other nations. In addition, there were 20 U.S. multinational banks, 13 European, 9 Japanese, and 3 Canadian.[6] These include the "Seven Sisters" (Exxon, Mobil, Standard of California, Gulf, Texaco, Royal Dutch Shell, and British Petroleum), auto manufacturers (GM, Ford, VW, Mercedes-Benz, Toyota, and others), electronics firms (ITT, IBM, Sperry-Rand, Philips, Sony, and others), and many food and cosmetic, marketing, and financial organizations. Of the U.S. MNCs, the top ten by gross annual sales are indicated in Table 15.1. In terms of net profits and assets, the largest are communications/electronics firms, auto makers, and, since 1973, the oil companies.

TABLE 15.1. Major U.S. Multinational Corporations (1981)

Company	Gross Sales (mil $)	Net Profits (mil $)	Assets (mil $)	Employees (000)
Exxon	108,108	5,567.5(2)	62,931(5)	180.0
Mobil Oil	64,488	2,433.0(4)	34,776(14)	209.6
General Motors	62,699	333.4(75)	38,920(12)	740.9
American Tel & Tel	58,214	6,888.1(1)	137,750(1)	1,042.1
Texaco	57,628	2,310.0(6)	27,489(22)	66.7
Standard Oil Calif.	44,224	2,380.0(5)	23,656(26)	41.8
Ford Motor	38,247	-1,060.0	23,012(28)	404.8
Standard Oil Ind.	29,947	1,922.0(8)	22,916(29)	57.5
IBM	29,070	3,308.0(3)	29,586(19)	348.1
Gulf Oil	28,252	1,231.0(13)	20,429(33)	58.7
Standard Oil Ohio		1,946.9(7)	15,743(43)	
Shell Oil		1,701.0(9)	20,118(34)	
Atlantic Richfield		1,671.3(10)	19,733(35)	
Bank America			121,158(2)	
Citicorp			119,232(3)	
Chase Manhattan			77,839(4)	

Note: All numbers in parentheses after data indicate rank among "Fortune 500" in 1981.
Source: Compiled from *Fortune*, May 10, 1982, pp. 203-309.

Why They Are Important World Actors

The data in Table 15.1 demonstrate that MNCs are formidable economic entities. It should be obvious that, by economic indicators alone, MNCs are powerful international nonstate actors. For example, were it possible to equate the annual gross sales of MNCs with the gross national products of nation-states,[7] one could have concluded in 1972 that General Motors was larger than Switzerland, Pakistan, and South Africa; that Royal Dutch Shell was bigger than Iran, Venezuela, and Turkey; and that Goodyear Tires was larger than Saudi Arabia.[8] Moreover, nearly 75 percent of the world's production is controlled by 200 MNCs. In some Western European markets, 70 to 90 percent of those markets is controlled by as few as four large corporations.

The immense economic power that characterizes most MNCs translates into significant amounts of political power and often serious problems for host-nation governments, especially for Third World governments.

Due to large investments, huge profits, and a concomitant magnitude of risk, MNCs have been tempted to shape or topple host-nation governments whenever they perceived the need or opportunity to do so. The activities of the United Fruit Company over several decades in Central America[9] and the 1973 effort of ITT to overthrow Salvador Allende in Chile[10] are well documented and frequently cited cases. ITT provides an example of more pervasive uses of power. In 1938, ITT bought 28 percent of Folke-Wulf in Germany. Later, that company produced German bombers used to attack Allied ships during World War II. Despite that fact, ITT was awarded $26 million by U.S. courts after the war, for damage done to its German subsidiary's plants by U.S. bombers.[11]

The men and women who control multinational corporations often argue that the ITT and United Fruit cases prove the exception rather than the rule and that their goals are not political but economic: namely, to satisfy their owners (stockholders), to attract new investors, and to create a loyalty to themselves on the part of their employees, customers, and society. The corporate strategy of controlled growth depends in large part on the ability of a given company to create a need or, better yet, a dependency for its product(s). Although this strategy may be considered sound, basic business theory,[12] it is the kind of practice that can lead to tragedy in very poor countries. Such a tragedy occurred in Africa when the Swiss Nestlé Corporation set out to convince mothers to cease breastfeeding their children in favor of baby formula milk produced by Nestlé. Many children died when their mothers could neither afford nor find the baby formula and, having stopped breast-feeding, the women could not provide their own milk for their children.

Proponents of multinational corporations argue that MNCs increase world efficiency, foster growth, and improve welfare.[13] MNCs provide Third World countries with investment capital, new technology, vital managerial skills, employment, and exports (especially of manufactured goods). In addition, they provide a bridge-building function among nations and increase global economic interdependence.[14] These perceived benefits are important to elites in developing states; without them MNCs could not operate in Third World countries. However, it is those characteristics for which MNCs are criticized that make them world political actors.

Critics of MNCs argue that these organizations are international oligopolies that lower efficiency and stifle growth. From an economic perspective, MNCs displace indigenous production by buying out existing industries designed to reduce dependency on imports, and they drive out of business indigenous competitors by increasing the foreign MNCs' share of the market.[15] Moreover, it is charged that the integrated subsidiary networks directed by MNC headquarters permit economic neocolonialism and facilitate home governments' use of MNCs as foreign-policy conduits. The United States, for example, has used export controls to interfere in or block trade agreements between a host country and a nation unfriendly to the United States. Ford-Canada and South Africa, IBM-France and France, a Belgian farm equipment company (U.S. subsidiary) and Cuba are examples. The United States has also selectively applied the Sherman and Clayton antitrust acts and its control of balance-of-payments policies to apply pressure through U.S. MNCs on other governments.[16]

From a sociological perspective, MNCs have been charged with fostering social hegemony, corruption, inequality, and pollution. Further, they have significantly increased consumer expectations while remaining indifferent to consumer interests.[17] One critic argues that MNCs are altering class structures by creating new socioeconomic and political divisions within the countries in which they operate. The new class structures create social conflicts that existing political and social institutions are ill-equipped to manage in developing countries.[18]

Critics of MNCs that employ a political perspective focus on the problems that multinationals cause governments and other actors (i.e., international organizations and labor unions). Relative to host governments and labor, MNCs have the great advantage of mobility; they can move capital, personnel, and equipment quite easily. This power of mobility has been used to threaten immediate "pull-outs," and thereby immediate unemployment and other (long-term) economic shocks, when governments and labor unions have made or threatened demands considered unacceptable by the MNCs. U.S. labor, for example, has been hurt particularly in New England (garment and footwear industries) by the tactic termed "runaway industries." U.S.-controlled MNCs have moved entire factories to places like Hong Kong, Taiwan, and South Korea, where labor and taxes are substantially cheaper. The responses of the AFL-CIO and international labor organizations to the tactic of runaway industries has been to pressure governments for protectionist policies against goods (re-)imported from those MNCs. In the United States, those policies have been high tariffs in most cases.[19] However, the MNCs have lobbied back, and tariffs have applied only to "finished products." This loophole in the law has engendered cases like the ladies' underwear corporation that made brassieres in Mexico (taking advantage of very cheap labor) and imported the product as unfinished (the snaps were sewn on in the United States) with very little tax penalty.

Transfer pricing is a problem for both home and host country governments. Typically, transfer pricing permits "vertical-monopoly" MNCs (those whose subsidiaries control a product from mining to manufacturing to marketing) to control (maintain and/or increase) retail prices of its products. The system also makes use of "tax haven" countries or "export platforms" to increase corporate profits. Consider the following hypothetical example: An MNC called Oxxon controls several subsidiaries (called Ossoil) engaged in the production, refining, transport, and marketing of petroleum and petroleum products. Ossoil (Kuwait), Oxxon's oil-pumping subsidiary, sells the petroleum to Ossoil (Panama), Oxxon's major oil-tanker company. Ossoil (Panama) then transports that petroleum to Rotterdam, the Netherlands. However, while in transit the oil is sold by Ossoil (Panama) to Ossoil (Bahamas). Ossoil (Panama) will sell that oil for very little or no profit (or, if deemed necessary, at a loss) to Ossoil (Bahamas), but the oil will continue its northern course up the East Atlantic and never come close to the Bahamas. Ossoil (Bahamas) therefore becomes a tax haven or export platform.[20] The company consists of a few small offices and a small administrative staff. Someone on that staff will sell that petroleum on the Ossoil (Panama) tankers to Ossoil (the Netherlands) at a substantial profit. It is done this way because taxes in the Bahamas are minimal and corporate "secrets" are well protected (a mutually beneficial arrangement, since the Bahamas get some corporate tax revenues it could get no other way). Ossoil (the Netherlands) then refines the crude petroleum and sells it at a modest profit (corporate secrets are also protected by criminal statute in the Netherlands) to Ossoil (Luxembourg), who will ship the refined products by rail to Ossoil (West Germany), the final (retail) destination. Should the West German government (or any other consumer state) wish to determine why the price its Oxxon subsidiary paid for gasoline is so high, it would have to trace the several transactions back through several uncooperative companies (Oxxon subsidiaries) and governments! Oxxon benefits doubly. It makes most of its profits where taxes are lowest and maintains an (artificially) high price for its product.[21]

One of the most cited criticisms of MNCs by leaders of Third World countries is the problem of transfer of technology. MNCs will sell their technology, but only when profits are sufficiently high and usually when they control the terms of the sales. Since the goals of MNCs are to recover research and development costs and increase revenues without losing their competitive edge, MNCs will transfer technology to subsidiaries in host countries, but with certain important conditions. Generally, the home company will not transfer "know-how" and patents that would make the subsidiary totally independent of the home company. Thus the home company may sell the technology for components that have no real market value since they are used in the manufacture of finished products produced in the home country; or, in the case of communications and data processing, the home country will sell hardware technology but continue to control software and systems analysts. In cases where the entire technical data package is transferred, the sale virtually always involves an outdated, superseded product.

MNCs have countered critics of transfer-of-technology policies by first pointing to the large volume of technology sales (without mentioning the quality of those sales) and then maintaining that technology transfer to developing countries is limited by the inadequate support of native universities for research and development activities.[22] In fact, MNCs contribute to that second difficulty by training the brightest local nationals and inviting them to work in the home nation company's laboratory (another kind of "brain-drain"). Generally, MNCs have deserved the criticism that they have created dependency relationships by keeping research and development solely within the home country and by providing inappropriate technologies (e.g., those only the elites can afford and use for labor-saving technologies that decrease employment in developing nations).[23]

Efforts to Control Multinationals

There are several techniques that have been proposed or applied successfully (on occasion) to control multinational corporations. Unilateral efforts have been restricted largely to the developing nations, since First World governments seldom see such actions in their own economic interests or, as in the United States, are reluctant to extend antitrust legislation enforcement beyond their borders. Third World governments are not powerless against the MNCs. They can threaten or carry out nationalization (expropriation) with full, partial, or no compensation (the latter is termed "confiscation"). But these methods are radical actions likely to thwart future investment and to strain relations with First World governments. Other traditional methods include the use of monetary policies, stock market regulations, and taxation. However, the great mobility of most MNCs have rendered these techniques long-term disasters. Techniques less radical (and therefore, less politically palatable for leftist governments) are joint venture and domestic content approaches. Joint ventures may occur in the form of limiting foreign investment to below 50 percent of equity in an enterprise (e.g., 1973 "Mexicanization") and "fade-out" ventures (as in Peru) where foreign capital is to be replaced over time by distributing part of the profits as shares to the workers.[24] The domestic content approach has been to insist that more stages of the production process be located in the host country, or that only local firms be used to supply certain component parts.[25]

Multilateral efforts to control MNCs include the "competition policy" and "abuse of a dominant position" rulings of the European Community (see Chapter 4) and Decision 24 of the Andean Group (discussed in Chapter 5). Perhaps the two best-known multilateral efforts are the voluntary codes of conduct produced by the United Nations and the OECD. The United Nations established the Center on Transnational Corporations and a Commission on Transnational Corporations (both in 1975). The Commission (consisting of ten developed states, five state-planning [Marxist] and twenty-three developing countries) will eventually produce guidelines for voluntary disclosure of information on operations, consumer and environmental protection, foreign-exchange operations, transfer pricing, and anticompetitive behavior.[26]

The 1976 OECD Voluntary Code of Conduct is similar to that being worked on in the United Nations in that it is perceived by most Third World governments as a litany of guidelines that all begin: "Wouldn't it be nice if only you would. . . ." The guidelines "require" that parent companies make their subsidiaries obey the guidelines; disclose complete information on operations (read, keep one set of books) to host governments; improve employment and industry relations (e.g., prohibit the movement of employees from one state to another during labor-management negotiations); and cooperate with host governments on national laws, especially those concerning taxation. A June 1979 review of the 1976 OECD Code (Declaration on International Investment and Multinational Enterprises) concluded that since there were no provisions for enforcing the Code, no assessment could be made on the conduct of individual companies.[27]

Not all activities of MNCs pose serious threats to Third World sovereignty (or that of the First World, for that matter), any more than all MNCs are corrupt oppressors and enslavers of the world's poor and downtrodden. For those MNC actions that do deserve such labels, national governments are easily disadvantaged in trying to deal with multinationals. MNCs are far more mobile and, of greater importance, more integrated than are nation-states. The weaknesses of the voluntary UN, OECD, and (older) ICC Codes attest to this. Stronger efforts in the EC and ANCOM are more often sources of dissension within those IGOs and, as with Chile's separation from ANCOM in 1975, a cause of disintegration.

Theories and MNCs

Chapter 3 of this text presented the argument that empirical description was not sufficient; that the goal of understanding political phenomena should be theoretical analysis based on explicit concepts and leading to significant generalizations. It was also mentioned in Chapter 3 that contemporary theories of international political integration were inappropriate to the study of multinational corporations. Attempts at such theoretical analysis are to be found in the body of literature associated with business management.

Theories of MNCs tend to fall within two distinct "schools": business/economic theories and political power theories. Business/economic theories stress the economic functions of MNCs (production, distribution, marketing, and research and development); political power theories concentrate on how MNCs use their size and mobility to "control" governments and the international economic system. Examples of business/economic theories of MNCs are the monopolistic theory of foreign investment (Kindleberger, Hymer, and Blair) and the product cycle model (Vernon and Moran). Power theories of MNCs include Perroux's "dominant economy" approach, Marxist and non-Marxist theories of imperialism (Hobson, Lenin, and Hilferding), and "dependency theory" (Galtung and Sunkel).

The monopolistic theory of direct foreign investment put forth by Stephen Hymes and Charles Kindleberger[28] is based on past explanations of why and how firms gain and maintain control over assets and subsidiaries in other countries. However, Kindleberger argues that foreign investment results from monopolistic advantages gained from departures from free market conditions in either supply or in marketing, from economies of scale, or by governmental actions. Although MNCs may absorb competitors and exploit their monopolistic advantage, they are generally beneficial to the world economy because they increase economic efficiency and widen the area of competition.[29] The product cycle model of Theodore Moran[30] and Raymond Vernon[31] is a variant of the monopolistic theory of foreign investment. Based on data for U.S.-based MNC activity for 100 years, the model postulates that the success of any MNC is dependent upon its ability to produce continually innovative products or a steady flow of differentiated products. Failing these, local competitors will arise and take away a firm's competitive advantage in any given market/country.[32]

Many of the "power theories" are based on Francois Perroux's seminal work (1947) on the theory of the "dominant economy," namely, his analysis of U.S. economic dominance over post–World War II Europe. According to Perroux, a "domination effect" may be present between two firms or national economies due to differences in size and/or bargaining power. An unavoidable feature of the world political economy, the domination effect elevates the firms of a dominant economy to a position of great advantages (domestic markets, set prices and terms of trade, and the like). Furthermore, Perroux argues, the advantages accruing to the dominant economy's firms are irreversible.[33]

An older and perhaps more influential body of thought is the theoretical literature on imperialism. The works of Hobson, Lenin, Hilferding, and others[34] have regained attention, particularly since the proliferation of newly independent states in the early 1960s. However, the Hobsonian/ Marxist concern with international political imperialism has been supplanted by neo-Marxist concerns with (economic) neo-imperialism. The major expression of this trend in the theoretical literature is "dependency theory," and the "father" of that school is Johan Galtung. In Galtung's scheme, a structural theory of imperialism is based on a bifurcated world system consisting of center (developed countries) and periphery (developing countries) held together tenuously by a complex network of dependencies. Galtung argues that MNCs are a form of economic imperialism in that scheme because they create asymmetrical dependency relationships among states and promote harmony between governments of First and Third World nations but disharmony between Third World states' governments and their respective peoples. He states further that MNCs exploit the "periphery" through commodity concentration and conditions of dependency.[35]

Other "la dependencia" advocates have built on Galtung's early work criticizing "marginalization" and "polarization" between center and periphery in the international economic order. Osvaldo Sunkel, who, like most dependency theorists, focuses on Latin America (but differs given his non-Marxist approach), argues that foreign investment diverts the attention of the domestic elite from development needs in their own countries. His "marginalization thesis" predicts that MNCs preempt the most dynamic sectors of the host nation economy and absorb local capital and existent local companies.[36]

The theories of MNCs are generally no more successful in explaining and forecasting the behavior of nonstate actors in world politics than are theories of international political integration. Both theoretical approaches suffer due to ideological biases, insufficient testing efforts, and very little consensus among the theorists. The efforts to develop explanatory theories (or, more properly, models/paradigms) of nonstate actors generally and multinational corporations specifically are easily criticized on qualitative grounds. Such efforts should be continued, however, if there is to be any hope of a truly systematic analysis of and appreciation for the impact of MNCs on world politics.

International Labor Unions

The nonstate actors best suited to control the abuses of multinational corporations are international labor unions. That might appear to be a logical assumption, but it is far from reality. Notwithstanding the fact that international labor transcends national boundaries and has (potentially) some of the mobility advantages of MNCs, there are several reasons that explain the unions' decided inability to control MNCs. First, labor organizations are weak (if they exist at all) in developing countries, and MNC executives have found them relatively easy to manage. Second, despite the rhetoric of international solidarity and brotherhood among workers' organizations, international labor is highly fragmented by ideology, nationalism, and "craft" orientation. Third, most U.S. labor unions have chosen to stay well away from international labor organizations.

The three largest international trade union groups are organized by ideology and political party alignments rather than around crafts (as in the United States: auto workers, steel workers, miners, and so on). They reflect Communist, Socialist, and "confessional-based" party orientations and ideology, and are often divided among themselves by internation economic rivalries. These organizations also differ as to size and scope of membership and organizational structure.

The World Confederation of Labor

The World Confederation of Labor (WCL) was founded in 1920 as the International Federation of Christian Trade Unions (IFCTU). Reconstituted with its present name in 1968, the WCL is the oldest yet smallest of the three large international labor unions. It has about 15 million members living in seventy-eight countries. Its central institutions are located in Brussels, Belgium. The WCL represents groups with strong ties to national Christian Democratic parties.

The institutional structure of the WCL consists of the Congress, General Council, Confederal Board, and Secretariat-General. The Congress is the supreme authority but rarely meets. Delegates from the member unions (national confederations and trade internationals) cast votes proportionate to the size of the organizations they represent. The functions of the Congress are to consider long-range planning and future programs, and to elect the Confederal Board. The Confederal Board consists of eight representatives from the national confederations and six from the trade internationals, as well as the twenty-two members elected by and from the Congress to four-year terms. The Confederal Board serves through its semiannual meetings as the WCL's executive body and manager of the Secretariat. The General Council is constituted much like the Congress; delegates from member-organizations are seated according to the size of the organization they represent. The General Council meets at least biannually to establish general policy for the Confederal Board and to establish the overall organization's budget.

In addition to its central institutions, the WCL operates several international institutes of trade union studies in Africa, Asia, and Latin America, and regional offices in Caracas, Venezuela; Manila, Philippines; Montreal, Canada; and Geneva, Switzerland.[37]

The World Federation of Trade Unions

The World Federation of Trade Unions (WFTU) is the largest international trade union, representing 73 affiliated national trade federations with approximately 190 million members total. Founded in 1945, it is the peak association group for all Communist party–related trade unions (hence, the large individual membership totals). The WFTU's central institutions—the World Trade Union Congress, the General Council, the Executive Bureau, and the Secretariat—are located in Prague, Czechoslovakia.

The WFTU Congress meets every four years to review and endorse work done in the other central bodies and to elect the General Council and Executive Bureau. Delegates represent national organizations, and the size of each delegation is proportional to the size of the member-unions. The General Council meets annually to consider the work of the Executive Bureau, plan the Congress agenda (in years when it meets), approve the budget, and elect the General Secretary. The General Council consists of 73 members and 72 deputy members elected by the Congress. The Executive Bureau consists of 28 members and meets three times per year. It serves as the executive arm of the WFTU. In addition to serving as the administrative support for the other central institutions, the Secretariat contains offices for economic and social affairs, national trade union liaison, press and information, the Trades Union Internationals, women's affairs, administration, and finance.[38]

The International Confederation of Free Trade Unions

The International Confederation of Free Trade Unions (ICFTU) was founded in 1949 by a split in the WFTU into communist and socialist groups. Composed of 126 affiliated national centers and individual unions in 90 countries (representing 70.3 million members in 1980), the ICFTU is the "socialist trade international" that represents unions closely aligned with socialist and/or social democratic parties in their respective nations. The Brussels-based central bodies are the World Congress, the Executive Board, the Permanent Committees, the European Trade Union Body, and the Secretariat. The Inter-Regional body is located in Paris.

The highest authority in the ICFTU is the World Congress. Like the WFTU Congress, this body meets every four years and consists of delegations whose size depends on the relative size of the national federation it represents. The Congress elects the Executive Board and Secretary General, examines the functioning of regional structures, and considers reports and proposals for future programs. The Executive Board meets semi-annually and consists of twenty-nine members plus the Secretary-General (ex-officio). The Board makes decisions as to operations, finances, membership applications, and "problems affecting world labor." It also elects a "subcommittee" that serves as a sort of crisis committee (if needed) between Board meetings. The permanent committees are Finance and General Purposes, Economic and Social, Education Policy, Joint Consultative, Migrant Workers, Multinational Corporations, and International Trade and Monetary Questions. The European Trade Union Body was founded in 1973 and represents trade unions in the EC and EFTA countries. The Inter-Regional Body represents trade unions in the OECD member-states.

In addition to the central bodies, the ICFTU has sixteen associated international trade secretariats and three regional offices (Monrovia, Liberia; Mexico City; and New Delhi, India), and operates the Asian Trade Union College in New Delhi.[39]

U.S. Labor and the Internationals

Labor unions in the United States have been perhaps the most nationalistic and least interested in international labor organizations. This is true particularly of the AFL-CIO. This organization once belonged to the World Confederation of Labor (WCL) but pulled out because it saw that most conservative of the three largest labor internationals as "too socialistic." Other factors contributed to the AFL-CIO's withdrawal from the WCL. The emphasis on very strong party ties and a labor-government rather than labor-management approach to handling workers' demands was foreign to U.S. labor. In addition, the preference of U.S. labor to organize around crafts differed importantly with the ideologically centered labor unions of Europe and the Third World.

The U.S. attitude toward the WCL, ICFTU, and the WFTU is important in and of itself. However, should international labor ever hope to exert at least a modifying influence on the activities of MNCs, the participation of U.S. labor groups would be important. This is so if only because the majority of the top 200 MNCs are U.S. firms. U.S. labor has not troubled itself with the rhetoric of world-wide worker solidarity. Rather, it has confined its interests in protectionist lobbies against foreign-MNC incursions that threaten U.S. jobs and against the "runaway industries" phenomenon.[40] For many reasons, international labor is ill-equipped to control or modify the dominant behavior of MNCs in host countries. The refusal of U.S. labor to join in any substantial way (i.e., to create transnational organizations) only exacerbates that problem, and is not the cause by itself.

Notes

1. These terms are often used interchangeably. However, many European scholars prefer "transnational corporation," and the British appear to prefer "transnational undertaking." Many scholars insist that a true transnational corporation has a multinational board of directors and that those that do not are multinational corporations.

2. Raymond Vernon, *Sovereignty at Bay: The Multinational Spread of U.S. Enterprises* (New York: Basic Books, 1971), pp. 4–25.

3. Ibid., p. 4.

4. Richard W. Mansbach, Yale H. Ferguson, and Donald E. Lampert, *The Web of World Politics: Non-State Actors in the Global System* (Englewood Cliffs, N.J.: Prentice-Hall, 1976), pp. 192–193.

5. Howard V. Perlmutter, "The Tortuous Evolution of the Multinational Corporation," *Columbia Journal of World Business* 4:1 (January-February 1969), p. 12.

6. Raymond Vernon, *Storm over the Multinationals: The Real Issues* (Cambridge, Mass.: Harvard University Press, 1977), p. 12.

7. Economists tend to bristle (in unison) at such a suggestion; many political scientists continue to employ the analogy anyway.

8. Richard J. Barnet and Ronald E. Muller, *Global Reach: The Power of the Multinational Corporations* (New York: Simon and Schuster, 1974), p. 15. Note that these comparisons were made before the 1973 oil price hikes.

9. See Thomas McCann, *An American Company: The Tragedy of United Fruit* (New York: Crown Publishers, 1976), especially Chapter 6. Most business leaders today claim that the once-favored strategems to shape or topple foreign regimes are no longer acceptable corporate practices. The U.S. Foreign Corrupt Practices Act inhibits payoffs for influence, for example. See Louis Kraar, "The Multinationals Get Smarter About Political Risks," *Fortune* (March 24, 1980), pp. 86–100.

10. Barnet and Muller, *Global Reach,* pp. 81–83.

11. Ibid., pp. 60–61.

12. See P. F. Drucker, *Technology, Management and Society* (New York: Harper and Row, 1970); and C. P. Kindleberger, *American Business Abroad: Six Lectures on Direct Investment* (New Haven, Conn.: Yale University Press, 1969), pp. 35, 192.

13. Joan Edelman Spero, *The Politics of International Economic Relations,* 2nd ed. (New York: St. Martin's Press, 1981), p. 109.

14. Mansbach et al., *Web of World Politics,* pp. 194–196.

15. Thomas J. Biersteker, *Distortion or Development: Contending Perspectives on the Multinational Corporation* (Cambridge, Mass.: MIT Press, 1978), pp. 51–52.

16. Vernon, *Storm over the Multinationals,* pp. 175–190; and Spero, *Politics,* pp. 115–117.

17. S. J. Kobrin, "Multinational Corporations, Sociocultural Dependence, and Industrial Need Satisfaction or Want Creation?" *Journal of Developing Areas* 13 (January 1979), pp. 109–125; and Vernon, *Storm over the Multinationals,* pp. 13–14.

18. R. W. Cox, "Labor and the Multinationals," *Foreign Affairs* 54 (January 1976), pp. 344–365.

19. Louis Turner, *Multinational Corporations and the Third World* (New York: Hill and Wang, 1973), pp. 175–209.

20. Barnet and Muller, *Global Reach,* pp. 282–284.

21. See R. Kaye, "Transfer Pricing," *Accountant* 182 (April 10, 1980), pp. 536–538.

22. See National Association of Manufacturers, *U.S. Stake in World Trade and Investment: The Role of the Multinational Corporation* (New York: NAM, n.d.), pp. 39–44.

23. Biersteker, *Distortion or Development,* pp. 54–58.

24. Mansbach et al., *Web of World Politics,* pp. 204–206.

25. In the early 1970s, the Ford Motor Company conceded some domestic content to Spanish industry in negotiations with the government of Spain. Finding furniture manufacturers to do auto upholstery was of little difficulty, but finding a Spanish company to produce steering wheels was a major undertaking. Finally, Ford had to settle on a company that made toilet seats.

26. "Multinationals—Comfortable Code," *Economist* 281 (September 12, 1981), p. 69.

27. R. Barovick, "Guidelines for Multinational Enterprises," *Business America* 2 (July 16, 1979), pp. 3–6. See also J. G. Crean, "Guidelines and Codes for Multinational Enterprises," *CA Magazine* 113 (March 1980), pp. 61–64.

28. Charles Kindleberger, "The Monopolistic Theory of Direct Foreign Investment," in George Modelski (Ed.), *Transnational Corporations and World Order: Readings in International Political Economy* (San Francisco: W. H. Freeman and Company, 1979), pp. 91–107.

29. George Modelski, "Theories," in Modelski, *Transnational Corporations,* pp. 86–87.

30. Theodore Moran, "Foreign Expansion as Institutional Necessity for U.S. Corporate Capitalism: The Search for a Radical Model," *World Politics* 25:3 (April 1973), pp. 369–386.

31. Raymond Vernon, "The Product Cycle Model," in Modelski, *Transnational Corporations,* pp. 108–117.

32. Modelski, "Theories," p. 87.

33. Ibid., pp. 88–89.

34. See James E. Dougherty and Robert L. Pfaltzgraff, *Contending Theories of International Relations: A Comprehensive Survey,* 2nd ed. (New York: Harper and Row, 1981), pp. 213–250.

35. Johan Galtung, "A Structural Theory of Imperialism," in Modelski, *Transnational Corporations,* pp. 155–171.

36. Mansbach et al., *Web of World Politics,* pp. 200–204.
37. Europa Publications, *The Europa Year Book 1981: A World Survey* Volume I (London: Europa, 1981), p. 279.
38. Ibid., p. 283.
39. Ibid., pp. 216–217.
40. Turner, *Multinational Corporations,* pp. 192–198.

16
Transnational Ethnic Groups

Of all nonstate actors, none have gained more notoriety in recent years than transnational ethnic groups. Unfortunately, this has occurred because of the tactics employed by these groups; their salience cannot be attributed to worldwide concern over the plight of the individuals who constitute these international actors. These groups are often referred to as terrorist organizations, "national-liberation-freedom-fighters," and the like. For the purposes of this chapter, the use of the term "transnational ethnic groups" is an attempt to avoid ideological predispositions toward characterization of any group or movement as good or right versus bad or wrong. As the term implies, these groups are nations of people (ethnically defined) who live in two or more nation-states (none of which they control). In addition, they exhibit at least one political organization and typically employ violent means in their efforts to attain goals ranging from local autonomy to the creation of a new nation-state. Finally, these groups as organizations are important world actors both as primary causes of political violence and international tension and as conduits of the policies of nation-states.

The Palestine Liberation Organization (PLO) is the best known transnational ethnic group. It is the only such organization that has been extended de jure recognition by certain (mostly Arab) nation-states and permanent observer status in the UNGA. The Israelis and others may refuse to negotiate directly with the PLO, but no one would attempt to explain the present situation in the Middle East without listing the PLO as a principal actor. Other transnational ethnic groups fall far behind the PLO in organization, scope of activities, and income, but several have the potential to rival the PLO as an international actor. Of the many groups mentioned in Chapter 1, the Kurds have been the most important. This group and the Basque peoples constitute the remaining foci of this chapter.

The Palestine Liberation Organization

The PLO was created formally on May 28, 1964, at the opening session of the first Palestinian National Congress in Beirut, Lebanon. The PLO's first leader, Ahmed Shukairy, declared that all Palestinians would "sacrifice their blood for the liberation of Palestine" and accept no substitute homeland.[1] The PLO was not the first organization created by refugee Palestinians, nor was it organized by "ideologue terrorists" but rather by moderate middle-class Palestinians. Indeed, the major force behind the PLO's inception was not Palestinian at all. Egypt's President Nassar willed its creation as a leverage device and as a means of controlling the Palestinians. By 1969, however, the PLO had become the umbrella organization of nearly all the Palestinian splinter groups and was dominated by the largest of these groups, Al Fatah. These groups are held together by a number of factors: ideologies including varieties of Marxism, Pan-Arabism, Islam, and perhaps most importantly, the goal of an independent Palestine. In a practical sense, the dominant cementing agent is the perception of a common enemy: Israel and its supporters.

The PLO is the only transnational ethnic group that has a formal charter of sorts, namely, the "Palestinian Covenant." The Covenant declares that Palestine, because its territory was constituted under the British mandate, is the "homeland of the Arab Palestinian People."[2] It further maintains that "armed struggle is the only way to liberate Palestine. . . . It is the overall strategy, not merely a tactical phase."[3] The Covenant places responsibility for the liberation of Palestine upon all Arab peoples and governments[4] and declares illegal the establishment of the state of Israel, the Balfour Declaration, the Mandate for Palestine, and anything subsequent based on these actions.[5] The Covenant makes it quite clear that the PLO is in favor of armed popular revolution to secure sovereignty over the territory it defines as Palestine and that it takes a rejectionist stance on all other possible outcomes.[6]

History and Development

The origins of the current PLO can be traced to the 1948 war that followed the withdrawal of the British and precipitated the creation of the state of Israel and the expulsion or flight of 600,000 Arabs to surrounding Arab states. From 1948 until 1956, Palestinian "fedayeen" operated out of the Gaza strip, Lebanon, Syria, and Jordan, but no real organization existed even among groups operating raids against Israel from the same country. That situation changed in 1956 with the creation of Al Fatah. However, until 1967, the Palestinians' efforts to regain their homeland remained localized, fragmented, and victim to several intergroup and internation rivalries: the Iraqi revolution (1958), the Lebanese civil war (1958), the dissolution of the UAR (between Syria and Egypt, 1958–1961), and the Sudanese and Yemeni civil wars.[7]

The 1967 "Six-Day war" was a watershed for the PLO. Prior to that war, the PLO strategy was to act as a catalyst to the confrontation between Arab and Israeli military forces. The 1967 war and the resultant humiliation of the Arab states' armies had two effects: (1) they left both political and military vacuums that would be filled with Palestinian groups, and (2) the new refugees from the West Bank and Golan Heights significantly increased the "Palestinian man-power pool."

By 1969, Yasir Arafat and his Al Fatah (the Syrian Palestinian group) gained control of the PLO and the numerous associated splinter groups. That control was tenuous, however, and more extreme groups like the Popular Front for the Liberation of Palestine (PFLP) and Black September operated with virtual impunity. In September 1970, civil war in Jordan broke out, in part due to King Hussein's attempt to restrain Palestinian extremists' activities. Eventually, PLO military units were driven out of Jordan into Syria and Lebanon.

The 1973 Yom Kippur war generated increased power for the PLO. Although Arab armies regained some degree of self-esteem, the PLO benefitted tremendously—economically as a result of OPEC's price hikes and politically as a result of OAPEC's oil embargo and the decision of the Arab states to extend de jure recognition to the PLO. In 1974, the member-states of the Arab League accepted the PLO as a full member and stated that the PLO should assume complete responsibility for all Palestinians at the national and international levels. Two years later, the United Nations extended to the PLO the status of permanent observer (i.e., with all the rights and privileges of a member except voting).

The PLO significantly expanded its power and influence in the late 1970s. Buoyed by petro-dollar contributions from OAPEC states, the PLO managed financial concerns in Europe and Africa as well as in the Middle East, established an annual operating budget of over $1 billion, and built a regular army of 20,000 in four Arab states and irregular forces of 40,000 in Lebanon alone. The PLO established its "home base" in Beirut and assigned diplomats to information offices and embassies in 117 countries.[8]

Lebanon was the ideal location for the PLO. It offered excellent terrain for guerrilla warfare, put forth no strong central authority following the 1975–1976 civil war, and featured a common border with and to attack Israel.[9] On June 6, 1982, however, Israel launched "Peace for Galilee," an operation that would deprive the PLO of its independent bases from which to launch attacks directly into Israel and scatter to nine different countries the military command structure and regular forces that had been in Beirut. With that, the PLO lost its command as well as supply and media centers. Arafat was forced to move his headquarters to its present location in Tunis.[10]

Structure

The institutional structure of the PLO consists of the National Council (PNC), the Central Council (PCC), and the Executive Committee. The PNC consists of 301 members and serves as a consulting assembly. The PCC is made up of 55 members and is the presidium of the PNC. The real power of the PLO resides in the Executive Committee, led by Yasir Arafat (head of Al Fatah) and fourteen others representing seven other subgroups. The Executive Committee manages the Palestine National Fund, seven functional bureaus, and the Palestine Liberation Army. (See Fig. 16.1.) Since it directly represents the "liberation groups" under the PLO umbrella, the Executive Committee is a policymaking body as well as the executive arm of the PLO.

There are eight subgroups represented in the Executive Committee. Fatah (as the Palestine National Liberation Movement) is the oldest and largest. Based in Syria, it has espoused not "pan-Arabism," but nationalism, self-sufficiency (no dependence on any Arab state), and anti-Zionism. Its military arm is Al-Assifa ("the storm"). The second largest group is the Popular Front for the Liberation of Palestine (PFLP). This group evolved in 1968 from the Arab Nationalist Movement and several smaller groups under George Habash. The PFLP is predominantly Marxist: it views the liberation of Palestine as part of a larger revolution in all Arab states, and it advocates unity first, armed struggle second. The PFLP has advocated "terrorist tactics" against any and all who did not support the front. It opposed Fatah until that struggle for control of the PLO was settled in 1969. Terrorist acts outside Israel committed by factions of the PFLP are condemned by the PLO (i.e., criticized and disavowed by Fatah).

Other rejectionist factions of the PLO are the Democratic Popular Front for the Liberation of Palestine (DPFLP), the Arab Liberation Front (sponsored by Iraq), the Popular Struggle Front, and the Palestine-Liberation Front. Splinter (command) groups include the Popular Front for the Liberation of Palestine—General Command (PFLP-GC), Al Saiqa (Syrian-based), Al-Ansar (communist parties), and Black September (the latter two are not represented directly in the Executive Committee).[11] (See Figure 16.2.)

The Basques

The Basques reside in an area from the Bay of Biscay west into the Pyrenees Mountains on either side of the border between France and

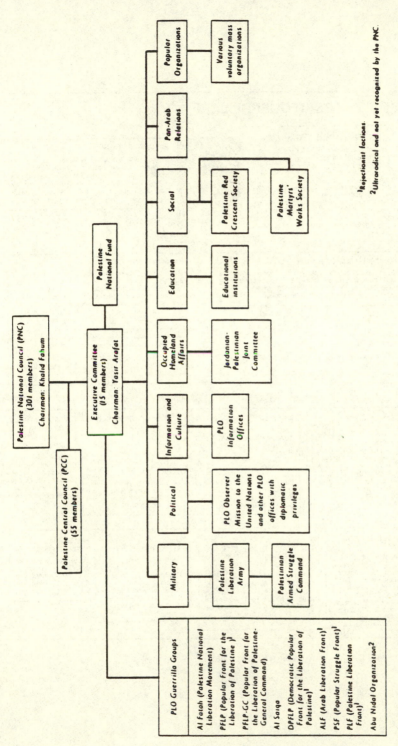

Figure 16.1 The Palestine Liberation Organization (1979)

Source: From Richard F. Nyrop, *Jordan: A Country Study,* courtesy of Foreign Area Studies, The American University. Washington. D.C.

224

THE PALESTINIAN GUERRILLAS

PALESTINE LIBERATION ORGANIZATION

Serves as umbrella organization for eight guerrilla groups, including four small ones that oppose any negotiated settlement of Middle East conflict. Formed in 1964. Came under control of Al Fatah, the main guerrilla organization, in 1969. Governed by 15-member Executive Committee dominated by Fatah and headed by Fatah leader, Yasir Arafat. Based officially in Damascus but actually in Beirut. Proclaimed by leaders of Arab countries at 1974 conference in Rabat, Morocco, as the only legitimate representative of the Palestinian people.

Yasir Arafat

EXECUTIVE COMMITTEE

Elected by P.L.O.'s legislative arm, the Palestine Liberation Council, with two of committee's 15 members from Al Fatah, one each from four other guerrilla groups including one of those that oppose peaceful Middle East settlement, and nine independents, most of whom back Mr. Arafat.

PALESTINE LIBERATION ARMY

Organization's regular army, numbering about 12,000 men, with units stationed in Syria, Egypt and Jordan. Headed by Yasir Arafat as "commander in chief of forces of the Palestinian Revolution."

PALESTINE NATIONAL COUNCIL

Palestinians' 295-member "Parliament in exile." Selected, not elected, for three-year term by Executive Committee from nominations made by Al Fatah and other member organizations. Roughly one-third from Fatah, one-third from other groups and one-third independents, most of whom back Mr. Arafat. Meets periodically in various Arab capitals.

PALESTINE ARMED STRUGGLE COMMAND

P.L.O.'s security or police organization, dominated by Al Fatah.

PALESTINE CENTRAL COUNCIL

A 55-member policy-making body selected by National Council to function while it is in recess. Based in Damascus.

P.L.O. GUERRILLA GROUPS

AL FATAH
About 10,000 members. Operates as fighting organization in Lebanon under name Al Asifah. Represented on P.L.O. Executive Committee by Yasir Arafat and Farouk Kaddoumi, the "foreign minister" of the P.L.O.

Farouk Kaddoumi

AS SAIQA
Perhaps 3,000 to 5,000 members, many of them Syrians. Represented on P.L.O.'s Executive Committee by its leader, Zuheir Mohsen, head of P.L.O.'s military department. Sponsored by Syria's governing Baath Party.

Zuheir Mohsen

DEMOCRATIC FRONT FOR THE LIBERATION OF PALESTINE
About 1,500 men. Led by Jordanian, Nayef Hawatmeh. Marxist oriented, pro-Soviet and close to Syria. Represented on P.L.O.'s Executive Committee.

POPULAR FRONT FOR LIBERATION OF PALESTINE—GENERAL COMMAND
About 500 men. Led by Ahmed Jabreel. Pro-Syrian. Represented on P.L.O.'s Executive Committee.

ARAB LIBERATION FRONT
Several hundred men. Led by Abdel Rahim Ahmed. Controlled by Iraq's governing Baath Party. Rejects peaceful Middle East settlement. Represented on P.L.O.'s Executive Committee.

POPULAR FRONT FOR THE LIBERATION OF PALESTINE
1,000 to 1,500 men. Led by Dr. George Habash. Rejects peaceful Middle East settlement. Quit P.L.O.'s Executive Committee in 1974.

Dr. George Habash

PALESTINE LIBERATION FRONT
About 150 men. Led by Abul Abbas. Backed by Iraq. Rejects peaceful settlement of Middle East conflict. Not represented on P.L.O.'s Executive Committee.

PALESTINIAN POPULAR FRONT
About 300 men. Led by Dr. Samir Ghosheh. Not represented on P.L.O.'s Executive Committee.

Figure 16.2 The Palestinian Guerrillas

Source: New York Times, February 21, 1978, p. 14. Copyright © by The New York Times Company. Reprinted by permission.

Spain. The four provinces in Spain (Alava, Guipúzcoa, Navarra, and Vizcaya) and three provinces in France (Labourd, Basse-Navarre, and Soule) constitute what is referred to in the Basque language as *Euzkadi.* This small region (ca. 20,000 km²) has been much in the news, due primarily to acts of terrorism committed against the Spanish government in the name of Basque independence. The population of some two million Basques, of whom one-third speak *Euskera,* has been the focus of much of the recent literature on ethnic nationalism and separatist movements.[12]

Scholars disagree as to the exact age of the Basque culture. However, there is sufficient evidence that it is older than any of the other tribes that formed the origins of other modern European ethnic groups.[13] The core of the Basque language is completely unlike any other European tongue.[14] The history of this group reveals a consistent effort to promote Basque culture and political autonomy and to resist outside domination. Although Rome dominated the Basques completely, the fall of the Roman Empire initiated several centuries of Basque autonomy, including a successful resistance against the Moorish invasion of the Iberian peninsula. Until the eighteenth century, the Basque region operated as a loose conglomerate of autonomous provinces and cities, each of which negotiated agreements with their more powerful Spanish and French neighbors (called *fueros* or *fors* in French).

The modern history of the Basque region is viewed best as two separate developments, that of the Basques in the Spanish provinces and that of the Basques in France. As early as the beginning of the eighteenth century, the Spanish Basque region had become important to the Spanish Crown. Iron-ore deposits and good natural harbors had contributed to Spain's growth as a colonial power, and these resources were an essential component of the Spanish economy. Consequently, Spain could no longer permit political autonomy to a region vital to its economic well-being. Spain began an incremental process to subjugate the Basques completely, and this brutal suppression under the Castilian monarchy was culminated by the end of the Second Carlist War (1876).[15]

During the latter 1800s, Spain attempted systematically to destroy Basque culture (especially the language and educational system) and nationalism by means of measures to force assimilation as Castilians. The first direct reaction occurred in 1893, when Sabino de Arana y Goiri established the Partido Nationalista Vasco (PNV). The PNV's initial goals were to restore Basque nationalism, to stop intermarriage between Basques and non-Basques, and to expel non-Basques from the region. During the first thirty years of the twentieth century, the PNV enjoyed substantial success, particularly in attracting large numbers of followers. With the advent of the Second Spanish Republic in 1931, the

PNV emerged from its underground activities, reestablished its organizational structure, and presented the new Spanish Parliament with a statute of autonomy. In 1936, the leftist government granted autonomy to the region, a coalition government was formed, and a president was elected for the Basque provinces. However, the Spanish Civil War ended autonomy almost before it began. In June 1937, Franco's forces overran the area and reinstituted a total repression of the Basques.[16] Franco's attitude was reflected in the words of his governor in Alava during the civil war: "These abominable separatists do not deserve a homeland. Basque nationalism must be ruined, trampled underfoot, ripped out by its roots."[17] The draconian measures and brutality of Franco's forces served to galvanize a generation of Basques who had been lukewarm toward the issue of Basque nationalism.

In the 1940s and 1950s, Spanish repression did not eradicate Basque culture, but it did succeed in diminishing the opportunity for expressions of Basque nationalism. The year 1960 marked a radical change. Labor strikes, clergy demonstrations, and direct violence against the Guardia Civile began what were to be continual occurrences throughout the decade of the 1960s. The youth arm of the PNV tired of inaction and broke away to form Euzkadi ta Askatasuna (Basque Nation and Freedom, or ETA). This group limited its activities to distributing pamphlets and displaying the illegal Basque flag, until violent raids ordered by the Franco regime against them drove them toward extremism and further underground. In 1962, the group's leaders proclaimed a new definition of the ETA: "a clandestine revolutionary organization with three fronts: cultural, political, and military."[18]

The ETA gained world attention in 1968 when some of its members "executed" Meliton de Manzanas, the chief of secret police of Guipuzcoa. The Franco regime redoubled its efforts to crush the ETA but, as before, the ETA was driven to greater militancy and into hiding. Franco's lack of success in eradicating the ETA was complicated further by dramatic increases in Basque lower-clergy activism. The Spanish authorities, without regard for the Concordat with the Vatican that required the prior consent of the arrested priest's bishop, began to arrest priests suspected of supporting the ETA. The extreme rift between church and state over this issue led as well to a rift between the lower clergy and the church hierarchy. A letter signed by 500 priests in 1969 to the Spanish Episcopal Conference decried the mild and equivocal attitude of the northern bishops.[19]

The ETA accelerated its "guerrilla" tactics in the Basque provinces during the early 1970s. By 1975, the Franco government faced its most dramatic internal crisis since the Spanish civil war. However, Franco's physical collapse and subsequent demise caused an amelioration in the

ETA's violent activities. The political reforms instituted by several governments since the ascendancy of King Juan Carlos did not end ETA violence. The new ideology of the ETA goes beyond expressions of nationalism and regional autonomy. Its leadership views the organization as one engaged in a class struggle, and the robberies, kidnappings, and assassinations continue.

The history of the French Basque people differs importantly from that of the Basques in Spain. Unlike the Spanish Basque region, the three French provinces have neither the excellent harbors nor mineral wealth that made the Basque provinces so important to Spain. Consequently, the French Basques enjoyed great autonomy through most of the nineteenth century by reason of neglect by Paris. Cut off from their more economically advantaged southern kinsman, the French Basques inhabited a bucolic, ignored, poor agricultural backwater of France, where mere survival took precedence over nationalistic activism.

Autonomy in the French Basque provinces ended abruptly after the 1789 revolution. The Jacobins responded to the religious-based resistance to the new regime by centralizing administrative control in the region and incorporating the three provinces into one department. However, successive governmental changes in France contributed to governmental amnesia, and the region soon regained its political anonymity. The creation of the PNV had no parallel in France. Little occurred until the Spanish Civil War, when hundreds of thousands of Spanish Basques fled into France. The French government assisted the refugees and went so far as to recognize the Basque government and extend "government-in-exile" status.[20] However, the World War II Vichy government was hostile toward the "Basque cause" and instituted severe repression and complete cooperation with Franco.

The post-war French Fourth Republic had little sympathy for fascism in Spain, and the French Basques were rewarded for their wartime resistance efforts by a return of local autonomy. However, the French government's attitude of benign neglect and its refusal to invest economically in the Basque region engendered the perception there that the Basques were the "bastard child" of France. For reasons of economic deprivation more than political repression, a French Basque nationalist party, Enbata, was formed in 1963. Enbata's founders called for an economic union of the French and Spanish Basque provinces, and accused the French government of deliberately restricting their economic development in order to use the region as a tourist park.[21]

By the mid-1960s, de Gaulle had decided to effect a rapprochement with Franco. In addition, increased ETA violence against Spanish law-enforcement officials began to foster an affinity among French authorities for their beleaguered Spanish counterparts. Those factors added to concern over local ethnic movements in Brittany, Occitania, Alsace, and Corsica, and the ETA's radicalizing effect in Enbata caused Paris to increase pressure on the Basque region. In 1971 and 1972, French police violently broke up celebrations of *Aberri Eguna,* the Basque national holiday. Basque cultural leaders were fired from teaching positions in state schools. Enbata leaders proclaimed that France had no meaning as a political entity and that the French-Spanish border was like the Berlin Wall: "a crime against nature and a wall of shame."[22] In 1974, Enbata expanded its scope of operations and claimed responsibility for several bombings in Lyon. The French government responded by officially banning Enbata and increasing political pressure over the region. Enbata was driven underground and into closer cooperation with the ETA, a situation not even contemplated in the 1960s.

The Kurds

The Kurds are (perhaps) 10 million "wild and unruly nomads"[23] who live in portions of Turkey, Armenia, Syria, Iraq, and Iran. They are a nation whose culture and language are very old, although there exists no hard evidence to trace the exact age. The modern history of the Kurds begins with the dismemberment of the Ottoman Empire and the 1920 Treaty of Sèvres that provided for local autonomy in most of the Kurdish region. That autonomy, however, was never permitted. Kemal Ataturk repudiated the 1920 treaty, and the 1923 Treaty of Lausanne he negotiated following his victory over Greece made no mention of the Kurds or their demands for local autonomy.

Expressions of Kurdish nationalism in the 1920s and 1930s took the form of uprisings in Turkey under the leadership of Mullah Mustapha Barzani. All of these uprisings were crushed with considerable violence. After the British and Soviets occupied Iran in 1941, the Soviets created the short-lived Kurdish Republic of Mahabad. When Soviet forces withdrew in 1945, however, the Iranian army defeated the tiny Mahabad army, executing the Republic's leaders and sending Barzani into a ten-year exile in the Soviet Union.

By the mid-1950s, the focus of Kurdish nationalism switched to Iraq. The Iraqi Kurds living in the mountain regions of Eastern Iraq claimed to have a population of one-quarter million, or just over one-fourth of Iraq's total population. Yet the Iraqi government totally ignored the Kurds, leaving them to primitive agriculture (mostly tobacco) while oil and jobs in the oil fields at Arbil and Kirkuk went completely to the Arabs. In 1954, the United Democratic Party of Kurdistan (UDKP) was formed and Barzani, still in exile in the USSR, was chosen party leader. Barzani was permitted entry into Iraq in 1958, and the UDKP was reorganized as the Kurdistan Democratic Party (KDP) under his leadership.

The 1960s are known in Iraq as the period of the Kurdish Revolt.[24] When in 1961 the Iraqis began a campaign of repression in the Kurdish region, Barzani and his KDP fled to the mountains. Barzani's forces defeated or coopted all rival Kurdish tribes and the KDP quickly grew in power. Barzani formed the Pesh Merga (or "they who face death") and fought major battles with Iraqi Forces in 1963, 1965, 1966, and 1969 (January and August). All of these battles ended in either stalemate or victory for the Pesh Merga. In March 1970, the Iraqis offered a 15-article peace agreement that would have granted Kurdish autonomy by 1974 and Barzani undisputed control over the KDP and most Iraqi Kurds. However, the Kurds repudiated the agreement for three reasons: (1) the "autonomous" administration was to have been appointed in Baghdad rather than elected by Kurds; (2) the Kurds would not be permitted to participate in the Iraqi national government; and (3) the oil fields in the Kurdish region were expressly excluded from the agreement.[25]

A local war broke out again in March 1974. The Kurds achieved military success initially, due largely to the secret support of Iran by supplying weapons and sanctuary. The KDP became a de facto government behind their "lines," establishing a slim but efficient government infrastructure (especially in education and health—areas largely ignored by Baghdad). However, the necessity to fight on three fronts forced Barzani to retreat again into the mountains. Early in 1975, the Iraqi Air Force began strafing urban Kurds with napalm and phosphorous bombs. An extremely harsh winter, a growing refugee problem, and governmental responsibility for areas hit by Iraqi terror raids (and an unwillingness to abandon completely civilians to Iraqi forces) made the Pesh Merga's guerrilla tactics increasingly problematic. The final blow to the fortunes of the Kurds occurred on March 6, 1975, at the Algiers OPEC conference. Iran and Iraq concluded a secret agreement by which Iran pledged to close its border to the Iraqi Kurds. Iran immediately stopped arms supplies to the Kurds, and Iraq sent three divisions (38,000 men) against the Kurds. Remarkably, Barzani's forces achieved the impossible, halting the Iraqi forces after seven days of fighting. On April 1, however, Iran formally and effectively sealed their border, cutting off all supplies and, more importantly, the use of their territory for safe haven. The resultant refugee problems and Iranian "treachery" forced a decision not to fight on. Barzani fled to Teheran where he was placed under house arrest.[26]

Fittingly, the focus of Kurdish nationalism shifted next to Iran in 1979. Iranian Kurds were most active first in the revolution to remove the Shah, then against Khomeini and his Islamic Constitution. (See the related discussion in Chapter 1.)

States of Integration

As with multinational corporations and international labor, theories of international political integration have little explanatory utility for transnational ethnic groups. There is, however, a relatively small body of "theoretical" literature on ethnic nationalism. C. R. Foster argues that when a central government responds positively to ethnic group demands, there is a concomitant lessening of tensions between the group or groups and the central government.[27] Milton M. da Silva's study on Basque nationalism refutes many of the theoretical assumptions of the political integration literature:

> The recent upsurge in Basque nationalism (1) runs counter to the generally accepted view that the level of ethnic discord varies directly with the degree of distinctiveness between groups; (2) raises questions concerning the widely held assumption that ethnic conflict can be explained in terms of economic inequality or class structure; (3) casts doubt on the hypothesis, closely associated with Donald Horowitz, that career aspirations constitute a major variable in ethnic struggles; (4) disputes the validity of the thesis that the level of ethnic dissonance is predictably influenced by the relative position of the state government on the authoritarian-democracy continuum; and (5) challenges the theory, most often associated with Karl Deutsch and Lucian Pye, that increases in social mobilization and communication have an integrating effect upon ethnically heterogeneous societies.[28]

For transnational ethnic groups, the extent and sophistication of organization do no necessarily correlate with the group's success in achieving its goals. Clearly, the PLO exhibits the greatest degree of institutional integration among the three groups considered in this chapter. Yet the primary nation-state government with whom the PLO has grievances, Israel, totally refuses to communicate with the PLO, and the PLO has consistently refused to recognize the state of Israel. In addition, the PLO experienced major setbacks in its organizational structure. In 1982, Israeli forces succeeded in driving out of West and South Lebanon a major component of the PLO army. In its expulsion from Beirut, the PLO lost a base of operations in which it could direct its political and economic operations with relative impunity from the Lebanese authorities. Perhaps more importantly, when Arafat moved the PLO "capital" to Tunis, the PLO forfeited a front-line state head-quarters. During 1983, Arafat had to contend with an uprising among the radical groups in his organization that threatened to depose and/ or assassinate him. PLO forces in East Lebanon felt that he was becoming too moderate toward Israel and refused to recognize his leadership, preferring instead to take their cues from the Syrian forces in Lebanon. The Syrians again pressed for control of the PLO by supporting the anti-moderates in the organization. Syrian President Al-Assad expelled Arafat from Syria, permitting him only six hours to leave Damascus. The internal disputes between radical and moderate PLO elements place not only Arafat's leadership in doubt, but PLO fortunes as well.

The Kurds have never had a true transnational organization. Nationalistic movements shifted from one nation to another over time: Turkey in the 1920s and 1930s; Iran in the 1940s; Iraq in the 1960s and 1970s; and Iran again in the 1980s. The most successful Kurdish organizations, the KDP and Pesh Merga, were confined largely to the conflict in East Iraq and did not spill over into the Kurdish regions of Turkey, Syria, and Iran. Indeed, rival Kurdish tribes in those countries wanted local autonomy, but thwarted Barzani's efforts to expand his organization. Following the Iranian Revolution, the Kurds have been used as foils by central governments, first by Khomeini to fight "satan" America (in part to diminish their grievances against Khomeini's repressive regime and Islamic Constitution), then by both governments in the conduct of the Iraq-Iran war.

Violent expressions of Basque nationalism diminished markedly following the death of Franco and the ascension of Juan Carlos. Post-Franco attempts by the Spanish government to recognize the cultural rights of ethnic minorities have served to deradicalize the population and to isolate the extremists. The evidence suggests that general support for the ETA has fallen dramatically. However, even the election of a Socialist government in Spain has not changed the intensity of ETA activities due to the increased ideological (i.e., Marxist) character of the ETA. Having experienced a loss of identitive appeal among the Spanish Basque population, the ETA has moved to strengthen ties with the French Enbata. In France, the benign neglect by Paris that exacerbates economic hardship in the region tends to amplify the voices of radical systemic change and to create an environment for increased transnational organization in the larger Basque region.

Notes

1. *New York Times,* May 29, 1964, p. 5, and May 31, 1964, p. 6.
2. Articles 1 and 2 of the Palestinian Covenant. The Covenant Articles are discussed in detail in Yahoshafat Harkabi, *The Palestinian Covenant and Its Meaning* (London: Valentine, Mitchell, 1979).

3. Article 9 of the Covenant.

4. Article 15 of the Covenant.

5. Articles 19–20 of the Covenant.

6. Article 21 of the Covenant.

7. See Peter Mansfield, *The Arabs* (New York: Penguin Books, 1978), pp. 277–316.

8. Grace Halsell, "Yasir Arafat: The Man and His People," *The Link* (July/August, 1982), p. 3.

9. Paul A. Jureidini and William E. Hazen, *The Palestinian Movement in Politics* (Lexington, Mass.: Lexington Books, 1976), p. 25.

10. Richard F. Nyrop (Ed.), *Jordan: A Country Study* (Washington, D.C.: American University Press, 1980), p. 174.

11. Richard W. Mansbach, Yale H. Ferguson, and Donald E. Lampert, *The Web of World Politics: Non-State Actors in the Global System* (Englewood Cliffs, N.J.: Prentice-Hall, 1976), pp. 109–118.

12. Cf. C. R. Foster (Ed.), *Nations Without a State: Ethnic Minorities in Western Europe* (New York: Praeger Publishers, 1980); R. P. Clark, *The Franco Years and Beyond* (Reno: University of Nevada Press, 1979); Rachel Bard, *Navarra: The Durable Kingdom* (Reno: University of Nevada Press, 1982); Patricia Elton Mayo, *The Roots of Identity: Three National Movements in Contemporary European Politics* (London: Allen, Lane, 1974); and Stanley G. Payne, *Basque Nationalism* (Reno: University of Nevada Press, 1975).

13. Clark, *The Franco Years,* p. 10.

14. Payne, *Basque Nationalism,* p. 9.

15. Ibid., pp. 72–73.

16. Clark, *The Franco Years,* p. 76.

17. Ibid., p. 80.

18. Ibid., p. 157.

19. Milton M. da Silva, "Modernization and Ethnic Conflict: The Case of the Basques," *Comparative Politics* (January 1975), pp. 234–235.

20. Mayo, *Roots of Identity,* p. 124.

21. da Silva, "Modernization," p. 236.

22. Ibid.

23. John Stathatos, "Indestructable Kurds," *Geographical Magazine* 48 (January 1976), p. 231.

24. For details on this period, see Edgar O. Ballance, *The Kurdish Revolt: 1961–1970* (Hamden, Conn.: Archon Books, 1973).

25. Stathatos, "Indestructable Kurds," pp. 231–235.

26. Ibid.

27. C. R. Foster, "The Unrepresented Nations," in Foster (Ed.), *Nations Without a State,* p. 3.

28. da Silva, "Modernization," p. 228.

Selected Bibliography

Atkins, G. Pope. *Latin America in the International Political System.* New York: Free Press, 1977.

Al-Otaiba, Mana Saeed. *OPEC and the Petroleum Industry.* New York: John Wiley & Sons, 1975.

Almond, G. A., and Coleman, J. S. *The Politics of the Developing Areas.* Princeton, N.J.: Princeton University Press, 1960.

Ansprenger, Franz. *Die Befreiungspolitik der Organisation fur Afrikanische Finheit.* Munich: Welforum Verlag, 1975.

Apter, D. E. *The Politics of Modernization.* Chicago: University of Chicago Press, 1965.

Ball, M. Margaret. *The OAS in Transition.* Durham, N.C.: Duke University Press, 1969.

Ballance, Edgar O. *The Kurdish Revolt: 1961–1970.* Hamden, Conn.: Anchor Books, 1973.

Banks, Arthur S., and Overstreet, William, eds. *Political Handbook of the World.* New York: McGraw-Hill, 1981.

Bard, Rachel. *Navarra: The Durable Kingdom.* Reno: University of Nevada Press, 1982.

Barnet, Richard J., and Muller, Ronald E. *Global Reach: The Power of the Multinational Corporations.* New York: Simon and Schuster, 1974.

Bastin, John, and Benda, Harry J. *A History of Modern Southeast Asia.* Englewood Cliffs, N.J.: Prentice-Hall, 1968.

Behr, Gerhard. *Judicial Control of the European Communities.* New York: Praeger Publishers, 1962.

Beer, Francis A. *Integration and Disintegration in NATO: Processes of Alliance Cohesion and Prospects for Atlantic Community.* Columbus: Ohio State University Press, 1969.

Biersteker, Thomas J. *Distortion or Development: Contending Perspectives on the Multinational Corporation.* Cambridge, Mass.: MIT Press, 1978.

Bozeman, Adda B. *Conflict in Africa.* Princeton, N.J.: Princeton University Press, 1976.

Call, Arthur. *Modern International Negotiation: Principles and Practice.* New York: Columbia University Press, 1966.

Calleo, David. *Europe's Future: The Grand Alternatives.* New York: Horizon Press, 1965.

Calmann, John, ed. *The Common Market.* London: Anthony Bland, 1967.

Cervenka, Zdenek. *The Organization of African Unity and Its Charter.* London: Hurst and Co., 1969.

Chime, Chimelu. *Integration and Politics Among African States.* Uppsala: Scandinavian Institute of African Studies, 1977.

Clark, R. P. *The Franco Years and Beyond.* Reno: University of Nevada Press, 1979.

Cobb, Roger W., and Elder, Charles. *International Community: A Regional and Global Study.* New York: Holt, Rinehart and Winston, 1970.

Coombes, David. *Politics and Bureaucracy in the European Community: A Portrait of the Commission of the EEC.* London: George Allen and Unwin, 1970.

Copley and Associates, eds. *Defense and Foreign Affairs Handbook.* Washington, D.C.: Government Printing Office, 1980.

Cottrell, Alvin J., ed. *The Persian Gulf States.* Baltimore: Johns Hopkins University Press, 1980.

Council on International Economic Policy. *Special Report: Critical Imported Materials.* Washington, D.C.: Government Printing Office, 1974.

Curtis, Michael. *Western European Integration.* New York: Harper and Row, 1969.

Department of Economic and Social Affairs. *Multinational Corporations in Work Development.* New York: United Nations, 1973.

Deutsch, Karl. *International Political Communities: An Anthology.* New York: Doubleday, 1966.

––––––. *Nationalism and Social Communication.* Cambridge, Mass.: Harvard University Press, 1966.

––––––. *Political Community and the North Atlantic Area: International Organization in the Light of Historical Experience.* Princeton, N.J.: Princeton University Press, 1957.

DeWitt, Peter R. *The Inter-American Development Bank and Political Influence.* New York: Praeger Publishers, 1977.

Dougherty, James E., and Pfaltzgraff, Robert L. *Contending Theories of International Relations: A Comprehensive Survey.* 2nd ed. New York: Harper and Row, 1981.

Drucker, P. F. *Technology, Management and Society.* New York: Harper and Row, 1970.

Etzioni, Amitai. *Political Unification: A Comparative Study of Leaders and Forces.* New York: Holt, Rinehart and Winston, 1965.

European Community Information Service. *The European Community: The Facts.* Washington, D.C., February 1974.

Falk, Richard A., and Mendlovitz, Saul H., eds. *Regional Politics and World Order.* San Francisco: W. H. Freeman and Company, 1973.

Feld, Werner J. *Non-Governmental Forces and World Politics: A Study of Business, Labor, and Political Groups.* New York: Praeger Publishers, 1972.

Feld, Werner J., and Boyd, Gavin, eds. *Comparative Regional Systems.* New York: Pergamon Press, 1980.

Fifield, Russell H. *Americans in South East Asia.* New York: Crowell, 1973.

Fitzmaurice, John. *The European Parliament.* New York: Praeger Publishers, 1977.

Foster, C. R., ed. *Nations Without a State: Ethnic Minorities in Western Europe.* New York: Praeger Publishers, 1970.

Friedrich, C. J. *Trends of Federalism in Theory and Practice.* London: Allen and Urwin, 1968.

Glasgow, R. *Die Arabische Welt: Geschichte, Probleme, Prospektives.* Freiburg: Verlag Ploetz, 1978.

Haas, Ernst. *The Uniting of Europe: Political, Social, and Economic Forces 1950–1957.* Stanford, Calif.: Stanford University Press, 1958.

———. *The Obsolescence of Regional Integration Theory.* Berkeley, Calif.: Institute of International Peace, 1975.

Halle, Louis J. *The Cold War as History.* New York: Harper and Row, 1971.

Harkabi, Yahoshafat. *The Palestinian Covenant and Its Meaning.* London: Valentine, Mitchell, 1979.

Hay, Peter. *Federalism and Supranational Organizations: Patterns for New Legal Structures.* Urbana: University of Illinois Press, 1966.

Hassound, H. A. *The League of Arab States and Regional Disputes.* Dobbs Ferry, N.Y.: Oceana Publications, 1975.

Hatem, M. Abdel-Kadar. *Information and the Arab Cause.* London: Longman Group, 1974.

Hazelwood, Arthur. *African Integration and Disintegration.* London: Oxford University Press, 1967.

Herman, Valentine, and Lodge, Juliet. *The European Parliament and the European Community.* New York: St. Martin's Press, 1978.

Houben, P.H.S.M. *Les Conseils des Ministres des Communautés Européennes.* Leiden: Sijthoff, 1964.

Hudson, Michael C. *Arab Politics: The Search for Legitimacy.* New Haven, Conn.: Yale University Press, 1977.

Jureidini, Paul A., and Hazen, William E. *The Palestinian Movement in Politics.* Lexington, Mass.: Lexington Books, 1976.

Kahin, George M., and Lewis, John W. *The United States in Vietnam.* Rev. ed. New York: Dial Press, 1969.

Kapoor, Ashok, and Boddewny, J. J. *International Business-Government Relations vs. Corporate Experience in Asia and Western Europe.* New York: Amacom, 1973.

Kelly, J. B. *Arabia, the Gulf, and the West.* New York: Basic Books, 1980.

Keohane, Robert O., and Nye, Joseph S., Jr. *Power and Interdependence. World Politics in Transition.* Boston: Little, Brown and Co., 1977.

Kindleberger, C. P. *American Business Abroad: Six Lectures on Direct Investment.* New Haven, Conn.: Yale University Press, 1969.

Kitchen, Helen. *Africa: From Mystery to Maze.* Lexington, Mass.: Lexington Books, 1976.

Larsen, Stanley R., and Collins, James L. *Allied Participation in Vietnam.* Washington, D.C.: Government Printing Office, 1975.

Le Vine, Victor, and Luke, Timothy. *The Arab-African Connection: Political and Economic Realities.* Boulder, Colo: Westview Press, 1979.

Levy, M. J., Jr. *The Structure of Society.* Princeton, N.J.: Princeton University Press, 1952.

Lindberg, Leon N., and Scheingold, Stuart A. *Europe's Would-be Polity: Patterns of Change in the European Community.* Englewood Cliffs, N.J.: Prentice-Hall, 1970.

Lindberg, Leon N., and Scheingold, Stuart A. (eds.). *Regional Integration: Theory and Research.* Cambridge, Mass.: Harvard University Press, 1971.

Liska, George. *Europe Ascendant: The International Politics of Unification.* Baltimore: Johns Hopkins Press, 1964.

McCann, Thomas. *An American Company: The Tragedy of United Fruit.* New York: Crown Publishers, 1976.

Macdonald, R. W. *The League of Arab States.* Princeton, N.J.: Princeton University Press, 1965.

Mangone, Gerald J. *A Short History of International Organization.* New York: McGraw-Hill, 1954.

Mansbach, Richard W., Ferguson, Yale H., and Lampert, Donald E. *The Web of World Politics: Non-State Actors in the Global System.* Englewood Cliffs, N.J.: Prentice-Hall, 1976.

Mansfield, Peter. *The Arabs.* New York: Penguin Books, 1978.

Moskowitz, Moses. *International Concern with Human Rights.* Dobbs Ferry, N.Y.: Oceana Publications, 1974.

Mayo, Patricia Elton. *The Roots of Identity: Three National Movements in Contemporary European Politics.* London: Allen, Lane, 1974.

Mazrui, Ali. *Africa's International Relations.* Boulder, Colo.: Westview Press, 1977.

Mitrany, David. *The Progress of International Government.* New Haven, Conn.: Yale University Press, 1933.

Modelski, George. *Transnational Corporations and World Order: Readings in International Political Economy.* San Francisco: W. H. Freeman and Company, 1979.

Morawetz, David. *The Andean Group: A Case Study in Economic Integration Among Developing Countries.* Cambridge, Mass.: MIT Press, 1974.

Morgan, Roger. *Western European Politics Since 1945: The Shaping of the European Community.* London: B. T. Batsford, 1972.

Musrey, A. G. *An Arab Common Market.* New York: Praeger Publishers, 1969.

Nash, Henry T. *American Foreign Policy: Changing Perspectives on National Security.* Homewood, Ill.: Dorsey Press, 1978.

National Association of Manufacturers. *U.S. Stake in World Trade and Investment: The Role of the Multinational Corporation.* New York: NAM, n.d.

NATO Information Service. *The Atlantic Alliance and the Warsaw Pact: A Comparative Study.* Brussels: NATO Information Service, 1980.

————. *NATO: Facts About the North Atlantic Treaty Organization.* Brussels: NATO Information Service, 1980.

————. *NATO Handbook.* Brussels: NATO Information Service, 1980.

Nye, Joseph S. *Peace in Parts: Integration and Conflict in International Organization.* Boston: Little, Brown and Co., 1971.

Nyrop, Richard F., ed. *Jordan: A Country Study.* Washington, D.C.: American University Press, 1980.

Organization for Economic Cooperation and Development. *Development Cooperation: 1981 Review.* Paris: OECD Secretariat, 1928.

Palmer, Michael, and Lambert, John. *Handbook of European Organizations.* New York: Praeger Publishers, 1968.

Payne, Stanley G. *Basque Nationalism.* Reno: University of Nevada Press, 1975.

Pentland, Charles. *International Theory and European Integration.* New York: Free Press, 1973.

Polach, Jaroslav G. *Euratom: Its Background, Issues and Economic Implications.* Dobbs Ferry, N.Y.: Oceana Publications, 1964.

Ramphal, Shridath, ed. *One World to Share: Selected Speeches of the Commonwealth Secretary-General.* London: Hutchinson Denham, 1979.

Remington, Robin A. *The Warsaw Pact: Case Studies in Communist Conflict Resolution.* Cambridge, Mass.: MIT Press, 1971.

Riker, W. H. *Federalism: Origin, Operation, Significance.* Boston: Little, Brown and Co., 1964.

Robertson, A. H. *European Institutions: Co-operation: Integration: Unification.* New York: Mathew Bender, 1973.

Rosenau, James N., ed. *Linkage Politics.* New York: Free Press, 1969.

Rosenthal, Glenda G. *The Men Behind the Decisions: Cases in European Policy-Making.* Lexington, Mass.: Lexington Books, 1975.

Rubin, Leslie, and Weinstein, Brian. *Introduction to African Politics.* New York: Praeger Publishers, 1974.

Sampson, Anthony. *The Seven Sisters: The Great Oil Companies and the World They Made.* New York: Viking Press, 1975.

Scheingold, Stuart A. *The Rule of Law in European Integration: The Path of the Schuman Plan.* New Haven, Conn.: Yale University Press, 1965.

Secretariat of the European Parliament. *Europe Today: State of European Integration.* Luxembourg: European Parliament, 1976.

Sewell, James Patrick. *Functionalism and World Politics.* Princeton, N.J.: Princeton University Press, 1966.

Slater, Jerome. *The OAS and United States Foreign Policy.* Columbus: Ohio State University Press, 1967.

Solem, E. *The Nordic Council and Scandinavian Integration.* New York: Praeger Publishers, 1977.

Spero, Joan Edelman. *The Politics of International Economic Relations.* 2nd ed. New York: St. Martin's Press, 1981.

Spinelli, Altiero. *The Eurocrats: Conflict and Crisis in the European Community.* Baltimore: Johns Hopkins Press, 1966.

Staar, Richard F. *The Communist Regimes in Eastern Europe.* Stanford, Calif.: Hoover Institution, 1971.

Sullivan, Michael P. *International Relations: Theories and Evidence.* Englewood Cliffs, N.J.: Prentice-Hall, 1976.

Sundelius, B. *Managing Transnationalism in Northern Europe.* Boulder, Colo.: Westview Press, 1978.

Taylor, Alice, ed. *Focus on Latin America.* New York: Praeger Publishers, 1973.

Taylor, Phillip. *When Europe Speaks with One Voice: The External Relations of the European Community.* Westport, Conn.: Greenwood Press, 1979.

Tharp, Paul, ed. *Regional International Organizations: Structures and Functions.* New York: St. Martin's Press, 1971.

Turner, Louis. *Multinational Corporations and the Third World.* New York: Hill and Wang, 1973.

UNITAR, ed. *Regionalism and the New International Economic Order.* New York: Pergamon Press, 1981.

Vernon, Raymond. *Sovereignty at Bay: The Multinational Spread of U.S. Enterprises.* New York: Basic Books, 1971.

———. *Storm over the Multinationals: The Real Issues.* Cambridge, Mass.: Harvard University Press, 1977.

Walker, Andrew. *The Commonwealth: A New Look.* New York: Pergamon Press, 1978.

Wardlaw, Andrew B. *The Andean Integration Movement: A Report Prepared Under Contract for the U.S. Department of State.* Washington, D.C.: Government Printing Office, 1973.

Wendt, F. *The Nordic Council and Cooperation in Scandinavia.* Copenhagen: Munksgaard, 1959.

Wiener, Friedrich, and Lewis, William J. *The Warsaw Pact Armies.* Vienna: Carl Veberreuter Publishers, 1977.

Willis, F. Roy. *France, Germany, and the New Europe 1945–1963.* Stanford, Calif.: Stanford University Press, 1965.

Abbreviations

AASM	Associated African States and Madagascar
ACCHAN	Allied Command Channel
ACE	Allied Command Europe
ACLANT	Allied Command Atlantic
ACP	African, Caribbean, and Pacific
AFCENT	Allied Forces Central Europe
AFNORTH	Allied Forces Northern Europe
AFSOUTH	Allied Forces Southern Europe
ALADI	Latin American Association of Integration
ALCOA	Aluminum Company of America
ANCOM	Andean Common Market
ANZUS Pact	Australia, New Zealand, and the United States
ARPEL	Assistencia Reciproca Petrolera Estatal Latinoamerica
ASA	Association of Southeast Asia
ASEAN	Association of South East Asian Nations
CACM	Central American Common Market
CAP	Common Agricultural Policy
CARICOM	Caribbean Community and Common Market
CARIFTA	Caribbean Free Trade Association
CENTO	Central Treaty Organization
CEPS	Central European Pipeline System
CIEP	Council on International Economic Policy
CINCHAN	Allied Commander-in-Chief/Channel Command
CIPEC	Conseil Intergouvernemental des Pays Exportateurs du Cuivre
CMEA	Council for Mutual Economic Assistance
COMECON	Council for Mutual Economic Assistance
COPA	Committee of Professional Agricultural Organizations
COREPER	Committee of Permanent Representatives
CSC	Combined Supreme Command

CSCE	Conference on Security and Cooperation in Europe
DAC	Development Assistance Committee
DDR	German Democratic Republic
DPC	Defense Planning Committee
DPFLP	Democratic Popular Front for the Liberation of Palestine
EAC	East African Community
EC	European Community
ECOWAS	Economic Community of West African States
ECSC	European Coal and Steel Committee
ECU	European Currency Unit
EDC	European Defense Community
EEC	European Economic Community
EFTA	European Free Trade Association
EMS	European Monetary System
ESC	Economic and Social Committee
ETA	Euzakadi ta Askatasuna (Basque Nation and Freedom)
Euratom	European Atomic Energy Community
GATT	General Agreement on Tariffs and Trade
GM	General Motors
GNP	gross national product
IBA	International Bauxite Association
IBM	International Business Machines
ICFTU	International Confederation of Free Trade Unions
ICJ	International Court of Justice
IDB	Inter-American Development Bank
IEA	International Energy Agency
IFCTU	International Federation of Christian Trade Unions
IGO	international governmental organization
ILU	International Longshoremen's Union
INGO	international nongovernmental organization
IOC	International Olympic Committee
IRA	Irish Republican Army
ITT	International Telephone and Telegraph
JDL	Jewish Defense League
KDP	Kurdistan Democratic Party
LAFTA	Latin American Free Trade Association
MBFRCE	Mutual and Balanced Force Reductions in Central Europe

MNC	Multinational Corporation
MNE	Multinational Enterprise
MPLA	Popular Movement for the Liberation of Angola
NADGE	NATO Air Defense and Ground Environment
NATO	North Atlantic Treaty Organization
NICS	NATO Integrated Communications System
OAPEC	Organization of Arab Petroleum Exporting Countries
OAS	Organization of American States
OAU	Organization of African Unity
OCAM	Common African and Mauritian Organization
ODECA	Organization of Central American States
OECD	Organization for Economic Cooperation and Development
OEEC	Organization for European Economic Cooperation
OPEC	Organization of Petroleum Exporting Countries
PCC	Palestine Central Council
PFLP	Popular Front for the Liberation of Palestine
PFLP-GC	Popular Front for the Liberation of Palestine— General Command
PLO	Palestine Liberation Organization
PNC	Palestine National Council
PNV	Partito Nazionalista Vasco
SACEUR	Supreme Allied Commander Europe
SACLANT	Supreme Allied Commander Atlantic
SEATO	South East Asia Treaty Organization
SELA	Latin American Economic System
SHAPE	Supreme Headquarters Allied Powers Europe
SPEC	South Pacific Bureau for Economic Cooperation
STABEX	Export Stabilization Program
STANAVFORLANT	Standing Naval Force Atlantic
TNF	Tactical Nuclear Forces
UDKP	United Democratic Party of Kurdistan
UN	United Nations
UNCTAD	United Nations Conference on Trade and Development
UNECA	United Nations Economic Commission for Africa
UNICE	Union des Industries de la Communauté Européenne
UNGA	United Nations General Assembly

UNSC	United Nations Security Council
UPEB	Union des Paises Exportadores de Banano (Association of Banana Exporting Countries)
UPV	Ulster Protestant Vanguard
USOC	U.S. Olympic Committee
WCL	International Confederation of Labor
WEU	Western European Union
WFTU	World Federation of Trade Unions
WTO	Warsaw Treaty Organization

Index

Moran, Theodore, 211
MPLA. *See* Popular Movement for
  the Liberation of Angola
Multinational corporations (MNE/
  MNC), 5, 13, 203–212
Mutual and Balanced Force
  Reductions in Central Europe
  (MBFRCE), 107

National Broadcasting Company
  (NBC), 13
NATO. *See* North Atlantic Treaty
  Organization
NBC. *See* National Broadcasting
  Company
Neofunctionalists, 34–38, 96, 122
Nestlé Corporation, 206
Nordic Council, 22–23, 191–195
North Atlantic Treaty Organization
  (NATO), 21–22, 105–124, 126,
  132, 137
  Eurogroup, 107, 120
  and Iran/Afghanistan crises, 9–11
Nye, J. S., 34–37, 187

OAPEC. *See* Organization of Arab
  Petroleum Exporting Countries
OAS. *See* Organization of
  American States
OAU. *See* Organization of African
  Unity
OCAM. *See* Common African and
  Mauritian Organization
Occidental Petroleum Company, 13
ODECA. *See* Organization of
  Central American States
OECD. *See* Organization for
  Economic Cooperation and
  Development
OEEC. *See* Organization for
  European Economic
  Cooperation
OPEC. *See* Organization of
  Petroleum Exporting Countries
Organization of African Unity
  (OAU), 22, 26, 153–163

Organization for Economic
  Cooperation and Development
  (OECD), 9, 12, 21–22, 63,
  86–87, 210
Organization of Arab Petroleum
  Exporting Countries (OAPEC),
  97
Organization for European
  Economic Cooperation (OEEC),
  48
Organization of American States
  (OAS), 5, 21–22, 141–152
  Inter-American Development
  Bank, 143
  and Iran/Afghanistan crises, 12
  Rio Pact, 141–143, 146, 149
Organization of Central American
  States (ODECA), 174–175
Organization of Petroleum
  Exporting Countries (OPEC),
  91–97, 100, 221
  and Iran/Afghanistan crises, 12

Palestine Liberation Organization
  (PLO), 5, 22–23, 185, 219–224,
  230–231
  Arab Liberation Front, 17
  and Iranian crises, 15
Pentland, Charles, 31, 32(n6)
Perlmutter, Howard, 204
Perroux, Francois, 211
PLO. *See* Palestine Liberation
  Organization
Pluralists, 32–34, 38
Popular Movement for the
  Liberation of Angola (MPLA),
  156
Pushtans, 14, 23

Scheingold, Stuart, 31, 39
Schmitter, Philippe, 34, 39–42, 60,
  72, 121, 170
Schuman Plan, 48–49
SEATO. *See* South East Asia Treaty
  Organization
Security community, 32–33, 36,
  121, 145